THINGS
MY MOTHER TAUGHT ME

Including Twenty Miraculous Encounters

To Rieta
with blessings from
Ps 78:3-4
Dec. 4, 2018
Wilf

WILFRIED HEIN

ISBN 978-1-64191-658-5 (paperback)
ISBN 978-1-64191-659-2 (digital)

Copyright © 2018 by Wilfried Hein

All rights reserved. No part of this publication may be reproduced, distributed, or transmitted in any form or by any means, including photocopying, recording, or other electronic or mechanical methods without the prior written permission of the publisher. For permission requests, solicit the publisher via the address below.

Christian Faith Publishing, Inc.
832 Park Avenue
Meadville, PA 16335
www.christianfaithpublishing.com

Printed in the United States of America

DEDICATION

In Honour of my mother

To my dear wife, Hedy, and my dear sons, Jeremy, Robert, and Adrian, with their families in appreciation and thankfulness for the good and blessed times God has given us.

ACKNOWLEDGMENTS

A special thank you goes to my dear wife, Hedy, who did the first proofreading, sometimes adding things I had omitted and other times recommending what not to include. Thanks also to Hildegarde Baerg who took the time proofreading this manuscript.

A special belated thank you goes to my dear mother who wrote me more than six hundred letters after I immigrated to Canada and gave me some valuable advice, which others might benefit from as well.

My final gratitude goes to God who granted me the health, energy, and the necessary self-discipline and persistence required to complete this biography.

Abbotsford, British Columbia, Canada
September 2017

CONTENTS

Foreword 11
Introduction 15
My Memoirs 19
Chapter 1: Birth and Maternal Ancestors (1940 and Earlier) 21
               Child Dedication 22
               My Mother 23
               The History of the Hege Family 27
               My Mother's Grandparents 30
               My Mother's Parents 34
Chapter 2: Childhood and Youth (1940–1955) 37
Chapter 3: Career and First International Travels (1955–1969) 59
Chapter 4: Our Love Story (1969–70) 81
               Our Engagement 85
               Our Wedding 92
Chapter 5: Drawing Nearer to God (1970–1975) 102
               Enthusiastic for the Lord 106
               Our First Child 116
Chapter 6: A Series of Miracles—Two Years in Germany
               (1976–1978) 122
Chapter 7: Enjoying Work, Family, and Traveling (1978–82) 130
               A Christmas Travel Story That Nearly Ended
               in Two Disasters 135
Chapter 8: Success in Career (1983–1986) 149
               The Golden Wedding 162

Chapter 9:   Some Joys and Sorrows (1987–1990) 168
             A Manager We Loved 171
Chapter 10: Faith Makes the Difference (1989–1990) 181
Chapter 11: Some Setbacks (1991–1992).................................194
Chapter 12: An Attitude of Gratitude (1993–1994)..................215
             My Speech for My Mother's Eighty-Fifth Birthday....218
Chapter 13: Transition to a New Life (1995–1997) 228
             Adrian's School Essay..239
Chapter 14: Some Gains and Losses (1998-2004) 241
             Robert and Jennyfer's Wedding 241
             Jake Sawatzky...244
             The Bread from Heaven Story 246
             Tina Sawatzky..249
Chapter 15: Ruins Speak Volumes (2005–2006) 258
             Turkey..258
             Greece 261
             Israel 262
Chapter 16: Two Weddings within Two Weeks (2007–2008)....274
Chapter 17: South America and Europe (2009–2010) 286
Chapter 18: Enjoying Family and Traveling (2011–2013) 304
Chapter 19: Golden Years (2014–2017) 324
             Mennonite World Conference, Pennsylvania 2015.....326
Afterword...345
Appendix..351
             Abbreviations 352
             Additional Historical Information about the Hege
             (Hegi, Hegy, Hagey) Families..............................353
             Family Tree of Lydia Hein 360
             Lydia Hein's Siblings 361
             Jake Sawatzky's Obituary 362
             Tina Sawatzky's Obituary 364
             Erica Suderman's Obituary 366

Al Willms Obituary..369
Wilf's Educational Background............................371
Wilf's and Hedy's Travelog 376
Resources 385
Bibliography of Wilf Hein......................................388
Index...391

FOREWORD

When I asked my brother Eckart to write a foreword for this book written in honour of my mother, he sent me the following letter. The English translation follows.

Lieber Wilfried.

Unsere Mutter haben wir Beide in dankbarer, schöner und liebender Erinnerung.

Als fürsorgliche Mutter, als sparsame, gesundheitsbewusste Hausfrau und auch als aktive, mitfühlende Pfarrfrau war unsere Mutter generationenübergreifend, vielfach als Tante Lydia, beliebt und anerkannt. Als Mutter waren die Sorge und Fürsorge oft gepaart mit etwas Ängstlichkeit vor dem Ungewissen und der Zukunft. Dies betraf insbesondere den jüngeren Wilfried, der dann ins ferne Kanada auswanderte. Die fürsorgliche Verbundenheit und das Miterleben dokumentieren sicherlich der umfangreiche Schriftverkehr und die zahlreichen Telefonate und vertieften die enge seelische Verbindung über viele Jahre und umfassten natürlich ihre zwei Schwiegertöchter Hedy und Helga mit ihren wachsenden Familien. Meine Kontakte konnten durch die persönlichen ca. vierwöchentlichen Besuche mit schönen, unterhaltsamen Ausflügen, Gesprächen und den gemeinsamen, auswärtigen Essen, lebendig, vielseitig und intensiv gepflegt werden.

Als überaus gastfreundliche Pfarrfrau, vielseitig in der Kinderarbeit und in der Gemeinde, auch als Organistin aktiv, waren die zahlreichen Verpflichtungen oft grenzwertig belastend, wurden zwar anerkannt, vielfach jedoch als selbstverständlich angesehen.

Als Mitmensch, zu jeder Zeit, in den verschiedenen Lebensabschnitten und Wohnorten war unsere Mutter stets eine gütige, liebenswerte und frohe Frau.

Ihr Leben war von Liebe geprägt. Sie war umsichtig, bescheiden, vielfach ausgleichend, kritisch, jedoch gerecht, sozial denkend, wahrhaftig und vielseitig interessiert. Hier soll noch ihre Freude an der Literatur und vor allem an der Musik erwähnt werden.

Bis zum Tod war unsere Mutter tief dankbar für alles Erlebte mit unserem Vater und ihren Söhnen. In der letzten persönlichen Unterhaltung sagte sie: Vieles Reden ist mir keine Hilfe, ich fühle mich gehalten. Es fällt Alles ab. Ich will Dir nicht traurig auf Wiedersehen sagen. Ich habe keine Angst, nur Freude.

Abschließend möchte ich noch einen Gedanken aus einem Brief vom 5.5.1971 von mir an unsere Mutter zum Muttertag erwähnen. Ich dankte für die Liebe, Sorge und das spürbare Gedenken einer fürsorgenden Mutter. Ein Gefühl, das noch heute spürbar ist.

Dr. Eckart Hein
Mühlheim, Germany

My brother's letter translated by Wilf Hein:

Dear Wilfried,

Thinking about what our dear mother meant to us evokes wonderful memories of love and thankfulness. Our caring mother was not only a frugal and health-conscious housewife, but she was especially loved and appreciated for her active involvement as a compassionate pastor's wife. The younger generations often addressed her as "Tante Lydia." Her caring sense was often associated with some apprehension of the unknown and the future. This applied especially to her younger son, Wilfried, who immigrated to "far away Canada." The extensive correspondence and numerous phone calls attest to a loving relationship and a spiritual bond that included her two daughters-in-law Hedy and Helga with their growing families. I will never forget the many good conversations I had with my parents during my monthly visits with them. Smaller excursions to surrounding villages and excellent meals in beautiful restaurants often created a conducive atmosphere for memorable discussions..

As a hospitable pastor's wife, my mother often invited guests to her home. Her extensive involvement in our community included [women's and] children's ministries and her playing the organ [or piano] during church services. The many obligations sometimes weighed heavily on her health. Her self-sacrificial work was recognized but often taken for granted.

My mother was not only able to make many friends throughout various stages of her life, but she was known to be a gracious, loving lady with a very positive and happy nature. Her life was marked by love. She was prudent, modest, alert, well-balanced, and able to evaluate things critically. She also was fair, conciliatory, judicious, socially minded, trustworthy, and a person of many interests, which included a love for literature and classical music.

My mother remained thankful for all her life's experiences with her husband and her two sons right to the end of her life. During the last conversation with her she said: "Much talking is not helpful to me. I feel constrained. Everything deteriorates. [What is essential, will remain]. I don't want to be sad when saying goodbye to you. I am not afraid, but only full of joy."

I would like to conclude with a thought I mentioned to my mother in a Mother's Day letter written on May 5, 1971. I thanked her for her love, concern, and the heartfelt thoughts [and prayers] of a caring mother. I still can sense this feeling to this very day.

Dr. Eckart Hein
Mühlheim, Germany

INTRODUCTION

My first book entitled *A Witness in Times of War and Peace* was written to honour my father who voiced his concerns about Nazi ideology in word and deed, and thereby risked his life. It also showed the great contributions he made as a Mennonite pastor, historian, and editor.

This book is written to honour my mother, from whom I learned so much. It was my mother who raised me for the first five years of my life, since my father had to serve in the German Army during World War II. Practically speaking, I knew my father only from a picture on my mother's night table. It was my mother who showed me so much love and understanding, not only during the first five years of my life, but throughout my teenage years and adult life. I could always approach her with any questions. She knew what was going on in my heart and mind, even when I did not know how to express myself as a child. She was the one who defended me and stood at my side when I ran into trouble. She was the one who cared for me like no one else could have done. A special bond between my mother and me existed throughout my entire life. She was a role model to me.

She tried to understand others of different faith orientations without condemning them, and when she was wronged, she was quick to forgive. After I immigrated to Canada, she would write four- to five-page letters every two weeks. I valued them so much that I filed the more than six hundred letters in twelve binders. They showed me that my parents cared for me and my family, that they were interested in our lives, and that they prayed for us. Her letters reflected her positive attitude in life. They were filled with encouragement and wisdom gained from her lifelong ministry as a pastor's wife. My mother laid the spiritual foundation in my life, passing on values one usually does not learn in school. The LOVE, FAITH, and HOPE that my mother instilled in me, helped and sustained me through the difficult times of my life.

When I applied the FAITH, which my parents had taught me, I experienced some wonderful incidents, which others might regard just as pure luck. To me, however, they were miracles, which I believe God allowed me to encounter, because I put my trust in Him. They are included in this memoir, since they are part of my life's story.

Another major purpose for writing this book was to leave something of lasting value to my children, grandchildren, relatives, and friends. Since my parents remained in Germany and our children had only limited opportunities to get to know them well, I would like to pass on some of the blessings we received from my parents. Even though my first book, which is a translation of my father's memoirs, contained a chapter about his family, this book is different, in that it adds my own life's experiences and the great impact my mother had on my life. It is intentionally laid out in a chronological order as it makes it easier to relive the wonderful times God granted to us as a family. I have included many of my mother's quotes from well-known writers and poets, since I believe others might benefit from them as well. As some of my mother's unique expressions sound so beautiful in German, I included them in their original form next to the English translation. For quick reference, most indexed items appear in **bold** within the text.

PS: All Bible references are given from the NIV version, unless otherwise stated.

THINGS MY MOTHER TAUGHT ME

Only be careful, and watch yourselves closely
so that you do not forget the things your eyes have seen
or let them slip from your heart as long as you live.
Teach them to your children and to their children after them.
—Deut 4:9–10

My Memoirs

CHAPTER 1

Birth and Maternal Ancestors (1940 and Earlier)

Since I was born during World War II, my parents named me *Wilfried*, meaning, "He desires PEACE." My mother nearly died after I was born. She wrote:

"During my time in the hospital I experienced God's presence, his goodness and grace in a new way. Since I was unable to breastfeed you, a nurse from the Thomashof took care of you during this time.... I would like you to know that the love of parents to their children is so great and deep that a mother is willing to endure difficult hours and days, when she is granted a healthy baby that brings so much happiness and joy into her heart and home."

In German:

"Während der Zeit im Krankenhaus erfuhr ich Gottes Nähe, Güte und Gnade erneut. Da es mir nicht möglich war Dich zu stillen, kümmerte sich eine Schwester vom Thomashof um Dich....

Weißt Du mein Kind, die Liebe der Eltern zu ihren Kindern ist so groß und innig. Ihr bringt viel Glück und Freude ins Herz und Haus. Eine Mutter nimmt schwere Stunden und Tage gerne hin, wenn sie danach ein gesundes Kindchen haben darf."

Geburtsurkunde

Standesamt Kaiserslautern

Daß der Geburts- Akt von Wilfried Hein

geb. Hege

Nr. 379 des Registers

den 28 ten Februar 1940 um 5 Uhr 15 Minuten

in die dazu bestimmten Register eingetragen worden ist, wird bescheinigt

Kaiserslautern, den 29 ten Februar 1940

Der Standesbeamte

I. A.:

Schein für den Herrn Geistlichen

WB. 5. 39. 5000.

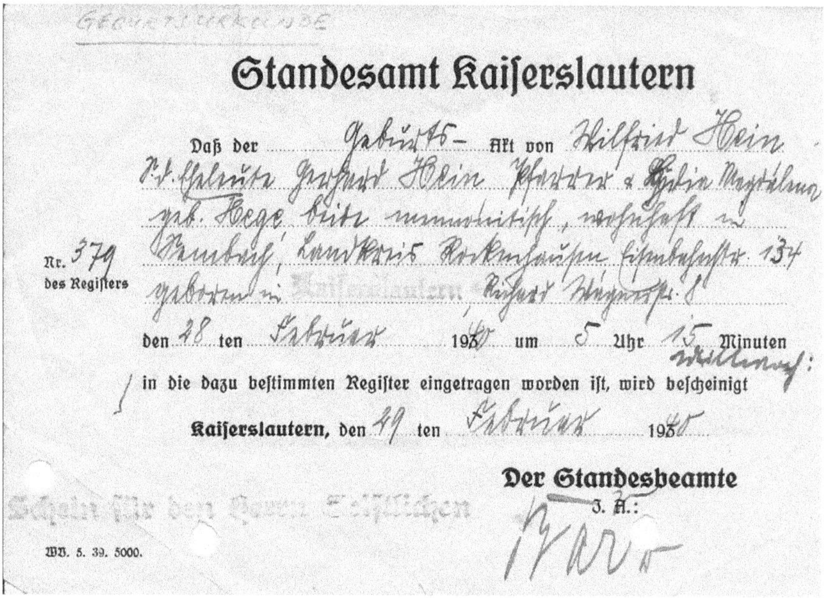

Wilf's Birth Certificate

Due to complications after the birth, my mother had to remain in hospital for nearly eleven weeks. We regarded her survival as a special gift from God. My father wrote: "God's grace prevailed over your birth, and this we should never forget." This divine grace my parents experienced was evident not only from the beginning of my life but also throughout my whole life, up to the present time. The hospital in which I was born was later bombed and reduced to a heap of rubble by American bombers.

Child Dedication

Since Mennonites practice adult baptism upon confession of faith and not infant baptism, many dedicate their babies to the Lord by praying over them.[1] When my Hege grandparents came to visit our

1 More about distinctions of Mennonites vs. Lutherans, including adult baptism, can be found in my book *A Witness in Times of War and Peace* (subsequently stated as *A Witness*), pp. 14, 267–268.

family on my grandfather's birthday, May 16, 1940, my father, knowing that he soon would have to leave his family to serve in the military, thought that this was the ideal time to dedicate me, his second son, to the Lord. Both my parents and grandparents prayed over me, to pass on their blessings, which have been meaningful to me to this day.

My Mother

Since my book *A Witness in Times of War and Peace* was dedicated to my father and contains *his* life's story, this book is written mainly to honour my mother, who was left alone to raise me for the first five years of my life, when my father had to serve in the military. For this reason, my relationship was always closer to my mother than to my father. I could ask her any questions, and she took time to listen to me, tried to understand me, and on many occasions, gave me some good advice.

My mother was the best mother I could wish for. She was a lady completely dedicated to the Lord. She taught me a wisdom that supersedes knowledge. It was a wisdom that can be summarized by the basic Christian fundamental values of LOVE, FAITH, and HOPE, as symbolized by the image on the cover of this book. They are values one often does not learn in school. More important to me was that she practiced these values, as the following chapters will demonstrate.

My mother, Lydia Hein, was born on August 29, 1908, the second oldest daughter of five girls to Mennonite parents Philipp Hege and Elise Funck. Her father was a successful estate manager of the Mueckenhaeuserhof near Worms, where she grew up. Her parents were committed Christians, who practiced what they believed Christians should be, above all, to show love and understanding toward others. Their children tried to follow their parents' teachings. As a fourteen-year-old teenager, my mother decided to be baptized, following the biblical command for those who want to become Christ followers.

My mother's certificate of baptism, dated April 1, 1923.

The scroll on top of the certificate quotes Jesus's words Mark 16:16: "Whoever believes and is baptized will be saved, but whoever does not believe will be condemned."

After graduation from high school in Worms, my mother studied home economics and then received her certificate from a nursing school in Stuttgart. The story of meeting her future husband, their courtship, engagement, and marriage is described in detail in my book *A Witness…* (chapter 3, page 68ff). During their time in Berlin (1958–1965), she was actively involved in many women's conferences, meetings, and retreats held at the Menno Home for ladies and children coming from East Germany. She also served as manager of the Menno Home from 1960 to 1965.

On several occasions, my mother was asked to serve as a conference speaker. For example, she spoke at the Mennonite World Conference in Kitchener in 1962 on the topic *Mennonite Women's Work in Germany* and at a women's conference in Thomashof, November 1970, where she spoke about *Peace and Prayer*. At another time, she wrote an article about *The Emancipation of Women* that was published in the Mennonite journal *Junge Gemeinde*.[2]

My mother Lydia Hein celebrated her engagement on October 1, 1933 (picture taken about 1935).

---

[2] Lydia Hein, Junge Gemeinde, 1/73, Januar/Februar 1973, 8–9.

My parents' wedding day: January 5, 1936

My parents were married at the Ibersheim Mennonite Church near Worms. It was the first and only Mennonite Church in Germany with a bell tower. Since it is the only church in town, it also hosts Protestant church services.

Ibersheim Menonite Church, built in 1836

Since my father's ancestry is thoroughly described in my book *A Witness*, I will include in this volume only my maternal ancestors.

The History of the Hege Family

The Hege family had its origin in Switzerland, where the name was spelled Hegi. A village and a castle named Hegi, dating back to the twelfth century still exist. The castle was owned by a noble family, the Knight von Hegi, and is located about five kilometers east of Winterthur (CH-1, 4).

The Hege Coat of Arms dates back to AD 1225

More important to me than the code of arms and their nobility is the fact that most of my ancestors were highly respected people, and many of them were lay pastors and very accomplished farmers. Four out of fifteen Hegi family members of Zurich Mennonites were pastors (CH-1, 4). Among my Hege ancestors were forty lay preachers and elders.³ The name *Hegi* was also found among the Anabaptists in the Aargau region of Switzerland.⁴

Due to the widespread persecution during and after the Reformation, many of the Swiss Hegis immigrated to south Germany, the Palatinate and Alsace, where they took on the name Hege in 1753 (ML, 271). Restrictions of freedom and persecution also existed in Germany in that no more than two hundred Mennonite families were permitted to live in the Palatinate (Kurpfalz; CH-2, 45). For this reason, many Hege families immigrated to the United States.⁵

My mother's grandfather Philipp Hege (see picture below) leased the Oberbiegelhof, an estate of more than 270 acres.⁶ For centuries, Mennonites were not allowed to own their own properties. They, however, were appreciated and widely known for their great achievements as accomplished and efficient farmers. Four generations of the Hege family leased and managed the Oberbiegelhof estate for nearly ninety years, from 1822–1910. Both Philipp and his father Ulrich were talented agriculturalists and lay preachers.⁷ Their surname fit the meaning of their primary and secondary vocation, for the imperative German word *hege* or its verb *hegen* means to take care or to tend (CH-1, 44–46).

Under the direction of the Heges, the Oberbiegelhof became a model of how an agricultural estate should be managed. Despite the achievements of the Hege family, the leaseholder decided to terminate the lease and rent it to a sugar factory (CH-2, 34). Part of the reason for this may have been the economic situation. When Napoleon stopped the import of sugar cane from the English colonies, German farmers switched their production to sugar beets, and the manufacturers likely offered a better deal to property holders (CH-2, 28).

---

3   Hege family members, who became pastors, are described in CH-2, 44–51.
4   Aargau is located about thirty-five kilometers west of Zurich.
5   Additional historic Information about the Hege (Hegi, Hegy, Hagey) families can be found in the Appendix.
6   Oberbiegelhof is located about twelve kilometers east of Sinsheim in south Germany (CH-1, 46).
7   More about Ulrich Hege and the accomplishment of his descendants can be found in the appendix.

My Mother's Grandparents

My mother's grandfather was also a Philipp Hege (1848-1909)[8]

My mother's grandmother Magdalena, nee Landes (1853-1920)

---

[8] They had two sons and four daughters. Their son Ulrich leased the estate at Markt near Augsburg, where he also served as a lay-preacher. The other son Philipp served as an elected elder at the Augsburg community. Their daughter Lina married a Peter Hege who settled at the Schafbusch estate near Wissembourg (now France).

My Mother Writes about Her Grandfather: "Grandfather Hege was an industrious farmer, who enjoyed raising animals at his farm. He was involved in seed research and served as a lay preacher. I remember it being said of him that he was a creative and musically talented person, who was interested in many things. He often played hymns on his pump organ by heart, occasionally improvising some songs. He also was a very generous person, with a good sense of humour."[9]

Hans Hege (see Appendix) writes about him: "He was my favourite uncle, a humorous person with charisma" (CH-2, 34).

My Mother Writes about Her Grandmother Hege (*nee Landes*): "She was a gracious, loving and hard-working mother. She also was a prudent and very modest person. Grandmother Hege had a beautiful alto voice. Her children wrote on her tombstone: '*Ihr ganzes Leben war Liebe*' (Her whole life was love). They had seven children."

Maternal Funck Great Grandparents

My Mother Writes about Her Funck Grandparents: "Grandfather Funck managed the leased estate Bonharthaeuserhof (Althof), near Bretten, Germany. He was a lay preacher and elder of the Mennonite church in Woessingen, in south Germany. They had six children."

---

[9] Notes from my mother's handwritten letter about her grandfather Hege.

My mother's grandfather Christian Funck

My mother's grandmother Magdalena nee Bachmann

As was the case with other Mennonite farmers, my great-grandfathers Funck and Hege, as well as my grandfather Hege, could only lease a large estate and not own it. These were the rules for many centuries, stemming from the after-effects of the Reformation in the sixteenth century, when Anabaptists were being persecuted and the state wanted to control their expansion (CH-2, 22).

When the lease of the Oberbiegelhof was terminated, the leaseholder, Count Viktor von Helmstatt, honored the Philipp Hege family for their hard and outstanding work. On May 18, 1910, he sent his delegate to deliver a thank-you letter and a silver cup in recognition of the Hege family's exemplary management of the estate (CH-1, 48).

Philipp Hege Jr., my grandfather, now needed to find a new acreage. Some property owners were not very impressed with their new leaseholders, the sugar factories. One of them was Baron Schilling from Hohenwettersbach, who owned a large estate near Worms.[10] Knowing of the accomplishments of the Hege family, he wanted to lease it to them. My grandfather was happy for this new opportunity and moved his family to this estate, the Mueckenhaeuserhof in 1910.[11]

---

[10] Hohenwettersbach is located about ten kilometers southeast from Karlsruhe.
[11] The Mueckenhaeuserhof is located about twelve kilometers north of Worms, near the Rhine River.

My Mother's Parents

My maternal grandparents, Philipp Hege and Elise nee Funck.
The picture was taken in about in 1910.

My grandparents Hege with their five daughters.
From left to right: Lydia (my mother), Helene,
Gertrude (Trudel), Martha, Liesel.

A table of my mother's lineage, including her siblings, is included in the Appendix of this book.[12]

After my grandfather had managed the Mueckenhaeuserhof estate for some time, the baron admired my grandfather's abilities and the yield of the sugar beet crop. He said: "I have never seen a sugar beet harvest like this before, not even among [other] Mennonites" (CH-2, 40-41).

My Mother Writes about Her Father:
"I appreciated and respected him very much. He was an authority figure in our family, distinguished in his mindset. He was also humble and remained calm in all situations. He was reliable, and people could trust him. When he spoke, he was always to the point, not using unnecessary words. I remember him being kind to his employees, helpful, socially minded, and a very generous person. Every Sunday morning father played two chorales on his pump organ. He was eager to learn and read much literature that helped him excel in his agricultural specialty."

About Her Mother, She Writes:
"Mother Hege was a very industrious lady, who knew how to manage and delegate tasks to people working in their household. She was a hospitable, helpful, and a very caring and generous person. She wanted to please others and make other people happy. She also had a good appreciation for beauty. She read her Bible daily, and was interested in naturopathic literature."

A broader picture of the Hege families, their persecution, immigration, and some of the better-known relatives is included in the appendix.

Gratitude for My Ancestry
Reflecting on my heritage, I noticed that three of my great-grandfathers were lay preachers. Jakob Hein was instrumental in bringing revival from South Russia to the Mennonite settle-

---

[12] A detailed description of the ancestors of my father's lineage is given in chapter 1 of my book *A Witness*.

ment in Alexandertal (also called Alt-Samara or Samara oblast) in the Volga region.[13] Philipp Hege, Sr. and Christian Funck, from my mother's side, were also lay preachers. All these ancestors were highly respected and hardworking people. They were committed Christians who prayed for their descendants.

As a child, teenager, and adult, I often felt God's blessings, his protection and guidance in my life, and I attribute that to my praying parents, relatives, and predecessors. The following Bible verse speaks about this promise given to all those who put their trust in the Lord:

"Know therefore that the LORD your God is God; he is the faithful God, keeping his covenant of love to a thousand generations of those who love him and keep his commands" (Deut 7:9–10).

---

[13] Jakob Hein's father-in-law, Dietrich Hamm, who immigrated to Russia in 1862 was also an elder in the Mennonite community in Alexandertal, besides being a teacher.

CHAPTER 2

Childhood and Youth (1940–1955)

In her diary, my mother mentioned that when my father left his family on June 21, 1940 for military service, my three-year-old brother, Eckart, already displayed his leadership qualities, saying to my mother: "Mutti, don't cry. I am your little daddy now, and I want to lead you." [1]

Not knowing what the future held, my father wrote in one of his first letters:

"We remain under God's guidance and protection"

In German: "Wir stehen unter seinem Schutz und Schirm"

For the first five years of my life, I didn't know my father, except for his occasional holidays when he visited his family for a short time. I knew my father more from the picture standing on my mother's night table than as a real person.

War Memories

Among my few wartime memories are the following:

- The screaming sirens waking us up, often during the middle of night. Then my mother came to pick us up to take us down into our dark, moist, dirt floor cellar. It was one of

---

[1] Lydia Hein diary entitled *Danke-Buechlein*

the few air raid shelters in our village, so that sometimes our neighbours joined us to have better protection.
- When the American tanks rolled through our village, I saw our neighbor lady wave the white flag from her window, welcoming the American soldiers. It was on March 21, 1945.
- My brother and I were making our homemade caramel candies when we heard a knock at the door. Two American soldiers commanded in German: "In zwei Stunden müssen Sie das Haus verlassen!" "You have to be out of your house in two hours!" We grabbed our essentials and walked to my mother's friend who lived on the hill directly above us from where we could observe all the activities in our yard.
- We noticed that we had forgotten the matches. My mother sent us back to ask for them. Thank God, they were very friendly, gladly fulfilling our request. My mother wrote: "After two days, we could return to our home." But for us boys, it was an eternity. Entering our home, we found everything in perfect order. Even our toys were neatly stacked away in the broom closet. I believe that the many religious pictures made the officers and soldiers realize that Christian believers lived in this home, sparing it from being ransacked. Not all were as fortunate since some homes were left in a big mess.

Wilfried, with his three-year-old brother, Eckart, in their garden in Sembach, Germany (1941).

By early spring 1945, everyone knew that the war would soon come to an end. There was no communication, there were no phone calls, no mail, and no trains running. For about four to five months, my mother didn't know whether my father was still alive, neither had my father any idea of what happened to his family after the Allies invaded. Keeping a diary, my mother wrote: "One of the most difficult decisions for me was to decide whether I should stay or move away with my two children. In the end, I decided to remain in our home."

A note in my mother's diary said:

"When I dress the children, I am thinking very much of you. I said to them: 'I hope Papa will come again, I am a little afraid.' Eckart's response: 'I am not!' This confidence by my seven-year-old son comforted me very much."

In German

"Beim Anziehen der Kinder denke ich viel an Dich. Ich sagte zu den Kindern: Wenn nur Papa wiederkommen darf. Ich hab ein bisschen Angst. Eckarts Antwort: 'Ich nicht!' Dies' zuversichtliche Kindeswort tröstete mich" (May 1945).

World War II came to an end with Germany's surrender on May 8, 1945. Six weeks later, on June 24, 1945, at about 4:00 p.m. as I looked through the bathroom window, I saw my dear father walking through our garden gate. My pants still halfway down, I ran down the stairs, shouting, "Papa is here, Papa is here!" My mother wrote: "God heard our prayers and requests and gave us our dear Papa back again."

Growing Up in Postwar Germany

The first few years after the war, we could only buy limited amounts of groceries in stores. Everything was controlled by food stamps. The limits of food rations varied in different provinces. In our area, the limit for bread was 500 grams and for butter and meat 125 grams per stamp.

Food stamps issued by German provinces limited each family to buy no more than the allowed ration.

As a six- or seven-year old boy, I still remember how happy I was when my mother allowed me to toast a piece of bread on top of our sawdust stove. This was all we could have for breakfast. But we, who lived in the country and had our own garden, were fortunate to always have something to eat. From our neighbours who lived on a farm, we could get some milk. But this was different in cities. A lady from Kaiserslautern, our nearest city, walked twelve kilometers twice and sometimes three times a week just to pick up two liters of milk. When she was standing outside in the cold weather, awaiting the milk truck, my mother invited her in. A friendship developed, and this dear lady often helped my mother with many household chores.

She faithfully kept on writing each one of us birthday letters until her very old age.

My mother wrote:

"Everything is wearing out and needs fixing. There is nothing we can buy yet. I wonder what will happen? But up to this point, God wonderfully provided. For this reason, we want to continue putting our trust in Him."

In German:
> "Alles geht kaput, zu kaufen gibt's noch nichts…
> Wie soll alles werden? Ganz wunderbar half Gott
> aber bis jetzt durch—und deshalb wollen wir
> Gott weiter vertrauen."

Soon after the war, generous and caring Christians in USA and Canada sent donations through the Mennonite Central Committee (MCC), which organized food distribution in postwar Germany. In an open letter, the mayor of Ludwigshafen thanked caring North American Mennonites for their generous donations and food supplies. Local food distribution was coordinated through the humanitarian agencies *Evangelisches Hilfswerk* and *Caritas*. Mayor Bauer writes that they could feed 7,300 starving and malnourished children. Eventually this number would be increased to 8,400. Mr. Bauer spoke about the immeasurable value of these contributions and what this all meant to them and their families.[2]

Personally, I would like to express my thanks and appreciation to my brothers and sisters in Christ in North America who sent thousands of care parcels to Germany. I remember when my parents helped distribute them to families in need, especially during Christmastime. Never will I forget when I found one of those towel-wrapped parcels under the Christmas tree and how happy I was finding a toothbrush, a piece of soap, a pencil, or a toy in it. A special thank you goes to my relatives in Canada who sent us many parcels in our times of need. Now I am often thankful that I could expe-

---

[2] Horst Gerlach, *Bildband zur Geschichte der Mennoniten* (Uelzen-Oldenstadt, Germany, Druck und Verlag Guenther Preuschoff), article entitled "Die Kinderspeisungs-Aktion der Mennoniten in Ludwigshafen/Rhein," 181.

rience such a time, because at no time in my life will I take things for granted but am thankful to God and other people who care and demonstrate their love to others. My parents-in-law were also saved from starvation when the Mennonite Central Committee (MCC) sent food to the starving people in the Ukraine in the early 1920s.[3]

In the postwar period, thousands of refugees arrived in West Germany mostly from East and West Prussia. We also accommodated a family until a new home could be found for them. Through the efforts and contributions of Mennonite Central Committee (MCC) and many Mennonite volunteer workers, especially the well-known "Pax boys" who came from North America, new housing developments (Siedlungen) were constructed in various areas throughout West Germany, where refugees would find their new homes.

We were so thankful that we could experience God's wonderful provision through people who cared, usually those who also were believers. Keeping the faith was very much in the center of our lives. Before tucking us into bed, my mother always prayed with us this prayer:

---

[3] See Jake Sawatzky's *Bread from Heaven Story,* 2.pdf

THINGS MY MOTHER TAUGHT ME

In German	In English
1. Müde bin ich, geh zu Ruh', schließe meine Augen zu. Vater, lass die Augen Dein Über meinem Bette sein.	Weary now, I go to rest, Close my eyes in slumber blest. Father, may Thy watchful eye Guard the bed in which I lie.
2. Hab' ich Unrecht heut' getan, Sieh' es, lieber Gott, nicht an. Deine Gnad' und Jesu Blut machen allen Schaden gut.	Wrong I may have done today, Heed it not, dear God, I pray. For Thy mercy and Christ slain Turns all wrong to right again
3. Alle, die wir sind verwandt, Gott, lass ruh 'n in Deiner Hand. Alle Menschen, groß und klein, Sollen Dir befohlen sein.	May my loved ones, safe from harm, Rest within Thy sheltering arm. All Thy children everywhere Shall find refuge in Thy care.
4. Kranke Herzen sende Ruh, müde Augen schließe zu. Gott im Himmel halte Wacht, Gib uns eine gute Nacht. Amen Alternative last stanza, which we usually prayed: Kranke Herzen sende Ruh, Nasse Augen schließe zu Lass den Mond am Himmel stehn Und die ganze Welt besehn. (Poem by Louise Hensel (1798–1876)	Send Thy rest to hearts in pain, Close the weary eyes again God in heav'n Thy vigil keep Grant us all a restful sleep. Amen (translated by Margret Loewen Reimer)[4]

---

[4] https://uwaterloo.ca/grebel/sites/ca.grebel/files/uploads/files/CGR-27-2-S2009-7-2.pdf

The melody of this beautiful children's evening prayer is given below.

– Selection # 534 in the 1965 Gesangbuch der Mennoniten

There is another prayer my mother taught me. She prayed it with us every morning before going to school:

In German	In English
Führe mich, o Herr und leite meinen Gang nach Deinem Wort. Sei und bleibe Du auch heute Mein Beschützer und mein Hort. Nirgends als bei Dir allein, Kann ich recht bewahret sein. (German Songwriter Heinrich Albert, 1604–1651)	Guide me, O Lord and direct my path according to your word [Please] remain with me today Protecting me and providing a place of refuge for me Nowhere else, but in you alone Can I find my true security.

I believe that God answered these prayers and protected and guided me throughout my life and even let me experience some miracles, which I would like to include in these memoirs.

My First Two Miracles

Miracle 1: Rescue from Drowning

In front of our house, next to our garage, we had a cesspit that normally was covered by a wooden lid about eight by six feet in size. Once or twice a year, a lady (Frau Lutzi) from our village came to help with various chores. One of them was to fertilize our garden with "organic" dressing. I believe I was about seven years old when I backed out my bike from our laundry and storage room. Not noticing that the lid was open, I fell into it. I remember thinking that I soon was going to heaven and saw my life replay like a video in split seconds. There was light all around me as I floated in this horrible liquid. A hand drew me out of it. My rescuer was a labourer who worked nearby and saw what had happened. He said that I held on to the edge, but I knew that I was floating in the about ten feet deep pool. When we looked at it afterward, we realized there was nothing I could have held on to since the top edges were somewhat rounded. Since my parents were not at home, a neighbor lady came to help. I took a bath, cleaned up, and thanked God that he kept me alive. Since I was embarrassed about this incident—as probably also my parents were—not much was said about it, and I am still sorry to this day that I didn't say thank you to my rescuer (Kurt Hoefli). May he accept my belated thanks, if this is possible. For me, it was a miracle and not just good luck.

Miracle 2: My Mother's Survival After a Stillbirth (May 1948)

My father was scheduled to speak at a conference in Hamburg in northern Germany, and since my mother was still in her eighth month and felt quite well, he risked attending it. It happened during these days of my father's absence. It was May 20, 1948, when my mother suddenly lost strength and lapsed into unconsciousness. Our neighbours rushed her to the hospital in Kaiserslautern, twelve kilometers away from our village. The doctors performed a Cesarean section, but it appeared that the baby had died due to a hemorrhage. They had given up on the mother's life and just wanted to keep her alive until her husband returned. However, after giving a blood transfusion, her condition unexpectedly improved. The physician said to my mother: "Dem Leben wieder zurückgegeben," meaning "Your life has been given back to you again." The head nurse mentioned that my mother already had the colour of a dying person. My mother writes:

> "It felt like heaven opened and a light ray came down and I could hear in my mind the words:
>   'Gottes Bruennlein hat Wassers die Fuelle'
> (Ps 65:9–10), meaning 'God's well has plenty of water.'"

She continued: "I sensed God's overflowing grace out of *His* great abundance. We were not allowed to keep our sweet little daughter. God has taken her to his heavenly kingdom as his little angel."

In German:
> "Unser süßes Töchterchen durften wir nicht behalten. Gott nahm es zu sich ins Himmelreich als sein Engelchen."

My parents planned to name her Erdmuthe, but now she was lying in her little white coffin decorated with beautiful sweet-smelling flowers. I still remember very clearly, as if it was yesterday, when we carried her coffin up the narrow trail on the west side of our house and made our way to the cemetery. After a short ceremony, we had to say goodbye to our dear little sister we initially were looking forward to so much.

Quoting Romans 8:28, my mother wrote:

"We know that in all things God works for the good of those who love him."

Even though we lost our little sister, we were so thankful that God had restored my mother's life. This event and my parents' attitude deeply affected me. The survival of my mother was a miracle to all of us.

When I needed a haircut, I patiently waited my turn at the barbershop in our village. The walls of his room were relatively bare, except for one picture with the following verse that stayed with me to this day. It said:

In German	In English
Wenn Du noch eine Mutter hast so danke Gott und sei zufrieden.	If you still have a mother, then thank God and be content.

Considering that many families had lost family members during the war, I indeed was happy and thankful to still have my parents, and so were my parents. One of my mother's letters attests to this:

"I am so happy with our dear Papa and our two precious boys, even though, they are not always so precious outside our home."

In German:
"Ich bin so glücklich jetzt schon mit unserm liebsten Papa und unsern zwei Goldbuben, auch wenn sie manchmal draußen gar nicht so nach Gold aussehen."

I am not sure of what possible misbehavior my mother might have been thinking. Was it the phraseology we used when playing with our friends, or was there some other misdeed? Perhaps it was our unauthorized construction of a playhouse in the big bush in our garden when we used the lumber lying around in our yard, without asking for permission. The result was that we had to tear down our beautiful "creation" that we had assembled with so much sweat and effort. The construction workers apparently needed the logs and timber for the conversion of our adjacent barn into a multipurpose worship center.

Our home in Sembach. Right side: The pastor's residence. On the left: The "Gemeinde Saal," a multifunctional church hall, completed with the help of some MCC volunteer workers in 1948.

THINGS MY MOTHER TAUGHT ME

From left to right: Wilfried, Eckart, with our friend Hans Friedrich, and our beloved companion "Racker."

Nevertheless, it seems that I was not always a bad boy since mother also wrote this:

"The last few months you were especially kind to me and a very loving child. What you can do and whatever we ask you to do, you perform with much love and joy. Your loving heart and mind is always open and needing to occasionally share what's on your mind or what is bothering you. This makes your Mutti very happy and she is thankful with her child."

In German:
"Du bist mir in den letzten Monaten ein besonders liebevolles Kind. Was Du mir von Liebe und Freude tun kannst, das tust Du willig. Gerne erfüllst Du jede Bitte und jeden Auftrag. Dein volles, liebendes Herzchen ist immer offen und muss sich ab und zu entleeren. Deine Mutti ist glücklich und dankbar mit ihrem Kind."

This relationship remained throughout my life. The following poem, written for Mother's Day 1950, expresses some of my appreciation toward my dear Mutti. I gave it to her together with some handpicked flowers from our garden when I was a ten-year-old.

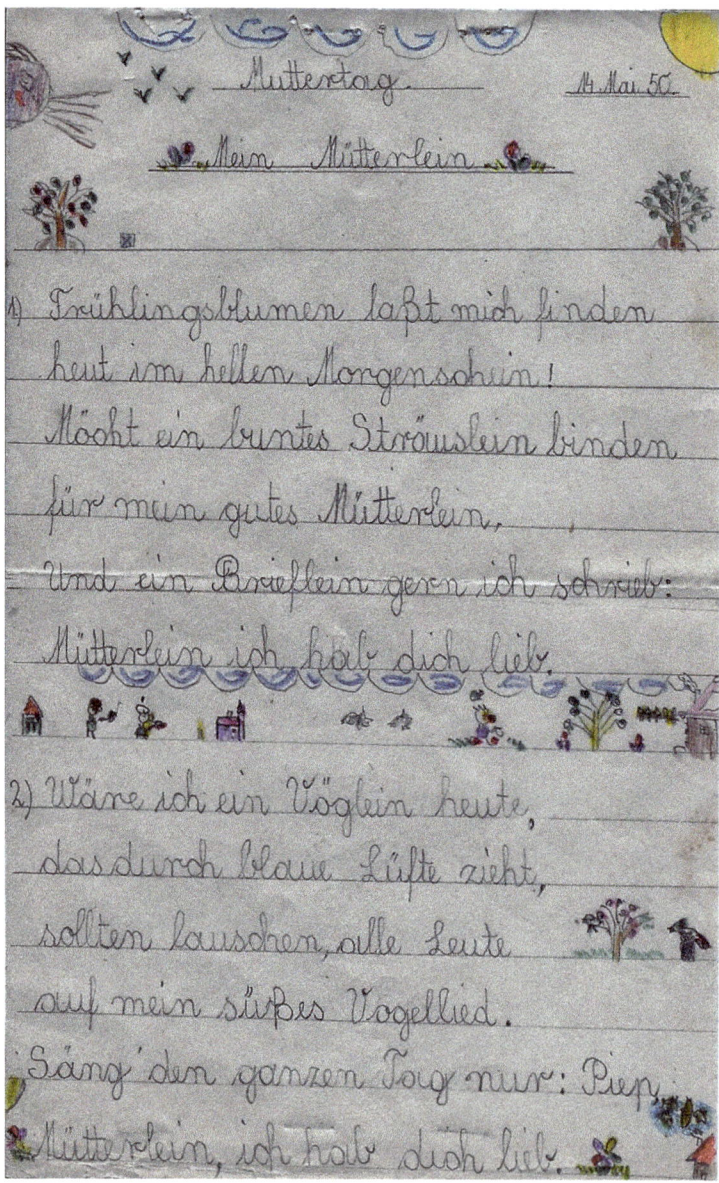

THINGS MY MOTHER TAUGHT ME

Translated to English
Mothers Day, May 14, 1950
To My Dear Mommy

1. Let me find some nice spring flowers
   today in this bright morning glow!
   I would like to collect a colourful bunch of flowers
   for my dear beloved mother
   and would like to write a letter to you with the words
   Mommy I love you dearly

2. Would I be a little bird today
   that can fly in the blue sky
   then all the people could listen
   to my sweet birdsong.
   Singing all day long only "Peep"
   Mommy, I love you dearly

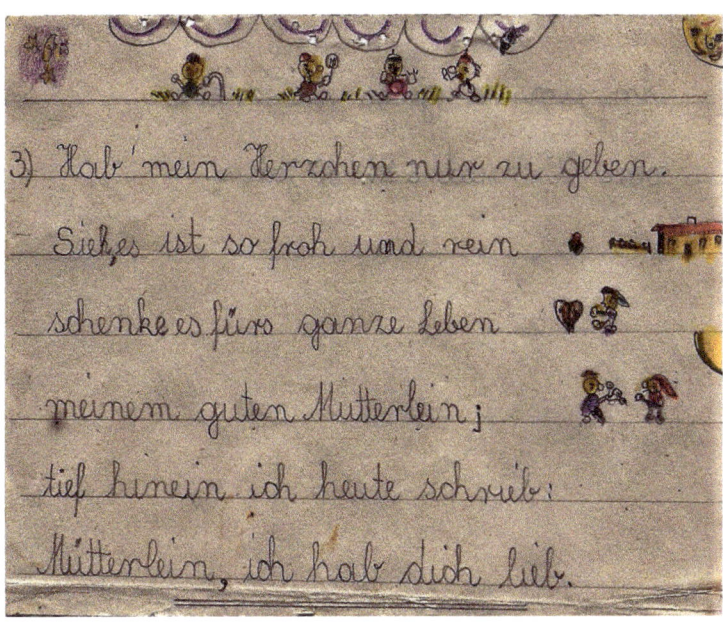

3. All I can give you is my little heart!
See it is so happy and clean
giving it to you for my whole life
to you my dear mommy.
Deeply I wrote in it today
Mommy, I love you dearly

A painting for my mother for Mother's Day
1951 from her eleven-year-old boy.

Surgery on Living Room Table (in 1950)

I had to spent my tenth birthday in bed due to a serious bilateral middle ear infection accompanied by high fever. We were told I needed surgery. In those days, physicians still paid house visits. Our large mahogany dining room table served as a perfect operating table. I still remember the doctor asking me to count, and besides crying like crazy, I believe I made it only to number five when the ether mask took effect. Both ears were punctured, and pus could now flow out freely. This was the procedure at that time. After spending about two weeks in bed, I was glad to be able to go back to school again.

School and Recreation

After five years of elementary school, my parents enrolled me in the *Altsprachliches* or *Humanistic Gymnasium* in Kaiserslautern. It was a high school specializing in the old classic languages of Latin and Greek. Unlike my brother, I experienced great difficulties especially in mathematics and Latin. There was, however, one subject I liked, and that was painting with watercolor. One of my paintings even won first prize in provincial school competitions. The theme given to us was "*The Great Sports Event*" (Das Große Sportliche Ereignis). I chose to paint the glorious victory of my home soccer team Kaiserslautern, which by beating Preussen Muenster 2:1, won the German championship.

My award-winning painting as an eleven -year-old boy

The prize consisted of a bottle of wine presented to me at the Volkshochschule in Kaiserslautern in September 1951.

During my high school years, I also took piano lessons and at one time participated in a school concert as soloist playing Schumann's "Soldier's March" from memory.

More enjoyable than studying for school was playing soccer and croquet and taking our dog on explorative walks around our village.

Having fun playing croquet in our yard with Wilf on the right.

My great friend, our second dog "Molli."

THINGS MY MOTHER TAUGHT ME

A New Direction in My Life

Due to increasing difficulties in high school, my parents decided to enrol me in an alternative vocational career. My father took me to the local employment services, where we discovered an opening existed for the "Drogist" profession, which was a mix between herbalist and chemical technologist. In April 1955, I entered a three-year coop program, which also involved some theoretical training at a local business school.

Wilf as a "drogist" apprentice at the Kloster Drogerie in Kaiserslautern.

My Baptism

As a teenager, I knew God had a special plan for my life and that there was much more to life than the physical aspect of well-being. I realized that there was also a spiritual dimension and that it was not enough to just call myself a Christian. I understood that to be a Christian means more than religion. It means to be a Christ follower, to have a personal relationship to Christ. Thus, it involved a personal commitment, which needed to be affirmed through baptism.

I consequently enrolled in a prebaptismal training course, taking place once a week over several months. Here we were taught about the basics of Christian faith, much about catechism and our Mennonite and Anabaptist forefathers who were martyred for what they believed was right. They wanted to practice adult baptism since they saw no scriptural basis in infant baptism. Among other things they stood for freedom of religion and nonresistance.[5] For these, their religious convictions, Catholics, Lutherans, and Calvinists alike declared them as heretics, worthy to die the martyr's death.

Studying Anabaptism in my retirement years, I came across a quote by Catholic theologian Franz Agricola who wrote about the character traits of the Anabaptists in 1582:

> "Under the existing heretical sects there is none that leads a life as decent and holy as the Anabaptists do. In respect to their public lives they are impeccable. Lying, cheating, swearing, fighting, offending language, overindulgence in eating and drinking could not be found in their lives. They are humble, patient, upright, peaceful, honest, self-controlled and open people that one would have to assume they are filled by the Holy Spirit."[6]

Many people in Germany did not know much about Mennonites since they constituted only a small minority of religions and often integrated with the Lutheran church. Most of them had immigrated to North and South America. In high school, this sometimes made me feel a bit of an outsider, and I remember that I did not want to

---

[5] More about the distinctions of Anabaptists and Mennonites can be found in my book *A Witness in Times of War and Peace,* pp. 266–279, and in the afterword of this book.

[6] Horst Gerlach, Das Mennonitische Gemeindeideal, Eine kurze Beschreibung einer christlichen Freikirche, ein Zitat von Franz Agricola's *Gegen die schrecklichen Fehler der Taeufer*; Traktat Christliche Mission der Mennoniten, Esch-Alzette, Luxemburg, p. 7 (no date given, probably 1956).

explain and answer any questions regarding my religion. Now this has changed, since I know more about my spiritual heritage and since Mennonites generally are very well respected in North and South America.

In our baptismal class, we had to memorize many Bible verses, which we had to quote in front of the audience during our baptismal ceremony. We were a group of seventeen teenagers (not all are on the picture) who were baptized at the Mennonite church in Sembach in the fall of 1955.

Even though I agree with the practice of adult baptism, I am not going as far as some Mennonites, who condemn infant baptism practiced by Catholics and Lutherans. Infant baptism can be just as meaningful to them as adult baptism to Mennonites. Peter Wiens cites an example in which a person lying on his deathbed could not be at peace because of his past sinful life. When Estonian Lutheran pastor and martyr Traugott Hahn (1875–1919) was called, nothing seemed to convince the dying farmer. Neither asking him to confess nor the reference to Jesus dying for our sins seemed to have an impact. But when he asked the question, have you been baptized, and he said, "Yes," he could die in peace.[7]

Our baptismal group with Wilf next to his father, September 4, 1955.

---

[7] Harry Loewen, Elisabeth L. Wiens, Elke and Peter Foth, *Warum ich mennonitisch bin,* (Hamburg:Kuempers Verlag, 1996), 293.

The pastor (my father) gave me the following Bible verse that has meant much to me for the rest of my life.

In German	In English
"Verlass dich auf den Herrn von ganzem Herzen, und verlass dich nicht auf deinen Verstand; sondern gedenke an ihn in all deinen Wegen, so wird er dich recht führen." (Spr. 3:5–6)	*"Trust in the Lord with all your heart and lean not on your own understanding; in all your ways acknowledge him, and he will make your paths straight."* (Prov. 3:5–6)

This verse expresses what I had seen practiced by my parents, and I wanted to put my trust in the Lord especially as I entered my occupational career.

CHAPTER 3

Career and First International Travels (1955–1969)

From apprentice in drugstore to pharmaceutical sales representative

The last six months of my three-year apprenticeship took place at the *Drogistenfachschule* (Technical Institute) in Neuwied.

Drogistenfachschule in Neuwied, Rh.

Wilf studying hard for his exams in 1958.

During this time, living away from home, I rented a room at some Mennonite friends who owned a farm in Neuwied, Germany. I graduated as *Drogist* in March 1958. It involved writing two exams, one about the medicinal use of herbs and the other about the properties and industrial use of chemicals.

Graduation certificate as *Drogist*.

WILFRIED HEIN

Overview of Occupational Career from 1960–1970

During these ten years, I gained much practical experience in the pharmaceutical industry as the following table illustrates:

Workplace	Function
Drugstore in Kaiserslautern	Apprentice in drugstore
Drugstore in Berlin (1960)	"Drogist" in a drugstore
Pharmaceutical Wholesale in Berlin (1961)	Filling orders in warehouse
German Institute for Medical Missions, Tuebingen (1962, see picture below)	Warehouse manager, supervising storage and shipments of mainly donated pharmaceuticals and medical supplies to various mission agencies in Third World countries
Bayer Pharmaceuticals, headquarters in Leverkusen (November 1962–December 1967)	Industrial sales employee: Having worked in various departments, I learned much about the pharmaceutical export business. Part of my responsibilites were cost calculation, the submission of tenders and supplying medical/scientific literature to subsidiaries in English speaking countries.
Merck Pharmaceuticals (January 1968–April 1970)	Pharmaceutical sales representative calling on physicians in South Germany (Stuttgart area).

During this time, while working for Bayer, a large pharmaceutical company in Germany, I was drafted and expressed my wish to serve in the Red Cross should I be needed. I received top marks in regard to my health evaluation, but since I was too old, I was never called up for military service.

Wilf getting ready the shipments of medical donations designated for mission stations in India and South Africa.

API

AUSBILDUNGSSEMINAR PHARMA-INDUSTRIE STARNBERG/SEE
INHABER UND LEITUNG: DR. MED. HORST GOHLKE

URKUNDE

Herr – ~~Frau~~ – ~~Fräulein~~ Wilfried Hein

geboren am 28.2.40 in Kaiserslautern

hat am 28.3.68

die Abschlußprüfung gemäß der Prüfungsordnung API bestanden.

Aufgrund dieser Prüfung ist er / ~~sie~~ berechtigt, sich als

ÄRZTEBESUCHER API

zu bezeichnen.

Starnberg, den 2.4.68

DER VORSITZENDE DES PRÜFUNGSAUSSCHUSSES FÜR DAS
API AUSBILDUNGSSEMINAR PHARMA-INDUSTRIE STARNBERG/SEE

(Dr. H. Gohlke)

API
Ausbildungsseminar
Pharma-Industrie
8130 Starnberg/See
Waldschmidtstr. 8

Certificate of graduation from the Seminary of the German Pharmaceutical Industry (API), approving me as a qualified medical sales representative (1968).

Occupational Advancement (1968)

Toward the end of 1967 when I still worked at the large Bayer plant in Leverkusen, I decided to explore further opportunities within the pharmaceutical industry. Checking the newspaper, I noticed an ad by Merck, which called for pharmaceutical sales representatives. This was the first time, to my knowledge, that any pharmaceutical company in Germany was looking for nonacademic people for this position. Merck decided to train their people at their own expense. I applied and was accepted.

Merck Pharmaceuticals sent us (about twenty young men) to an independent seminar of the German Pharmaceutical Industry (API) for a three-month training course in Starnberg, Bavaria. After completing this course, another month of product specific training followed at the head office in Darmstadt. Now I was ready to start my new job as "Aerztebesucher" or pharmaceutical sales representative, calling on medical doctors to promote specific medications. In retrospect, I find it interesting to recall a friend of my parents saying to me once as a young teenager, "I believe you will become a commercial consultant ("Kommerzienrat"), a prophecy which came true.

I enjoyed my work and regarded this promotion as God's wonderful direction in my life. My mother wrote: "I want you to know that I am very happy and thankful that you have achieved so much. By continuing to work hard and trying to do your best, God will grant you further success." She concluded her letter with the following beautiful poem:

In German	Approximate English meaning
"Leit uns in allen Dingen Lass Rechtes uns vollbringen! Tu uns treulich beraten, Stärk uns zu guten Taten!"	Direct us in all we do Help us to do the right things Please keep on advising us and give us the strength to perform good deeds

WILFRIED HEIN

From Local Excursions to International Travels

Biking with a friend across the Rhine River near Ludwigshafen en route to a youth retreat in the Odenwald, 1957.

Moped ride with a teacher who invited me on a day trip from Koenigsfeld/Blackforest to the Bodensee in 1957.

In summer 1958, I had an opportunity to join some young people on a drive to Holland (Friesland), where we attended a youth retreat organized by Pastor Postma.

Visiting a family in Holland, Wilf on the left in 1958.

Menno Simons monument in Witmarsum Holland, his birthplace. The monument was erecteed 1879 near the old hidden church in Pingjum.

In the same summer (1958), I participated in a Mennonite Voluntary Service (MVS) assignment in Vienna, Austria, where I helped renovate a school destroyed during the war. The school was located at the Karlsplatz, in the center of the city. Hitchhiking home some nine hundred kilometers, I remember staying overnight at the Salvation Army in Stuttgart, sleeping next to some snoring colleagues who had been picked up from the street the night before. Shortly after my arrival at home, we moved to Berlin, where my father had taken on a new position (more about my father's ministry in Berlin is described in chapter 5 of my book *A Witness*). Having only recently received my driver's licence, I drove my first long stretch of about six hundred kilometers to Berlin, together with my mother.

The *Mennoheim* on Promenadenstrasse 15b in Berlin, with my father's Lloyd car and my 98 cc Miele motorcycle.

Menno Home (garden view)

One Year as Trainee in USA (1959–1960)

While living with my parents in Berlin, I heard about a one-year overseas trainee exchange program sponsored through the Mennonite Central Committee (MCC). Finding the idea of travelling to the United States exciting, I applied and was accepted. The first six months I stayed with a Beachy Amish family (Aaron Glick) at a farm in Lancaster County, Pennsylvania. The second half year I spent on a farm belonging to a GC (Mennonite General Conference) couple (Frank and Helen Kennel) who lived near Roanoke in Central Illinois.

Wilf on the manure-spreader in Lancaster county, Pennsylvania, 1959. Other chores included helping to milk the cows, taking care of the pigs, and feeding three thousand chickens.

During my holidays, I joined some friends to travel to Key West in Florida. On another occasion, my friend Uwe from Holland and I booked a bus roundtrip from Illinois to Vancouver, Canada, where we visited my relatives and returned via California. After sightseeing the beautiful city of Vancouver, I thought at that time, that this would be the ideal spot to live and spend my retirement. My dream came close to fulfillment in my later life.

Having lived away from home for more than a year, I composed the following poem for my mother on Mother's Day 1961:

| In German: | Approximate meaning |
| Meiner lieben Mutti zum | in English: |
Muttertag 1961	To my dear mother on Mother's Day 1961
Ein ganzes Jahr lang unter Fremden bracht mich zur Einsicht doch bald sehr- Wie schön war's doch von Mutters Händen gehegt zu werden und noch mehr! Drum möchte ich für Alles danken Und wünsche für die nächsten Jahre dass Gott Dir gebe weitre Kraft Gesundheit und den Lebens Saft!	A whole year among strangers soon brought me to the realization How nice it was to be cared for by dear mother's hands, and so much more! For this I would like to thank you And I wish you for the following years That God may grant you further strength And much health and vitality!

Vacationing in Holland and Belgium (1963)

In summer 1963, I decided to bike through Holland and Belgium. My three-fold purpose was to visit a friend in Friesland, to attend a youth retreat in Holland, and to participate in a Mennonite Voluntary Service (MVS) camp in Belgium, where we had to lay the foundation for a new church construction. The youth retreat on the Dutch island of Texel took place at an old barn near the North Sea. Besides attending lectures, we had lots of fun hiking the dunes, swimming in the ocean, playing volleyball, and riding our bikes across the small island. In a letter to my parents, I reported some of my experiences. I am including some excerpts (from a letter dated July 30, 1963):

> Dear parents,
> After supper, we usually had an open mike session. Each participant was expected to contribute in some way left up to the individual's own creativity and imagination. I tried to compose a poem, which I presented to them. Even

though it may not be quite perfect, I will attach it below. We sang my verses in the melody of the well-known German folksong "Horch was kommt von draußen rein.

Since it sounds much funnier in German, I will include the German text for readers who might understand it. After each line, we sang the refrain "*Hollahi-Hollaho!*"

In German	Approximate meaning in English
Heute ist der vierte Tag Der uns wieder Freude gab Dafür danken wir Euch all Und wir singen noch einmal…	Today is the fourth day Which again gave us much fun For this, we thank all of you And, therefore sing again…
Gestern sprachen wir vom Wein Und wir sagten er ist fein Auch in Holland schmeckt er gut Steigert Geist, gibt frischen Mut	Yesterday we spoke of "wine" Concluding that it tasted fine Even to the Dutch it tasted good Enhancing spirit, raising mood
Nach dem Thema Trinken kam Auch das Rauchen bald daran Fasst ein jeder wusste was Aber Keiner kennt das Maß	After drinking, the next topic was discussing smoking Everyone knew something about it But nobody knew at which point to stop
Doch von allem was wir hörten Wollen wir das Best verwerten Und wir wünschen für die nächsten Tage Freude, Glück und Wohlbehagen. (composed by Wilfried Hein)	Of everything we have learned We want to apply only the best And we wish you for the days to come Joy, happiness and well-being

For the last night of our youth retreat, I composed the following three verses:

In German	In English
Unsre Zeit ist nun vorüber meine Schwestern und ihr Brüder. Drum sage ich Euch nochmal Dank für gute Speise und den Trank.	Our time now has come to an end my dear sisters and valued brothers. That's why I like to express my thanks for the fine food and the good drinks
Doch wichtiger als dieses war mir Eure Gastfreundschaft, fürwahr. Wir haben Vieles besprochen und gesungen etwas zu verstehn, ist mir gelungen.	But much more important was your hospitality, indeed. We discussed many things and sang together and I even have understood some of it.
Doch wenn ich wieder Euch besuche dann braucht kein Dolmetscher Ihr zu suchen. Ich wünsche Euch nun allesamt, macht aus dem Rat die Tat bekannt! (Composer: Wilfried Hein)	But when I come again to visit, you don't need to find an interpreter. I now advice all of you to transform what we learned into good deeds!

Inspired by the beautiful surroundings, I sent a postcard to my colleagues at Bayer, Leverkusen with the following rhyme I composed:

In German	In English
Das Wandern ist die Lust vom Hein besonders bei strahlendem Sonnenschein. Jedoch per Fahrrad reist's sich besser mit wenig Geld und einem Messer.	Hiking is lots of fun for Hein especially during brilliant sunshine. Travelling by bicycle is a lot better with little money and a knife
Ich radle durch die Benelux und habe schon die zweite "Buchs". Daneben spür ich alle Glieder und freu mich auf Q 30 wieder	I am biking through Benelux and already wear my second pair of pants Besides this, I can feel all my joints And I am looking forward to Q30 again.[1]

A Trip to Moscow (Summer 1969)

    A unique opportunity arose in 1969 when a large German travel agency advertised the first tourist flights to Moscow. Initially, my father thought of visiting his two surviving sisters in Kazakhstan in Siberia. But his sisters suggested that they were willing to meet him in Moscow. My proposal for our whole family to go found ready approval. After our decision, my father's sister from Canada (Anna Kroeker from Abbotsford, British Columbia) also expressed interest in joining us in our flight to the Soviet Union.

    Our two aunts met us at the Moscow airport. Since they were not allowed to come into our Intourist hotel, we met them every day in the nearby Gorki Park, where we soon noticed that we were under surveillance by Soviet guards. These were the days before the Iron Curtain came down. My brother Eckart and I decided to still take a trip to St. Petersburg, Russia's cultural center and its second largest city. At that time, it still was called Leningrad. Among points of interest, we visited the Hermitage Museum and took a cruise along the Neva River. When we returned to Moscow, our cousin Heinrich Wiens had arrived from Kazakhstan since he also wanted to meet us

---

[1]   Q30 was the abbreviation of the office building I worked in.

before our return to Germany. He was later interrogated by Soviet security personnel and asked many questions about why he met with German clergymen. He subsequently faced some problems in his workplace since they found out that he was a Christian. I was thankful that I could live in country that allows personal freedom and that God protected us during this trip and brought us home safely.

Protection During Two Car Accidents

Miracle 3: Car Accident Near Berlin (December 1961)

While working in Tübingen in south Germany, I decided to visit my parents in Berlin over Christmas. It was in December 1961, shortly after I had bought my first used car, a two-seater Heinkel with only three wheels. The distance from Tübingen to Berlin was about 650 kilometers, and I hoped to reach my destination in one day. The roads that December morning were very icy, and I figured that I probably wouldn't be able to drive more than 50 kilometers per hour on the average. While travelling along the Autobahn corridor through the then-separated East Germany and still having to travel about 50 kilometers to reach Berlin, it started snowing. Suddenly I found myself in the ditch. Since I was overtired, I must have fallen asleep at the wheel. It was close to midnight, and there was hardly any traffic on the freeway. Since my car was about the smallest one could get, it was easy for me to lift it back on to the road. Without a scratch, I continued my trip, when I unexpectedly faced some armed Soviet soldiers. I was at the wrong border crossing. With a malfunctioning heating system and the gas pedal right behind the noninsulated front door, my feet felt half frozen. Finally, I arrived at home unharmed, after some fourteen hours of driving. I thanked God for his gracious protection and a warm bath I could take.

My first car in Tübingen, a three-wheeler Heinkel, 1961

Miracle 4: Protection from Car Accident in South Germany (Winter 1969)

During winter 1969, when I lived in Schwaebisch Hall, in Baden-Wuerttemberg, I left one morning to make some doctor calls in neighbouring villages. The roads were icy and very slippery. Heading down toward the village entrance, the road became narrower and near the curve a trailer was parked, stacked up with parcels about three meters high. There was oncoming traffic in the left lane, and I needed to slow down. Tapping my brakes slightly, my VW Beetle started to slide toward the trailer. In my mind, I could already see parcels flying all over the street. In desperation, I let the steering wheel go, saying a prayer. Lo and behold, the steering wheel flipped to the opposite side and my "Beetle" happened to turn just in the right direction. I couldn't believe it but thanked God again for this protection. My mother had taught me that it is very important to remain thankful.

THINGS MY MOTHER TAUGHT ME

Correspondence with Parents

During summer 1962, when I lived in Tübingen, my mother wrote me an encouraging letter, which showed me that she cared and continued to pray for me. Enclosed are some portions from it:

> My dear Wilfried,
> Our prayer request is, that God may help you find the right vocation for your life and continue to direct your path. May He continue to bless you and make you a blessing to others. We hope and pray that you enjoy your work, no matter what or where this might be. May you be able to find some friends who will support you in your plans and endeavours. We hope and pray that they are genuine Christian friends. Our sincere prayer is that God may help you find the right girl at the right time, and that you someday will experience a very happy family life. God can make it possible!
>
> Wilfried, remain the same way as you were to me, when you were a little boy. When I was expecting our little daughter (your stillborn sister), you were just eight years old and a real gentleman to me. When it was difficult for me to move around, you brought the blankets for me and placed them on the lounge chair in our garden, and you untied and took off my shoes. I will never forget your helpful and kind attitude. You were a very caring child. Try to be the same way to your future wife, and she will appreciate it.
>
> Often, I am thinking that I should have done much more for you children, when you were young. I should have read more stories to you, but the years are past and you are adults now. Much of what should have been done, remained undone. No doubt, mistakes were

made, but they were not done intentionally. We, as your parents, need forgiveness from our children, whom we love with all our hearts, as only parents can do. I want to let you know, my dear child, that your mother's love will be with you to her last hour. I thank you for all that you have done for me. Our prayers will not be in vain. You will experience God's rich blessings! This, I believe with all my heart. My heart's desire is that you two brothers will remain connected, despite your different natures. May God's word be the guideline for your faith and lives. May you be able to think in love of your parents, once we are no longer with you. (My mother's letter was dated July 18, 1962.)

During my father's illness, I wrote him a letter in March 1965 of which I am including some segments as well. I believe that my father had suffered a burnout, likely due to taking on too many responsibilities. More about his work and the circumstances leading to his illness is explained in greater detail in my book *A Witness* in chapter 5, in the section "My last four years in Berlin."

My dear dad,
    Mutti mentioned to me that you are presently not doing very well. This doesn't surprise me, since I recognize that hardly any human being can take on such an enormous workload, connected with so much stress over a longer period.
    Be assured Papa, that besides God, there are some people who recognize your hard work. Among those are your two beloved sons. As your youngest son, I care about you and what is happening in your life. For this reason, I would like to write to you this personal letter. When a per-

son does not feel well, new strength is needed for the recuperation process.

Even though, we as your sons might not comprehend at this point the whole scope of what you have accomplished, through your historic research, your writings, and your pastoral work, we want to let you know that we are proud of you! We also want to thank you for the Christian values you have passed on to us, and for the love and understanding you have shown to us. You, our parents, have demonstrated the fundamental Christian values of faith, love and hope to us again and again. I believe that they are simply the "alpha" and "omega" of life. May they take on a new meaning for you Papa, in your present condition.

No one is perfect and we all have our shortcomings. We all experience certain disappointments in our lives at certain times. My hope and wish is that you may regain new strength, vitality and new joy of life. Perhaps a good holiday may be needed to bring about the necessary changes. I will be praying for you and your soon recovery. We hope that we still can have you as our loving father for many more years to come.

Greetings, your son *Wilfried*

Blessings Experienced

During my many inspirational walks as a young man, I sometimes experienced special blessings that are hard to describe. They happened especially during the time when I lived in Leverkusen (1963) and in Schwaebisch Hall (1968). While going for my regular walks, I sometimes experienced what felt like a gentle electric current flowing from the top of my head down my spine, radiating warmth throughout my whole body. It sometimes came in waves, creating a pleasant, tingling feeling all over. It felt as if God was pouring out his blessings upon me, and I was made aware of God's presence and his love for me. I believe that it was a gift from the Holy Spirit, likely being passed on to me through my praying parents and ancestors. The verse from Deuteronomy 7:9 comes to my mind in this connection:

> *Know therefore that the* LORD *your God is God; he is the faithful God, keeping his covenant of love to a thousand generations of those who love him and keep his commands.*

I was now twenty-nine years old, and I knew it was time to do some shopping around, trying to find the right girl. Little did I know that my parents had met my future wife about four weeks before I would meet her.

CHAPTER 4

Our Love Story (1969–70)

Before We Met: Wilf in Germany

It was in 1968 when a twenty-eight-year-old bachelor in Germany started looking seriously for the right girl for his life. The way young people usually met friends of the opposite sex was on the dance floor. But I knew that was not the place where I would find my future wife. I wondered, *How can I know which of the many good-looking girls will be the right one for me for the rest of my life?* There were some girls in my teenage years who attracted me, but it seems that I was a bit shy and maybe not imaginative enough to approach them in a unique, attention-getting way. On the other hand, there were some girls who were interested in me, but I couldn't care less. In one case, even a mother thought that I would make a good son-in-law. As I was lying on the beach on the Italian Riviera, she came up to me and said, "I dreamt that your name was J'espair" (the French word for "I hope"). They had a daughter and even invited me for a sightseeing tour, but it was not meant to be. One day, I thought, such an important decision needs to be prayed about. I remember the day when I knelt at my bedside, committing that whole "right girl" question into the LORD's hand. I also knew that my parents, and especially my mother, prayed for me. A few months later, when I went for my regular inspirational walks through the forest, alongside fields and meadows in Schwaebisch Hall (in south Germany), I suddenly heard an inner voice, saying, "You will meet your future wife at your parents' home!" It was like someone whispering this into my ear. My immediate reaction: But how can this be? Here, I am living about two hundred kilometers away from my parent's home, and I usually visit them only on their birthdays or at Christmas. Then I dismissed this experience.

Hedy from Canada to Germany

In the meantime, a young beautiful Mennonite girl in Canada was studying music in her third year at UBC in Vancouver. She heard about an existing government-sponsored exchange program for students enrolled in German language studies. Having grown up in a German-speaking home and wanting to do some international travel, she signed up for the German course, and this exchange program and was accepted.

Students needed to arrange their own trip to Montreal from where the tour started. In summer of 1969, Hedy took the train from Vancouver to Montreal, where she met with the rest of the group. After their arrival in Frankfurt, the young people traveled on a sightseeing tour to Berlin, where they received their prospective destinations. It happened that this secular placement agency assigned Hedy to work in a Christian-run hotel in Koenigsfeld in the Black Forest. It was the "Christliches Erholungsheim zu Doniswald" operated by the "Herrnhuter Bruedergemeinde," also known as Moravian Brethren.[1]

It also happened that my father, a Mennonite pastor, had been asked to come to this place to conduct the morning and occasional evening devotions. My mother was invited too. In turn for their service, they were given free room and board.

Retelling the story of how my parents met this Canadian Mennonite girl, my mother wrote, "Among the kitchen staff helping serve food to the guests, was also a young Canadian girl. We noticed her kind and calm manners. Papa thought right away that she may be a Mennonite girl and it turned out to be true. This, of course sparked the interest of a Mennonite pastor, who had a brother living

---

[1] The Moravian Brethren were the first Protestant missionaries sent overseas in the early eighteenth century. They are known for their daily devotionals called "Losungen."

in Canada. Further communication revealed that Fräulein Sawatzky knew my dad's brother (Dietrich Hein and his family). Aunt Anna [Anna Kroeker, a sister to my father from Canada], who was visiting and accompanying us even said a prophetic word. 'This nice girl may perhaps be suitable for one of your sons'. I responded: 'Our sons are old and independent enough to pick their own girls and I—as their mother—don't want to interfere.'"

My parents found out that Ms. Sawatzky's time in Koenigsfeld was soon coming to an end and that she planned to travel through southern Europe. They invited her to visit, mentioning that they would be happy to show her Worms, the historic Luther-city. Since Worms is not too far from the Frankfurt airport, the young lady asked my parents whether they could take her suitcase along so that she wouldn't have to bother with too much luggage during her travels.

Miracle 5: How We Met (Summer 1969)

Weeks went by, and my parents started wondering what happened to Fräulein Sawatzky until one day they received a postcard saying that she would be arriving on August 29. This happened to be my mother's birthday, the day when their youngest son came home for a visit.

Our meeting place: My parents' home, the pastoral residence in Monsheim, near Worms, Germany.

Some relatives had already arrived for the birthday party. When I walked in the door with flowers in my hand, I saw a young lady sitting at the table having "Kaffee und Kuchen." My first impression: "Not too bad." We had a fantastic time together, showing slides from our Moscow visit and singing various songs together. We all noticed the beautiful voice of that young Mennonite girl from Canada. As evening drew near, I invited Ms. Sawatzky for a walk, trying to practice my English by telling her a bit about my work. Returning home, we chatted a bit more, had a glass of wine, and soon were per "Du," the informal address among friends. A somewhat sleepless night followed, since my heart kept on beating at an accelerated rate.

The following day, my father offered to take Ms. Sawatzky for a ride to show her some of our beautiful surroundings, as he had promised her earlier. I responded: "This is my responsibility," and that was it. We drove to the nearby Donnersberg, the highest mountain in the Palatinate, where we had lunch in a beautiful restaurant. Returning home, both of us had to leave, I for a convention in Karlsruhe, where I had to man a booth, and Hedy to Frankfurt for her return flight to Canada.

Hedy & Wilf who fell in love in 1969

We started corresponding, and I knew that this case should be followed up soon. In one of my first letters to her, I mentioned that

I would like to visit her during the Christmas holidays. The message to my parents was, "I am planning to visit my relatives in Canada," but they had a hunch as to what the real reason might be.

Our Engagement

One of the least expensive flights to Vancouver was a flight departing from Brussels with stops in New York and Toronto. Trying to make a good impression on the person I fell in love with, I shaved and put on my best "after shave," about an hour before landing in Vancouver. Having picked up my luggage, I looked around, but there was no Hedy. To my surprise, an old man (her father then fifty-nine) approached me, asking "Sind Sie (are you) Wilfried Hein?" Excusing himself, he explained that Hedy couldn't make it since she had to direct a children's choir at a Sunday night's church service. I felt like turning around and flying back home again. To make things worse, he took me to his youngest daughter's place (Ingrid and Ed Suderman) in Vancouver where the rest of the family was congregated. What a welcome! All these people, strangers to me, were sitting in a circle waiting for our arrival. When Hedy finally arrived, everyone seemed interested in how these two young people would greet each other since they had previously met for only two days. Fortunately, things started improving gradually. In retrospect, I now say, it was worth it to remain patient and enduring.

Hedy still had to work at Woodward's in Vancouver a few days, demonstrating piano keyboards, while I stayed at my uncle's place (Dietrich and Susa Hein). During this time, I checked out some future work opportunities, just in case things turned out well, as I was expecting. Before Christmas, the Sawatzkys invited me to stay at their place. By New Year's Eve, we were engaged. I phoned my parents around midnight (about 8:00 a.m. New Year's morning in Germany) to relay the good news. They passed on their best wishes for our future and were very happy with us.

Some might think this was all coincidence or pure luck. But to me, it was a miracle. I regarded it as an answer to prayer and a fulfilment of Jesus's words:

Ask and it will be given to you; seek and you will find; knock and the door will be opened to you. (Matt 7:7)

Wilf and Hedy on New Years day 1970 in front of the Jacob Sawatzky home in Abbotsford, British Columbia, one day after their engagement. Aunt Anna's prophetic pronouncement a few months earlier became a reality.

After our engagement, my mother wrote:

"We as your parents would like to pass on to you our best wishes and many blessings for your engagement. We firmly believe that God has brought you two together, 'the right girl at the right time!' [as my mother had always prayed for]. God has implanted the love towards each other into your lives. May you be able to live a life together under God's guidance. May he bless you with a happy marriage filled with much love, joy, and courage. Make sure to include some humour into your lives, and try to take minor differences not too seriously. May God create in you a cheerful heart, an inner peace, and an ability to keep on trusting in the Lord. Can you recognize God's wonderful hand in the direction of your lives? Papa said: 'The angels played a part in all of this.'"

My mother concluded her letter with the poem that became so meaningful to her before her engagement thirty-six years earlier.

In German	In English
Gott muss man in allen Sachen, Weil er alles wohl kann machen End und Anfang geben frei! Er wird, was Er angefangen, Lassen so ein End Erlangen, Dass es wunderherrlich sei. (Stockfleth (1643–1709))[2]	Submit all matters to God Since he can make them succeed Grant him the beginning and end of your life And he will complete what he has begun In a most wonderful way!

On my thirtieth birthday, while still living in Germany, my mother wrote me these beautiful words about love:

In German	In English
"Liebe ist das Einzige das wächst wenn wir sie verschwenden" (Ricarda Huch).	"Love is the only thing that keeps on growing, when it is given away generously."
"Ohne Liebe ist der Reiche arm, den Armen macht sie reich" (Augustinus).	"Without love the rich are poor, [but through love] the poor will be made rich."
"Der Lohn der Liebe ist, dass dein Wesen Liebe ist" (Brunn).	"The reward of love is, that your character will become love."

My father added:

"We wish and hope that you will find the spiritual dimension in your new home country, that you missed in Germany. We are

---

[2] Heinrich Arnold Stockfleth, *Gesangbuch*, Ludwigshafen, Konferenz der Sueddeutschen Mennonitengemeinden, e.V., 1972 (hymn 388, stanza 4).

convinced that God will bless you richly . . . May your marriage reflect a ray of God's love. May God be gracious unto you and may you be able to pass his divine gifts on to others as well. After all, we Christians are made for the purpose to let our light shine and be salt of the earth!"

In response to these beautiful parental wishes, I would like to say this:

Reflecting on our forty-seven years of marriage, at the time of this writing: "I believe that there is power in parental prayers and their sincere wishes. Yes, I did find a new spiritual home in my new country, when we became members of Willingdon MB Church in Burnaby and later at Bakerview MB Church in Abbotsford, British Columbia. We were recipients of many blessings, and it is our hope that we can pass on some of these blessings to others as well."

Immigration on May 5, 1970

Returning after my Canada visit to Germany January 2, 1970, I showed my engagement ring to my boss (Dr. Schultz) in Stuttgart and mentioned that I was planning to emigrate in the beginning of May. He was very kind to me, giving me as much freedom as possible, and added: "You can work with us until your departure, just as it suits you best. Just drop off the company supplies and medical samples before you leave." This was quite unusual since the procedure for employees resigning from the sales force was usually immediate. As I had learned from my mother, I did not take these things for granted and was very thankful.

Much needed planning and arranging during the months before my emigration. Most belongings needed to be sold. The essentials I packed into a wooden box, delivering it to the harbor in Bremen together with my brand-new VW Beetle which I had waiting for me at the VW factory in Wolfsburg.

On May 1, 1970, the Sunday before my departure, my parents organized a farewell party for me, which we celebrated in the youth center, adjacent to the pastor's residence in Monsheim. My parents had invited all my uncles, aunts, and cousins with their wives, altogether about twenty-five people. They helped in preparing the food, decorating the rooms with flowers, and displaying various pictures. My brother brought along his special company projector that allowed us to project black and white pictures from different stages of my life.

Farewell party for Wilf Hein with his parents in Monsheim, Germany, on May 1, 1970. My Canadian sweetheart was some eigth thousand kilometers away from us, waiting for my soon arrival.

Then my parents shared the story of how we met, and we sang some folk songs. My father had composed a poem which we sang to the melody of one of my favourite children songs. "Frau Schwalbe ist 'ne Schwaetzerin" (Mrs. Swallow Is a Talker) was a song my mother sang to me as a child, of which I never could get enough. This beautiful day will always remain among my treasured memories. Embarking on a new future in a new country, I valued the good wishes and prayers of my parents and relatives.

My parents brought me to the Frankfurt airport on May 5, 1970, from where I said my *Auf Wiedersehn* to them and to my home country. Fortunately, it turned out not to be the final good-bye. In a letter my mother gave along, she wrote these inspired words:

German	Approximate English meaning
Geh im Frieden mein lieber Sohn- Geh mit Freude und Zuversicht- Geh im Vertrauen auf die verheißende Gnade!	Go in peace my dear son— Go with much joy and confidence in your heart- Go in the assurance of God's promised grace!
Bleibe in Aufrichtigkeit und Wahrheit- Bleibe in Dankbarkeit und Hoffnung- Bleibe in Liebe zu Menschen-in Ehrfurcht vor Gott!	Remain standing for what is right and true- Remain in gratitude and joyful anticipation- Remain loving people- [and keep on serving] our awesome God!
Wisse, dass die Liebe Deiner Eltern Dich weiterhin im fernen Lande umgibt- Wisse, dass ernste Gebete in Treue Dich weiterhin begleiten- Wisse, dass wir alle, Du dort, wir hier, unter der Allmacht und Barmherzigkeit unsres himmlischen Vaters bleiben! Deine Mutti	Know, that the love of your parents surrounds you even when you are far away from us Know that earnest and consistent prayers will always be with you- Know that we all-you in Canada- and we in Germany- remain under the protection and grace of our almighty heavenly Father!" Your mother

With these motherly encouragements, I entered a new country. I would soon get married and need to find a new job. Before departing from Germany, I had arranged for some job interviews with pharmaceutical companies in Montreal. My car shipped from Germany had arrived safely and was waiting to be driven the longest stretch I ever drove, some 4,500 kilometers to Canada's most western province. My fiancée decided to meet me at the home of her friend near Calgary. Starting out from cold and windy Montreal and driving through snowy Alberta, we finally arrived in sunny, beautiful British Columbia, an ideal setting for a young couple in love. When I mentioned this to my mother, she responded this way:

"May this BC sunshine stand as a symbol for your life together. May the sunrays keep you warm, and bring you much joy and happiness. May your mind, soul and body experience the wonderworks of

God's creation, and instill happiness into your hearts, so that you can pass some of it on to others! May God fill your hearts with an overflowing joy and gratitude that will radiate from you unto others. May God fill your heart with his grace and love and make you a blessing to each other and to your friends. May He bless your marriage with happiness, and much joy."

Since our wedding date was nearing rapidly, I received some additional motherly advice:

> My dear son!
>
> Your wedding will be in a week and then a new period of life will begin for you. You are already thirty years old—a good age! Some time ago, you mentioned to me "I pretty well got used to my own lifestyle." This seems to me a unique and fitting expression for a bachelor. But now, all this will change, and one needs to get used to life together, with your wife who is always around you, and who certainly will surround you with much love. You must try understanding each other, and learn to accept each others' points of view. There may be a need to change some of your thinking and ways you used to do things. There may also be times, when you find that some things had been better before. But make sure that you remain open and keep on loving and trusting each other. Please don't get angry at each other and leave no room for anger in your heart, since a small thing can easily develop into something bigger. Learn to forgive each other and don't let the sun go down in an angry state of mind. Wilfried, please have always an ear and heart for the needs of your wife! Always try to understand her and be willing to support her! Keep on appreciating and respecting her and try to remain polite. It is important to stay tactful

towards each other and be in control in critical situations. Finally stand together in love, care and faithfulness, no matter what happens.

Hedy's Graduation on May 27, 1970

Hedy graduating with a bachelor of music degree at UBC on May 27, 1970.

Our Wedding

Our wedding ceremony took place at Bakerview Church in Abbotsford, British Columbia, on May 30, 1970. Hedy and her family had planned everything to the smallest detail. Except for my father who played an active role as the officiating minister, the rest of the Hein family (my mother and brother) had no obligations,

THINGS MY MOTHER TAUGHT ME

being able to fully enjoy the service. My father spoke some words in German about my chosen theme, "Faith, Hope, and Love" from 1 Corinthians 13:13 and conducted our vows. Reverend Jacob Quiring, our senior minister, presented the message and prayed with us. This way, we received doubled blessings. A choir and orchestra contributed much to make our wedding ceremony a special memorable event for many (see program below).

The marriage of
Wilfried Hein and Hedwig Sawatzky
Bakerview Mennonite Brethren Church
Clearbrook, B.C.
Saturday, May 30, 1970
3:00 P.M.

"This is the Lord's doing; it is marvellous in our eyes. This is the day which the Lord hath made, we will rejoice and be glad in it."
Psalm 118:23, 24

PROGRAM

Prelude
Processional — "Largo" — Haendel
Giving away of the Bride
Choir: "O Rejoice Ye Christians Loudly" — Bach
Message: Rev. Quiring
Choir and Duet: "Von Deiner Guet' " — Haydn
Vows: Rev. Hein
Choir: "O God Thou Faithful God" — Bach
Recessional: "Trumpet Tune in D" — Purcell
Postlude

Officiating Minister —	Rev. Gerhard Hein Monsheim, Germany
Assisting Minister —	Rev. J. Quiring Clearbrook, B.C.
Organist —	Mrs. Irene Schmor Vancouver, B.C.
Parents of Bride —	Mr. and Mrs. Jake Sawatzky Abbotsford, B.C.
Parents of Groom —	Rev. and Mrs. Gerhard Hein Monsheim, Germany

BRIDAL PARTY

Matron-of-Honour —	Mrs. Ingrid Suderman — sister of bride
Best Man —	Mr. Art Hein — cousin of groom
Ushers —	Mr. Helmut Sawatzky Mr. Ed Suderman Mr. Henry Suderman Mr. Abe Warkentin

Choir

Mrs. Hildegarde Baerg	Mr. Rudy Baerg
Mrs. Rita Thiessen	Mr. John Thiessen
Mrs. Helga Stobbe	Mr. Abe Olfert
Mrs. Linda Letkemen	Mr. Victor Friesen
Miss Rose Loewen	Mr. Henry Wiebe
Miss Lorraine Olauson	

Orchestra

Violins	Viola
Mr. Frank Dyck	Mr. John Klassen
Mrs. Nancy Dyck	Mr. Ernie Neufeld
Mr. Jim Thompson	
Miss Beverly Penner	Cello
Mr. Robert Martens	Miss Audrey Nodwell
Mr. Walter Suderman	Mr. Jake Olfert

Many of my bride's friends were qualified musicians, who were willing to sing in the choir and play in the orchestra. My mother commented: "It was a delight and joy to listen to this beautiful music, which contributed much to make your wedding a very special celebration." She added: "I believe that I have never experienced such a beautiful wedding celebration".

In German:

> "Ich glaubte noch nie solch eine wunderschöne kirchliche Trauung erlebt zu haben"

Coming from a pastor's wife who attended many other weddings, it was quite a compliment to us.

Wilf and Hedy Hein, the newly married couple in May 1970.

THINGS MY MOTHER TAUGHT ME

In her letter, my mother described my bride as "schlank und rank" (slim and trim). Admiring her long white dress with a cotton lace and the beautiful veil, she commented: "You can be thankful and proud of your loved one!" (In German: "Du kannst dankbar und stolz auf Deine Geliebte sein!")

Wilf, who never had any sisters, gained four beautiful sisters-in-law. What a treat!

After the reception at church, the gift-opening took place on the deck of Hedy's parents' farm in beautiful sunshine. Among the cards and congratulations were also letters from my aunts Lene and Hanni in Russia, who sent some spiritual poems and many good wishes for our future as well. Our hearts were full of joy and thanksgiving, and we appreciated the many good wishes. My father had composed the following poem, which we sang together to the melody of one my favourite children's songs.

Verse	In German	In English
1.	Die Hedy kommt aus Kanada, Ein weites, fernes Land. Der Wiwi aus der deutschen Pfalz Dort drüben kaum bekannt *Refrain: Die Hedy-der Wiwi,* *Was das wohl werden mag?*	Hedy comes from Canada A great and faraway country "Wiwi" from the German "Pfalz" Is hardly known abroad *Refrain: Hedy . . . [and] "Wiwi"* *How will this turn out?*
2.	Die Hedy will Europa sehen, Zieht über Land und Meer Der Wiwi sieht sie vor sich stehen Will keine andre mehr *Refrain: Die Hedy-der Wiwi. . . .*	Hedy wants to see Europe Travels across the ocean and several countries Wiwi sees her stand before him And desires no one else *Refrain: (like above)*
3.	Die Hedy, ein fein's Maegdelein So schlank und rank und zart Der Wiwi hat sein' Freude dran Selbst sportlich und behaart! *Refrain*	Hedy is a fine girl Slim, trim and delicate To the joy of Wiwi sporty and full of hair! *Refrain*
4.	Die Hedy singt und musiziert Das klingt so rein und fein Der Wilfried hört mit Freude zu, Stimmt gern wohl auch mal an. *Refrain*	Hedy sings and makes music That sounds so clear and fine Wilfried listens with [much] joy And often sings along *Refrain*
5.	Die Hedy lehrt und dirigiert Die Schüler folgen still Der Wilfried Ärzte informiert auch er weiß was er will *Refrain*	Hedy teaches and directs [the choir] [her] students follow quietly Wilfried informs the doctors He also knows what he wants *Refrain*
6.	Die Hedy merkt's dem Wilfried an: Dem Mann kann ich trauen Der Wilfried weiß es ganz genau: Auf Hedy kann ich bauen. *Refrain: Ja Hedy, ja Wiwi,* *Wie schön das werden mag!*	Hedy senses of Wilfried This is a man I can trust Wilfried knows for sure Hedy's the one I can build my future upon *Refrain: Yes Hedy, yes Wiwi* *How beautiful that will be!*

THINGS MY MOTHER TAUGHT ME

Newspaper Announcement in Abbotsford News

Parents attend from Germany

Rev. and Mrs. Gerhard Hein came from Monsheim, West Germany, to be present for their son's wedding. Afternoon nuptials on May 30 united in marriage Hedwig Helen Sawatzky, daughter of Mr. and Mrs. Jake Sawatzky of 1327 Clearbrook road, and Wilfried Hein.

Double ring ceremony was performed in the Bakerview Mennonite Brethren Church by Rev. Gerhard Hein for his son and bride. Organist was Mrs. Paul Schmor.

Given in marriage by her father, the bride chose a full length white crepe wedding gown, with train, and fashioned with a cowl collar and long sleeves. Lace adorned the cuffs of the sleeves, the bodice, and in a front panel down the skirt. Floral headpiece held the bouffant shoulder length veil and the bride carried a cascading bouquet of deep red Forever Yours roses, accented with white stephanotis and white feathered carnations.

Mrs. Ed Suderman was the only attendant for her sister and she wore a pink organza gown with a bodice of lace daisies. She wore a lace daisy headpiece and her cascading bouquet was of white chrysanthemums and pink sweetheart rosebuds centered with a line of white daisies.

Art Hein was best man and ushering the guests were Ed Suderman, Helmut Sawatzky and Henry Suderman.

Ed Suderman was master of ceremonies at the reception which was held in the basement of the church. Prayer was given by the father of the bride. Mr. and Mrs. Abe Neufeld served the head table guests.

Rose Loewen was in charge of the guest book.

Out of town guests present for the wedding, besides the parents of the groom from Germany, included Eckart Hein, brother of the groom of Dortmund, Germany; Mrs. Ronald Thiessen, sister of the bride, of Winnipeg, and Erika Wiebe of St. Catharines, Ontario.

Following a wedding trip to Hawaii, the young couple will be making their home at 319-1016 Howie avenue, Coquitlam.

Mr. and Mrs. Wilfried Hein (nee Hedwig Helen Sawatzky)   (Clearbrook Photo Studio)

Honeymoon in Hawaii

We had our airplane tickets and were at the boarding gate but almost didn't make it. I had the Canadian immigration papers but did not realize that I needed a US visa to fly to Hawaii. My bride had tears in her eyes already, thinking that our honeymoon would have to be canceled. Fortunately, one of Hedy's university friends worked at the counter and was able to get an approval for us.

After one week in Honolulu, we spent the second week of our honeymoon in this hut at Maui Lou Resort in Maui. June 1970.

Returning home from our honeymoon, we were welcomed at the airport by relatives and friends holding up a big banner, saying, "Willkommen Herr und Frau Hein." Our nice apartment in Coquitlam that we had furnished before our wedding was now waiting for us. Before my parents returned to Germany, my mother gave me the following letter (dated June 24, 1970):

My Mother's Departing Words
    We will return to Germany in a few hours. Our four weeks of vacation in Canada have come to an end. We still could experience your return from your Hawaiian honeymoon. The last five days were especially meaningful and beautiful for us. You invited us several times to your lovely new home. Through this, we got to know, love and appreciate Hedy, our dear daughter-in-law even more. Our excursion with you yesterday was a wonderful "finale" to our Canada visit. We

admired the picturesque surroundings of your new homeland, the magnificent mountains, the beautiful lakes, forests, meadows with the great blue sky which spans the continents and our lives.

We leave with much gratitude in our hearts. Thank you for all your love. I will now pass on to you, my dear son, the two journals I kept, documenting your life, the first of which I started shortly after you were born. Maybe you will enjoy reading through them as they bring back childhood memories and experiences up to this very day.

My desire and prayer for you is that our heavenly Father may grant a rich fulfilled life and that your love and trust relationship will grow towards each other. May you experience God's richest blessings. When difficult times arise in your lives, please don't lose hope, but rather keep on relying on God's wonderful promises. May you also learn and practice carrying each other's burdens (Gal 6:2). I would like to conclude this departing letter with the following two Bible verses:

> *"Delight yourself in the Lord and he will give you desires of your heart"* (Ps 37:4) and
> *"Commit to the Lord whatever you do, and your plans will succeed"* (Prov 16:3).

With much love to my dear good son!

Your Mutti.

*****

Motherly Marital Advice

After my parents' return to Germany, my loving mother passed on some good marital advice:

It is so good that we have seen the place where you live with your loving wife, since we likely will not meet again for a long time. Maybe we will never see you again, we don't know. But our wishes are that you may experience much joy and happiness in your new home. May your lives be filled with much love and understanding towards each other. As you live together and get to know each other better, there—no doubt—will be times of misunderstandings or some difficulties. Please make sure that you forgive each other quickly, and don't let anger take a hold of you. Remember, happiness involves two people that can forgive each other. Look in each other's eyes the way you did, when you first met and loved each other. Assist each other, and remain united. Please think of us, your parents sometimes as well. Even though we are far away from you, our love will always remain with you. We know that God loves you and we commit you to his divine grace, guidance and protection. Our thoughts and prayers will always be with you. Our heavenly father indeed has blessed us abundantly in the past. Our inner bond of love will always remain!

Your Mutti!

Reflections

Now, as I write these memoirs forty-seven years later, I see more clearly God's wonderful guidance in my life and his answer to prayers. When reflecting upon finding the right girl for my life, the wise words of King Solomon come to my mind:

THINGS MY MOTHER TAUGHT ME

"Who can find a virtuous and capable wife? She is more precious than rubies" (Prov 31:10, NLT).

In retrospect, I would like to express thanks to my parents-in-law for accepting me, a foreigner from Germany, like their own son, into their home.

Hedy's parents Jacob and Tina Sawatzky (picture taken in 1984).[3]

---

[3] For more about Jake and Tina Sawatzky, see chapter 15 and appendix.

CHAPTER 5

Drawing Nearer to God (1970–1975)

My experience of finding the right life partner in such a miraculous way strengthened my faith in God tremendously. In addition, finding a vibrant church community that I could call my spiritual home helped me to grow spiritually. While living in Germany and having attended many church services, I was always looking for something more. I was looking and searching for a certain dimension, which even I didn't know how to describe. God has led me to a place where I found what I was searching for. It was the Willingdon Mennonite Brethren (MB) Church in Burnaby that became my new spiritual home. Later, when we moved to Abbotsford, we joined the Bakerview Mennonite Brethren Church, where we also found the same warmness and receptivity. During my time at Willingdon Church, I helped along in the Boys Brigade program, sang in the choir, and was appointed the representative of the German periodical *Mennonitische Rundschau*. At Bakerview MB Church, I also became actively involved in teaching a Sunday school class to Laotian refugees, serving on the missions committee, and coordinating our parking lot security. Trying to analyze what it was that made the difference between churches in Germany and our new church in Canada, I now believe it was the active involvement of church members and their sincere commitment trying to live as Christians.

As new immigrant, I realized that I needed to improve my English, especially my technical and medical terminology, in order to become successful in my career within the pharmaceutical field. While Hedy found a teaching job, I went to Douglas College and UBC to further my education for the next four years.

Our first Christmas in our new apartment in Coquitlam in 1970. Hedy unwrapping a set of silverware, a gift from my parents.

A happy young married couple in their first apartment in Coquitlam, British Columbia, in 1971.

While I took a summer course (1971) at Douglas College, Hedy participated in a music camp sponsored by Jeunesse Musicales held at Shawnigan Lake School on Vancouver Island, where she took courses taught by well-known violinist Ruggiero Ricci. I visited her during weekends.

My sweetheart in Victoria, summer 1971

After I sent this picture to my parents, my **mother wrote**: "Wilfried, you indeed have chosen a precious treasure!"
In German:
"Wilfried Du hast Dir aber auch einen kostbaren Schatz ausgesucht!"

Mother's Teachings on Encouragement

"We are so happy that Hedy loves classical music so much. Good music enriches one's life tremendously. I will never forget the moment when Hedy and you picked us up at the airport in Vancouver before your wedding, and when I saw Hedy at your side with her sparkling eyes, radiating so much inner beauty. Make sure, you pass on this same happiness to your loved one as well. The choice of the right partner is of such immense importance, because of the great influence a couple has upon each other."

She concluded her letter with the following poem and wise saying:

In German	Approximate English meaning
Du Vater, du rate, lenke und wende, Herr, Dir in die Hände sei Anfang und Ende sei alles gelegt. Eduard Mörike (German Poet and Pastor 1804–1875)	Father [in heaven], advise, steer and direct Lord, into your hands I commit the beginning and end and everything else
Sei Deines Willens Herr Und Deines Gewissens Knecht M.v. Ebner-Eschenbach	Be master of your mind and a servant to your conscience

In the year after my immigration, we were already fortunate to be able to celebrate Christmas together with my parents in Germany.

Christmas 1971 with Wilf's parents in Germany

Miracle 6: Passing the Calculus Course (1972)

Mathematics and especially calculus was my weak spot. It was one of the required courses for acceptance into the school of pharmacy at UBC. Wanting to know at the end of the semester whether I had passed it or not, I phoned my professor to ask him about it. He said, "Sorry you didn't pass it." I mentioned to him that I was planning to repeat it since I needed it for entering the science program at university.

When I picked up my record a day later, I could not believe what I read. I saw a "P" for pass and wondered, *Was this a printing mistake?* But I accepted it graciously. Since I had received quite a good mark in the first part of this course, it had averaged out just enough to be accepted at UBC. To me, it was a miracle.

Enthusiastic for the Lord

In summer 1972, I had the opportunity to join a group of young people from Willingdon Church to attend the *Explo 72* evangelistic conference in Dallas, Texas. This event was sponsored by Campus Crusade for Christ. Among the main speakers were Billy Graham and Bill Bright. Most of the participants were young high school or college students. It is hard to describe the impact thousands of young enthusiastic people can have upon a participant. One needed to be there. Never in my life had I been set on fire for the Lord, as I was during this event.

The Cotton Bowl Stadium in Dallas Texas during the Explo 72 conference held on June 12–17, 1972. An estimated eighty thousand young people coming from seventy-five countries participated in this great evangelistic event.

One evening after our meeting, one of the young people told me that he witnessed of what Christ meant to him to three people. All three of them accepted Christ as their Lord and Saviour. I was sorry that I couldn't tell him a similar story but was determined that I would give it a try. I went to my hotel room and prayed that God would help me say the right words to the right person. As I walked along the street, I saw a bar with the inscription "Where food is good and girls are better". Immediately I thought, *This probably is an environment in crucial need of some mission outreach.* At the street corner, I saw a man, perhaps fifty years old, walking toward me. I asked him: "Have you heard of the *four spiritual laws?*" His name was Vernon. He invited me to come into the bar with him and talk about it.

At the conference, we were given some small *Four Spiritual Law* booklets that explain in easy-to-understand language how one can become a Christian. At the conference, they encouraged us to talk to some nonbelievers about it and share the gospel with them. But

I had given all my booklets away to a black person who also wanted some copies for his friends. Fortunately, Vernon had received a copy of the *Four Spiritual Laws* from another conference participant the same morning. Vernon showed me the illustration that represents his life and told me the desired circle he would like to be in. It was the diagram, where Jesus Christ is the center of one's life. Now I decided to do something, which I never would have had the courage to do before. I prayed with him, sitting with him at the bar counter at 1:00 a.m., asking Jesus to enter his heart. After we had prayed, Vernon took a piece of paper and a pen, dated it, and wrote down four points:

1. You are what you feed your mind.
2. Read Galatians 5:14 twenty times so that you understand it. (This passage says:
    "*Love your neighbour as yourself.*")
3. Pray to receive wisdom from Jesus Christ.
4. Write to your mother.

Suddenly his facial expression changed, and his eyes that had looked so sad and dull before lit up and radiated joy. A little while later, they became red and started twitching. I asked, "What happened?"

"Don't worry, I had a heart attack last Sunday, the same thing happened to me before. Yesterday I was released from hospital," he replied.

Since it was already early in the morning, he intended to hang out and then go directly to his early morning shift. However, I phoned a taxi for him. Two of the cab drivers did not want to take him since they thought he was drunk. I explained to the third driver that it was his health condition and that he was not drunk. He took him home, and Vernon waved good-bye with a thankful and joyful expression in his eyes.

This was just one example of the great spiritual movement that swept through that city. We could see many young people sharing the gospel and praying with nonbelievers in city parks, on street corners, or other places in Dallas.

In an article about this experience that was published in the German journal *Mennonitische Rundschau*, I summarized my impressions of this conference with the three sentences:

- It was through God's love that we gain forgiveness of our sins.
- We need to have faith in God and accept him not only as our Saviour but also as our Lord.
- Believers need to be enthusiastic and encourage each other to be witnesses for Christ.[1]

Two Months in Europe (1973)

Being independent with no children as yet, we wanted to do some more traveling. My father had retired from his ministry as a Mennonite pastor in Monsheim, and we planned to be part of his farewell ceremony and help my parents with their move to a new retirement home in Bad Bergzabern.

Representatives from across Germany came to attend my father's farewell service on July 1, 1973, to honour him for his contributions as pastor, editor, and historian. Among the speakers expressing words of recognition were delegates of the Lutheran Church (Evangelische Kirche) and the local mayor. A choir from the neighbouring community sang, and my wife Hedy played a violin solo. (More about this event can be found in my book *A Witness*, pp. 157 and 253.)

We noticed some reasonable flights to Bulgaria advertised in the newspaper and decided to spend a two-week holiday in Varna, a resort city on the Black Sea.

---

[1] *Mennonitische Rundschau*, July 12, 1972, 95. Jahrgang, Nummer 28, 9; heading "Explo '72."

Wilf and Hedy peddling on the Black Sea in Varna, Bulgaria, summer 1973. From here, we booked a tour to Bulgaria's capital, Sofia, and a cruise to Istanbul, Turkey.

My parents' friends had an old Mercedes parked in their barn, which they no longer used. They gave it a tune-up and let us use it for a roundtrip to Switzerland, Italy (Milan, Venice, Florence, Rome, and the Italian Riviera), Monaco, France (Paris), and Holland (Amsterdam). There we picked up my wife's parents to show them some beautiful parts of Germany.

The Leaning Tower of Pisa, Italy, summer 1973.

Kaiser Wilhelm Gedächtnis Kirche, in Berlin.

We of course also visited some of our friends, relatives, and my parents in Bad Bergzabern.

My Parents: An Example of Staying Active and Remaining Thankful

After our visit, my mother wrote:
> "We are so thankful and happy to be able to spend our old age in this lovely place (Bad Bergzabern) with its beautiful surroundings. We enjoy our regular walks through the forest and city park ("Kurpark") admiring God's wonderful creation. Our usual one-hour walks are very energizing.

Part of the beautiful Kurpark in Bad Bergzabern
my parents enjoyed so much.

Some of our favourite activities are playing scrabble, reading a book, and singing together. Life is never boring for us. We've never regretted our decision to come to this ideal place" (from 1973–1974 correspondence).

The activity levels of my parents in their retirement years impressed me very much. They occasionally attended lectures, slide presentations, concerts, or theater performances. They were involved in Bible studies and took part in ecumenical meetings. They also resumed their English lessons by listening to lectures on tape, together with another couple (fall 1974). They invited friends to their home and visited neighbours, friends, and the sick in hospitals and care homes.

My mother continued:

> "We want to be sensitive to people who need help.... When we act upon small things in life, we sometimes can experience bigger things .... We would like to get more and more involved in counseling and listening to the burdens others have to carry, while we keep our own inner peace and gratitude. It is important to practice love, care and compassion towards others. We want to be a blessing to others. This is our God given task! Albert Schweitzer said something like this: 'We must all participate in the grief and sorrows of this world. When we do this, then we will be doing the will of Christ.'"

My father wrote:

> "Besides singing in a choir in the local Lutheran church and some occasional preaching, I am teaching Russian in a local high school. A gentleman from the German army recently contacted me. He wants me to teach some of his officers and soldiers the Russian language. I enjoy teaching them, not only to earn some extra income, but also to make some new contacts, which may enrich our lives. Often conversations arise about different worldviews, faith and spiritual matters. Recently we talked about the Russian poet Solzhenitsyn. We always start our lessons with prayer."

My father also started teaching religion for one hour in a school for children with special needs (Sonder Schule), reading Bible stories and singing songs with them. Another activity that kept him busy was trying to help his relatives from Russia emigrate to Germany. It took several applications and much paperwork before the Braun family was allowed to emigrate from Russia (from correspondence in 1974).

From University to the Workforce (1974)

My studies at UBC became increasingly more difficult, to the extent that they affected my health negatively. I was under great stress and experienced some nightmares and anxiety attacks. It became clear to me that I needed to withdraw from the pharmacy program. Lacking high school years and everything being taught in a language still foreign to me were probably the major reasons for the difficulties. I also found that the curricula requirements can sometimes hinder a student's ambitions.

My aunt Liesel Hege, who had served as a missionary nurse in the Tayu hospital in the Pati region of Java from 1950 to 1968 and who later lived at the Thomashof retreat center near Karlsruhe, was one of my aunts who faithfully prayed for me.[2] When she heard about the difficulties I faced at university, she wrote me:

"Even though we may not understand certain difficult situations we face in our lives, God's blessings are [often] wrapped up deep within them."

In German:
"In allen unverständlichen Führungen unsres Lebens ist tief drinnen der Segen Gottes eingewickelt."

Both my mother and my father wrote me a letter. Without knowing ahead of time what each one would write, they sent me the same encouraging verse for my thirty-fourth birthday.

---

[2] Testing Faith and Tradition, 278.

Parents' Advice When Facing Anxiety:

In German	Approximate meaning in English
Er ist ein Fels, ein sichrer Hort, und Wunder sollen schauen, die sich auf sein wahrhaftig' Wort verlassen und IHM trauen. Er hat's gesagt, und darauf wagt mein Herz ist froh und unverzagt und lässt sich gar nicht grauen.[3]	He is a rock, a secure refuge, and those who trust in Him and in his true word will experience miracles. He said it, and for this reason I dare to remain cheerful and fearless and will not yield to any anxiety.

These encouraging words helped me keep a positive outlook on life. Planning for our family, we bought our first small home in Coquitlam in September 1973.

Our first own home in Coquitlam (September 1973).

---

[3] Karl Johann Philipp Spitta (1801–1859), *Gesangbuch* (Ludwigshafen, Konferenz der Sueddeutschen Mennonitengemeinden e.V., 1972), Hymn 365, stanza 2.

To supplement our income, I started driving taxi. My mother wrote: "I am convinced that your taxi driving will be a blessing to many people." Having been encouraged by our church to be active witnesses to those who seek meaningful lives, I sometimes picked up customers who needed spiritual advice. Some of them welcomed being prayed for. I then stopped my taxicab and prayed with them.

In one instance, a customer asked me for a ride to the nearest priest. He told me that he had taken a drug overdose and wanted to end his life. I complied with his wish, found a priest not too far away, and accompanied him into his office. When the priest did not want to take him to the hospital, I volunteered to take him to emergency in my own car and helped get him checked in.

During my cab-driving time, I always kept my eyes open for a way to get my foot back into the pharmaceutical industry. Checking with Upjohn in Vancouver, I was offered some work in their warehouse. In fall, the same year, Canadian Hoechst offered me a position as technical service representative to promote their diagnostic tests (of the Behring subdivision) to hospital laboratories in Western Canada. This much-better paid position came at the right time, as we were looking forward to establishing a family.

Our First Child

Many people from Willingdon Church had prayed for us, especially since our first child was stillborn (April 1973). This birth, on August 29, 1974, was nothing but a miracle to me. Suddenly there was another person, an individual with his own will, equipped with everything, and everything functioning well. The family was complete, and our hearts were full of joy and thanksgiving. We named our son Jeremy, meaning "appointed by God," and his second name David means "beloved by God."

THINGS MY MOTHER TAUGHT ME

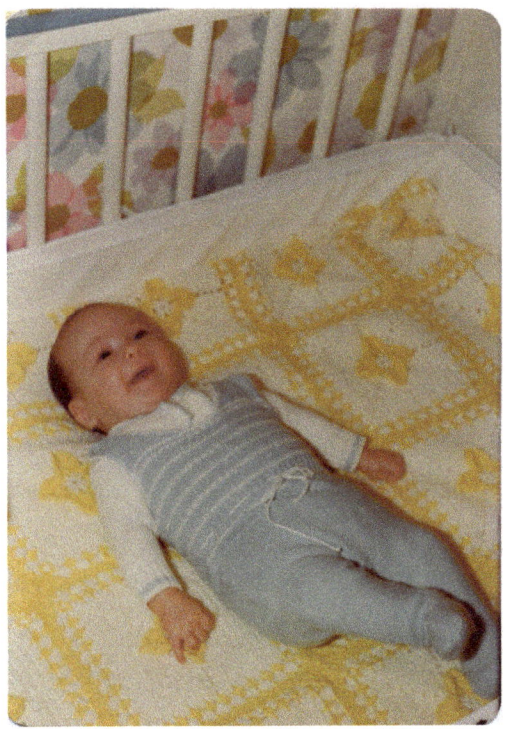

Jeremy, our first child, was born on August 29, 1974, on my mother's birthday.

When I sent the first pictures to my parents in Germany, my mother commented:

"He indeed is a lovely and cheerful child, despite being a real boy. Does your sweet little one thrive well?"

In German:

"Es ist wirklich ein liebes und sonnig-frohes Kindchen, dabei ein rechter Junge"… Gedeiht das süße Kleinchen weiterhin gut?"

My father added: "We admire, again and again, the great progress your 'wonderchild' (*Wunderkind*) is making. Children are a gift from God, who will bless all those who fear Him—small and great alike" (Ps 115:13).

Parents Visit (1975)

For some time, we had considered selling our home and perhaps moving to Abbotsford, where homes were less expensive and where Hedy's parents and other family members and relatives lived. When our Coquitlam home sold, we bought a new spec-house in Abbotsford, still under construction. We moved into our new home in spring 1975, and after having lived there for a few months, our son Jeremy developed breathing problems and allergies. We checked everything that could possibly trigger these symptoms, cleaning the window frames of any mold accumulation, vacuum cleaning often, and trying to keep our home dust-free as much as possible. One day I thought I should check the air ducts of our forced air heating system. They were full of construction dust. I could remove handfuls of dust by just reaching into it. After having the ducts cleaned professionally, our son's symptoms improved. I believe that our building contractor should have mentioned this to us in the beginning.

Our first new home on 32660 Geneva Avenue in Abbotsford, British Columbia.

We moved into it in March 1975.

Having extra space in our partially finished basement made it possible to accommodate my parents who came to visit us in the summer 1975.

A family trip to Victoria with my parents in Summer 1975.

Miracle 7: Meeting an "Angel"

One sunny day during my parents' visit, we took them for a ride to Vancouver. We were traveling along the freeway near Langley when I sensed a problem with the motor of my new company car. I slowed down and took the next freeway exit. I had barely stopped my car when a pickup truck coming from behind stopped right in front of us and a man got out. I hadn't even opened the hood of my car yet, nor had I said anything to this man, who said: "Your car needs oil." He grabbed a can of oil, the only item in the back of his truck, and poured it into my engine. When I wanted to pay him, he wouldn't accept anything. To this day, I can still see his radiant eyes in my mind as he left. My car started normally, and we continued our trip without any further incident. I then realized that I had forgotten to check my oil regularly and said to my parents: "This man was an angel to me. Maybe I can be an 'angel' to someone else some other time."

Miracle 8: A Flight Rescheduled

One of the major reasons my parents visited Clearbrook now was my father's involvement as speaker and coorganizer of a reunion of Mennonites coming from the Ufa region in Russia. About a week before my parents' return flight, my father received a note from the airline, telling him that their departure time from Vancouver had been rescheduled. Their plane was now going to leave a day earlier. This new time made it impossible for my father, as the initiator of this conference, to present his concluding talk. We prayed and sent telegrams to the airline, mentioning that this conference was the major reason my father had booked this flight with them and that he needed to be there to conclude the conference. We prayed, waited, and hoped for the best. After a few days, we received another notification, a new departure time, which now made it possible for my father to wrap up the conference and still have enough time to get to the airport. This new rescheduling meant that the airline had to inform all the passengers once more. Again, I regarded this occurrence as a miracle and an answer to our prayers.

During these days neither e-mails, nor Skype existed, but we kept my parents up-to-date with letters, pictures, audiotapes, and periodic phone calls. My mother always knew how to say some kind, encouraging words. I am including some examples.

My Mother's Ability to Encourage Others

In German:

> "Liebe Hedy, Du bist uns ja eine solche eine liebe Schwiegertochter. Wie gern geben Eltern ihren Sohn einer Frau, die ihm so liebend und helfend zur Seite steht."

In English:
> "Dear Hedy, you are such a dear daughter-in-law. We are so happy to give our son to a girl who surrounds him with so much love and supports him in his duties."

She continued: "We are fortunate and thankful that our children are so kind to us. Experiencing the love of our children in our old age, makes our lives beautiful. We are pleased that in this aspect we don't have any burdens to carry."

She concluded her letter with these words:

"Now, at our age [she was sixty-seven] we need to be prepared for the end of our lives. We need to be willing to follow Him. When the last call comes, it will only be one step over 'the threshold' that brings us to the Kingdom of Light. May the Lord be near to us, whether we live or die."

In German:
> "Es gilt jetzt, sich mehr denn je mit dem letzten zu befassen—bereit zu werden, wenn der letzte Ruf kommt, ihm auch gerne zu folgen, weil es ja nur ein Schritt über ‚die Schwelle' ist, die uns in ein neues Reich des Lichtes führt.—Wir wünschen uns allen fürs Leben und Sterben das Nahesein unsres Herrn!"

Wilf's comment: It turned out that my mother, who had been given up by doctors three times after each pregnancy, still lived twenty-two years after she wrote me the above-mentioned words. She even survived my father, reaching the blessed age of eighty-eight before our Lord called her home. To us, this also was a miracle.

CHAPTER 6

A Series of Miracles—Two Years in Germany (1976–1978)

Miracle 9: Finding Reliable Renters for Our Home

In spring 1976, I was working for Behring Diagnostics, responsible for introducing new diagnostic tests to major hospitals in the three Canadian western provinces. This meant often being away from my family. Without giving a reason, the company told me in April 1986 that I was no longer needed. Maybe my manager felt that I had difficulty managing such a large territory. We were planning to visit my parents in Germany and had already bought our airplane tickets with a charter company. Two years earlier, I had asked Hedy: "Would you be willing to move to Germany for perhaps two years so that my parents can get to know you and our grandchildren a bit better?" She immediately agreed with this idea. Now, I thought, was the right time for this adventure since I needed to find a new job, be it here or in Germany.

We advertised our place for rent, and one of the first people who came to our door was a teacher who, finding rents too high in Richmond, was looking for a furnished home in Abbotsford, which he with his family could rent for two years. This was exactly the time frame we were planning to stay in Germany. From the first moment on, we felt that this was a trustworthy person. We signed an agreement and left our home as it was, with all the furniture, including our piano. We kept our airline tickets and just did not use up the return flight portion. As we found out later, a one-way flight would have been even more expensive at that time. We departed as scheduled from Vancouver mid-May 1976.

Within four weeks, from the time I had lost my job to the time of our departure, we found some renters, who were willing to live at our place for two years, the period we planned to stay in Germany. We regarded all of this as God's wonderful provision. To us it was a miracle.

Miracle 10: Finding a Place to Live in Germany

Friends of my parents, living in the small community of Deutschhof only about four kilometers from my parents' place in Bad Bergzabern, had built a new home. They lived upstairs and planned to rent out their basement suite, which they had just finished furnishing. Everything was in it, including pots and pans, dishes, cutlery, and bedding, etc. When my mother inquired about it, they offered it to us for free, even though my mother wanted to pay the rent. We had known this family for many years. We felt like the biblical promise had come true for us: *"Before they call, I will answer"* (Isa 65:24).

Miracle 11: Finding a Job in Germany

The day after our arrival, the telephone rang, and a pharmaceutical company asked whether I could come for an interview. Unknown to me, my brother had contacted about a dozen different pharmaceutical companies, sending them a short resumé and asking whether they had an opening. The second company I applied to offered me a product manager position in Bielefeld in the northern part of Germany, which I could start six weeks after our arrival from Canada. I regarded this not as pure luck, as some would define it, but as God's wonderful direction in my life!

Miracle 12: Finding a Suitable Place Near My Work

My wife, who was expecting our second child, remained with little Jeremy at the place near my parents' home in Bad Bergzabern, while I shopped around for suitable accommodation for our family in Bielefeld, near my new workplace. All the condos I had seen were unfurnished. They didn't even contain any appliances, carpets, or curtains. Everything needed to be bought. But I could get some very good deals in estate sales. Most of the items could be transported in my recently acquired used station wagon. My aunt Liesel loaned me some money to cover all my initial expenses. When Hedy arrived two weeks later, the place was fully furnished with all the essentials being there.

A few weeks after I started my work, my boss asked me: "Mr. Hein, you had many expenditures with your move, please write down all your expenses, including carpet and curtains, and I will see what we can do for you." It turned out that the company helped pay for all my expenses. I never expected this.

Miracle 13: Difficulties Turned into Blessings

Since I had no working experience as a product manager, I found it somewhat difficult to fulfill the expectations at my new workplace. In addition, I had lived in Canada for six years and needed to again get used to the German ways of doing things. My boss approached me one day mentioning that it seemed unfortunate that things weren't working out as well as they had expected. I agreed with him and asked: "Do you have a position as pharmaceutical sales representative, perhaps in one of your subsidiaries, since this is my area of expertise?"

He phoned his affiliates who said to him: "We have started a training course and need one more man. Can he come tomorrow?" I packed up my material, had an interview in Biberach in South Germany, and was accepted. I knew that it was my heavenly Father, *Jehovah Jireh* in Hebrew, who provided for me again. While in Bielefeld, our second son Robert was born.

Miracle 14: All Expenses Paid for and Some Great Experiences

When I left the company in Bielefeld, they offered to pay me five months salary in advance. This was quite different from my previous job in Canada. When I was let go, no mention was made about any remuneration. I had worked for this company in Bielefeld for only five months, and they treated me so generously. At the same time, I received a second salary from the new company in South Germany. During the four-month training course, our group of young men lived in hotels paid for by the company. Wanting to bring my family to this place, I looked around for alternative accommodation and found a newspaper ad, saying: "Vacations on a farm" (i.e., "Ferien auf dem Bauernhof"). This place was a furnished apartment on a ranch, just outside the town of Biberach, and cost even less than our hotel. Explaining the situation to my boss, I asked whether it would be possible to bring my family from Bielefeld and live at this place instead of staying in a hotel. He gave me his approval. The renters in Bielefeld allowed us to store our furniture and belongings at their place until my course was finished. With the baby crib tied to the top of our Renault, we sailed down the "Autobahn" to romantic Biberach an der Riss. In less than six months, I had paid off all my debts and knew that this was more than luck. To me it was a miracle.

While living in Biberach not far from the Alps, we decided to explore the surrounding area. On one nice Sunday afternoon, we packed up the children and drove to Liechtenstein in the Alps for a coffee break. This sixth smallest country in the world borders Switzerland and Austria and was less than a two-hour drive from where we lived.

After completing the training course, we could select a territory we wished to work in. I chose the Rhine-Mosel area for calling on medical doctors to promote our pharmaceuticals. Searching for a place to live, I found a new condo that met our expectations in a quiet cul-de-sac in a suburb of Koblenz. A transport company agreed to pick up our furniture in Bielefeld without having to be there. We felt very much at home right from the beginning, possibly because we made new friends at a Baptist church in Koblenz who welcomed us warmly. During this time, we welcomed several visitors, among them Hedy's two Canadian uncles and aunts, Jake and Elsa Redekopp and George and Helene Neufeld, whom we took on some local excursions. While in Koblenz, Hedy taught three children violin through the provincial school system.

Our main purpose for moving to Germany was, of course, to be able to visit my parents more often. We even spent two holidays with them—one was a winter holiday in the Black Forest, near Neustadt, the other, a summer holiday together with my parents-in-law on the small Spanish island of Ibiza. Here our son Robert, who was born in Germany, risked taking his first steps.

During our time in Koblenz, we had another major family celebration. My brother, Eckart, married Helga Bassner in Dortmund on June 4, 1977. My father, Gerhard Hein, who married them, based his message on Psalm 36:6–10 and 1 Corinthians 13. Hedy played Beethoven's Romance in F as a violin solo with organ accompaniment. She and I also sang a duet by Gluck "Come O Thou Fount of Every Blessing" (in German, "Komm, O Du Quell des Ewgen Lebens.")

When Hedy's parents visited in the summer of 1977, we took them on a trip to Switzerland. To have enough space for all of us, we rented a white Volkswagen bus. As we traveled down the Autobahn, we were suddenly stopped by the police who marched around the van with their machine guns drawn. We wondered what was going on. We did not know that the police were looking nationwide for a white VW bus. At that time the Baader-Meinhoff gang, a terrorist organisation known for assassinations and kidnappings, were on the run in a white VW bus. When they saw a young smiling, though somewhat apprehensive, family with their old parents, they let us go without even checking our papers. With relief, we continued on our way.

We felt fortunate and blessed to be able to see quite a bit of Europe during these two years.

Jeremy and Robert building castles on the Spanish island of Ibiza. A day later, a severe thunderstorm wrecked the whole beach (1977).

Jeremy and Robert, our two sons, 1977

From left to right: My brother, Eckart, with his wife, Helga, my parents, Lydia and Gerhard Hein. Wilf, holding Robert, and my wife, Hedy, with Jeremy (Germany, 1977).

Miracle 15: Getting Rid of Our Stuff

Our tenants in Abbotsford sent us a letter, requesting to end the lease agreement a little sooner than anticipated. They wanted to move out in March, instead of May 1978. We agreed and started planning our move back to Canada. Placing an ad for a garage sale into the newspaper, we sold almost everything to the last item. This surprised me, since many Germans usually want new things and not old, used furniture and appliances. But during this time, many refugees and immigrant families were looking for used items. We got everything wrapped up in time and soon were on our return flight to beautiful British Columbia. Our hearts were full of thanksgiving to our Creator, whom we knew takes care of those who love Him.

Miracle 16: Finding a New Job in Canada

We arrived back home in Canada in March 1978. It was a time when the economy had a downturn and unemployment was relatively high. Not many companies were hiring new people. But shortly after we arrived, I noticed an ad in the newspaper calling for a pharmaceutical sales representative to which I applied. The manager interviewed me four times, then told me, "I have had sixty interviews, and now it is down to two, a pharmacist and you!" When I heard this, I was 90 percent sure that I would never get the job since I thought I could not measure up academically. The manager called me a few days later, saying, "The job is yours, and you can start next month." I was speechless.

Later my manager said he hired me because he thought I was more teachable and that I would stay with the company longer. I ended up working twenty-four years for this company until retirement. First it was Squibb Canada, which was later bought by Bristol-Myers, to become Bristol-Myers Squibb. During this time, I was privileged to have the best boss I had ever worked for, Vic Miller. I enjoyed my work and excelled in it.

Some skeptics might say all these experiences are pure coincidence. My response to them is that I see it differently. To me they are wonders and miracles provided by the One who blesses all those who put their trust in Him. The fact that God allowed me to experience his wonderful provision, strengthened my faith as I began my new job in Canada.

CHAPTER 7

Enjoying Work, Family, and Traveling (1978–82)

When my parents heard that I had landed a job within four weeks of our return, they were overjoyed and sent me some valuable advice. I am enclosing some excerpts.

Parental Advice on Work Attitude

My mother wrote:

"The school of life does not know any vacation. The **learning process continues**, and we hopefully keep on maturing. This holds true for young people, as it does for us in our old age" (from a letter in 1981).

Speaking about the same topic, my father expressed it in slightly different words:

"Your new job may also come along with some burdens and difficulties. Trials and tests never seem to end during our lifetime here on earth. We **need to keep on learning** until we are old and grey, and even then, the learning process continues. We are in *His* [God's] school which is a continuous learning process. We are certain that you and your family are under God's grace."

He continued:

"We have to prove ourselves, especially when we face difficult and imperfect situations. There will be a time when the imperfect will give way to perfection. Being aware of this can be a great consolation to us. Meanwhile, it remains important that we **keep on trying to do our best** no matter which situations we are facing. We are to tackle any problems head-on and are to do it with a happy and positive attitude. God has promised us *His* help and *He* will keep *His* word, as *He* has done in the past."

My father concluded his letter with the encouraging words of this poem:

Das Dunkel Muss Vergehn	*The Darkness Must Vanish*
Geh deinen Weg und zweifle nicht, der Herr wird mit dir gehen. Er ist in jeder Nacht *Dein* Licht Getrost, du wirst es sehen!	Go your way and do not doubt It is the LORD who will accompany you He will be your light during each night Be assured, you will see it!
Geh deinen Weg und klage nicht, das Dunkel muss vergehen. Bald wirst du, wenn der Tag anbricht, Im Glanz des Morgens stehen.	Go your way and do not complain, The darkness must disappear. Soon when the daylight dawns, You will stand in the splendor of the morning.
Geh deinen Weg und säume nicht, du sollst ihn fröhlich wagen! Und wenn es dir an Kraft gebricht, wird Gott dich liebend tragen.	Go your path and do not forget, Attempting to be cheerful! And should you lack the strength, Our loving God will carry you through it.
Geh deinen Weg und danke nur. Im Danken liegt der Segen. Am Ende deutet dir die Spur: Gott war auf allen Wegen! Albert Bartsch, Neukirchner Kalender, 19-3-1978	Go your way and remain thankful Blessings arise from being greatful. In the end, you will clearly recognize: That God was with you in all your ways Translated by Wilf Hein

I found that we all need some encouragement at different stages of our lives. Wondering which Bible verse I could pass on to my mother when she turned seventy, the following verse from Nehemiah 8:10 came to my mind: *"The joy of the Lord is your strength!"* My mother responded with these words:

"When you phoned and quoted this Bible verse, it meant very much to me and I would like to tell you why it was so meaningful to me. After you were born, I became severely ill for several months and had to stay in the hospital in Kaiserslautern. During this time, I was searching for spiritual strength and found it in this verse. It filled my heart with so much joy and gave me new strength, like I never experienced before. The fact that on my 70th birthday you mentioned the same words that became so meaningful to me thirty-eight years ago, is a special gift for me today. May these words equally fill your heart and enrich your life."

Our children also brought us much joy, and we were thankful to the Lord for our family. I am including some pictures.

Our two boys: Jeremy and Robert Christmas 1978

THINGS MY MOTHER TAUGHT ME

Our family Christmas in 1978

Motorhome trip with my parents to Lake Louise, Alberta (summer 1979).

Jeremy at age five painted his memories of our motorhome trip through the Canadian Rockies.

Adrian, seven months old, November 1979. My mother called him "Unser Wunderkind" (our wonder boy).

Jeremy's first school day, 1980

Miracle 17: Healed by Prayer (1979)

Our Sikh neighbour, who had injured his lower back in a sawmill accident, asked me one day whether I could take him along to a Christian healing service. I promised him I would do this next time I hear about such a service. One evening in 1979 I went to the Abbotsford Pentecostal church to hear Dr. Richard Eby speak on his near-death experience. He was an American gynecologist who shared his testimony of coming back to life, after having fallen from the third floor of an apartment building on to the concrete below. Apparently, his head was split open, and he had been declared dead. Just before hospital staff was going to take him to the morgue, the EEG (electroencephalogram) showed some signals that he was coming back to life again. Dr. Eby told the audience that God had allowed him to see heaven and hell and that he was given the task to tell people his story. At the end of his testimony, an announcement was made that a healing service would follow. I remembered the promise to my neighbour and drove home at about 9:30 at night. I knocked on his window and asked him to come along to a healing service. First Mrs.

Eby prayed over him, but nothing happened. We persisted. Then I asked Dr. Eby to pray for him. My neighbour told me that he felt something like an electric current rushing down his spine and that he no longer had any pain. A few months later, I met my neighbour in the park, and he said, "Ever since the healing service, I have been free of back pain problems and have been able to return to work."

*****

When our family traveled to **Germany** for **Christmas 1980,** we never thought we would come to two near-disasters. Sixteen years later, when my wife listened to a CBC radio classical music show, the commentator encouraged listeners to send in an interesting Christmas travel story, together with their favourite music request. My wife immediately thought of our 1980 Christmas experience. She submitted our story with her request (see below), and CBC aired it a few weeks later.

Miracle 18: Surviving Two Near Disasters (Christmas 1980)

A Christmas Travel Story That Nearly Ended in Two Disasters
Written by Hedy Hein on December 8, 1996

It was December 22, 1980, and our family was on the way to spend Christmas in Germany with my husband's family. We were strapped in our seats, our young sons fairly content, and my husband and I hoping the flight from Vancouver to Frankfurt would be congenial and not too strenuous for any of us. As we were cruising down the runway, picking up momentum, the plane inexplicably started slowing down. "What's going on?" we wondered as the plane turned on to an adjacent runway. We heard the engines being revved. Finally, the pilot spoke over the intercom and said that they had tested the engines separately two times, and everything checked out fine, and we would be on our way. Off we went to the main runway again. Then, as we gathered speed, just before takeoff, there was a sudden loud bang and a flash outside the window. We strained against the seatbelts as the plane braked furiously. Fortunately, the pilot could slow down the plane in time. What a scare! He then announced that there was a problem, and we would have to return to the terminal.

So there we were, back in the airport waiting lounge at 9:30 in the morning with three little boys ages six, four, and one and a half, wondering if we'd get to Germany for Christmas. The airline told us to report back at twelve noon. Just in case we'd have to wait longer, my husband went to the different airline counters to see if he could arrange another flight. No success! He telephoned his family to let them know we'd be later than anticipated. At lunchtime, the airline issued us food vouchers and told us the plane would be ready later in the evening.

My husband kept trying different airlines and finally got a flight for 7:00 p.m., but on stand-by. We thought we'd try it. We kept the kids entertained until it was time to go through the gate once more, this time at the other end of the terminal. While we were waiting there and boarding had already started, we heard the announcement that our original plane was ready and could be boarded at 7:00 p.m. Not wanting to risk not leaving that day, we decided to go back to the original flight, at the other end of the airport. What a race to get there in time! They delayed the plane for us, changed the tickets, and whisked us aboard. What a relief to finally be on board.

But that was not the end of the excitement. We were scheduled to stay overnight in a Toronto hotel where we arrived sometime after midnight. Early the next morning, we heard a small little voice yelling in German, "Feuer, Feuer" ("Fire, Fire"). It was our four-year-old. Ever the early riser, he discovered the matches in an ashtray and decided to experiment with a Kleenex tissue on the floor while the rest of us slept. My husband rolled out of bed in a flash, smothered the tiny fire with his hand (he was not burned), and sternly reprimanded the miscreant. That roused the rest of us. It was time to continue our trip. Without further mishap, we finally arrived in Germany, early on December 24, exactly 24 hours later than anticipated.

As we were reviewing the events of that trip, we realized that twice on the same trip, we were very close to disaster. We are very thankful that our Christmas celebration turned out well.

We believe our guardian angels were watching over us. My special request was to hear my favourite Vancouver soprano, Ingrid Suderman, sing "0 Divine Redeemer" from her new CD *Hear My Prayer*.

THINGS MY MOTHER TAUGHT ME

*****

Due to the delay of our plane, we arrived in Germany a day later than scheduled but still could celebrate Christmas Eve together with my parents.

Christmas 1980 in Germany

My parents called them "Goldkinder"

Even though my parents were beginning to experience some signs and symptoms of old age, they remained thankful and gracious, as the following extracts from their letters demonstrate:

My Mother's Observations about Old Age:

We are so thankful now in our old age that our two children care, love and support us.

Now Papa can't be as active as usual, but this shouldn't be necessary. **People deserve to enjoy life without having to achieve anything!** This is the privilege of old age. It seems that some people need to learn how to switch off, and step back, and be thankful for the remaining health the Lord has given them.

When Papa speaks of his sons, he often cries, because of love and thankfulness. Now at my age 74, I feel my limitations more and more and I realize that we need to be ready when the last call comes. I wish that the Lord's grace will be with us when this happens. **It is less important what we do, but much more important what we are!** It remains essential to be open to God's word and let him speak to our soul. We should forget about doing unnecessary things but rather utilize our time for letting God's word richly dwell in our heart and mind (from a letter in 1982).

THINGS MY MOTHER TAUGHT ME

Hein family in Germany, 1980

Expressing her gratitude, my mother concluded her letter with the following poem defining GRACE.

In German:	In English
Gnade ist es frei von manchen Dingen zu werden, Eine große Gnade ist es, wenn ein Menschenkind von der rechten Liebe erfüllt ist, die das sucht, was des Andern ist—nicht sich selbst. Author unknown	**Grace** is to gain freedom from some things [that might restrain us] Greater grace exists, when a human being is filled with godly love, A **love** that seeks to please others—and not oneself.

On my fortieth birthday, my **mother** encouraged me to keep my **FAITH** with these words:

In German	In English
Und auch im neuen Jahreslauf Schlägt Gott Dir seine Türen auf An jedem Tag aufs Neue. So tritt ins Tor, ins neue Jahr Und **glaub!** Gott führt Dich wunderbar Gelobt sei Seine Treue. (Albert Bartsch)	In your new year of life God will open his doors for you [He will do this] every day anew. March on through the gate into the new year And **have faith**! God will direct you in a wonderful way Praise him for his faithfulness.

My **father** included a prayer that also speaks about **trust and submission**.

In German	In English
Du Vater, Du rate, Du lenke und wende, Herr, Dir in die Hände, sei Anfang und Ende, sei alles gelegt!" Eduard Mörike (1804–1875)	[Dear heavenly] father, [please] advise, and direct [the events of my life] Lord into your hands I commit the beginning and the end [of my life] and everything else!

My mother sent me the following ***Seven Choices for Each Morning*** which I would like to include since I found them worthy of contemplation.[1]

---

[1] *Sieben Angebote für Jeden Morgen* was published in a monthly newsletter of the Obersuelzen community.

THINGS MY MOTHER TAUGHT ME

In German: Sieben Angebote für jeden Morgen	In English: Seven Choices for Each Morning
Du kannst den neuen Tag in der Furcht Gottes beginnen— Und Du wirst Deine Angst vor den Menschen verlieren.	**You can** start the new day in the fear of the Lord— and you will lose your fear of people
Du kannst Deine Schwierigkeiten und die schwierigen Menschen in Deiner Umgebung heute in Dein Gebet einschließen— Und Du wirst ihnen offener begegnen können als gestern.	**You can** pray today for the problems and difficulties when dealing with people— and you will be able to be more open and communicate better with them than yesterday.
Du kannst Dich heute unter die Vergebung Jesus Christi stellen— Und Du wirst nicht bei jedem Fehler verzagen, der Dir oder andern passiert.	**You can** submit your life today to Christ who forgives you— and you will be able to better cope with the mistakes you or others commit.
Du kannst die Probleme dieses Tages von Gott her sehen zu lernen— und Du wirst ihre Lösung gelassener entscheiden oder auch abwarten können.	**You can** learn to see today's problems from God's perspective— and He will help you to make the right decision or find a solution be it now or later.
Du kannst Deine Fähigkeiten als Gaben Gottes annehmen— Und Deine Minderwertigkeitsgefühle werden allmählich aufhören.	**You can** accept your talents as a gift from God— and your inferiority feelings will gradually cease.
Du kannst Deinen Nächsten Gott anvertrauen— Und Du wirst ein Augenmaß dafür bekommen, was er wirklich braucht.	**You can** entrust your neighbor and fellow human beings into the Lord's hands— and you will be able to discern their true needs.
Du kannst Dein ganzes Leben in Gottes Hand legen— Und Deine Tage werden aufstrahlen im Morgenglanz der Ewigkeit. (by D. Schneider)	**You can** commit your whole life into the Lord's hands— and your days will radiate the glory of eternity.

During the 1980s, it was not yet possible to communicate with my parents via e-mails, texts, or Twitter messages. But we phoned them periodically and sent them pictures of our family, our vacations, and special events. I am including a few.

Wilf with his three boys enjoying God's beautiful nature in Victoria, spring 1980.

Robert, 1981

THINGS MY MOTHER TAUGHT ME

Adrian loves driving his tractor, 1981.

Vacations

Family Camp vacation in Cannon Beach, Oregon, summer 1981.

Jeremy feeding deer on campground in Washington, summer 1981.

In spring 1982, my wife and I were asked to participate with a group of musicians who sang in various Mennonite churches in Austria, Switzerland, and Germany and at the Mennonite Brethren European Conference in Vienna. Music instructor and choir director Rudy Baerg had selected a group of fourteen people and arranged the program in conjunction with pastor J. J. Toews from Neuwied, Germany. Our choir sang in various Mennonite churches including the churches of the German-speaking Mennonites from Russia, who through the help of the German government had recently settled in Germany, the so-called "Umsiedlergemeinden." I was asked to read some suitable Scripture verses in German.

Wilf and Hedy in **Vienna, Austria,** at Schloss Schoenbrunn, May 30, 1982—their twelfth wedding anniversary.

Hedy on "Klein Scheideck" mountain in Switzerland, located about eighty kilometers southeast of Bern (June 1982).

Some Special Events (1982)

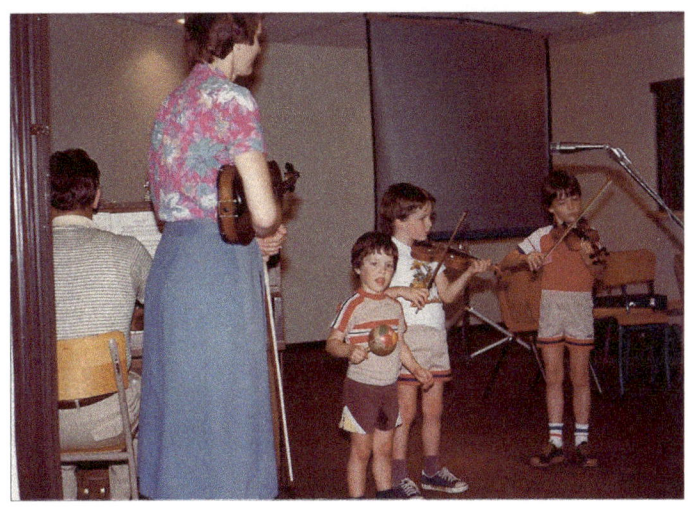

Our family performing at the Wiebe Reunion Trinity Western University in Langley, July 1982.

Hedy with her four sisters and her mother singing during Herta Thiessen's twenty-fifth wedding anniversary in Edmonton in August 1982. From left to right: Erica Suderman, Alice Willms, mother Katharina Sawatzky, Hedy Hein, Herta Thiessen, and Ingrid Suderman.

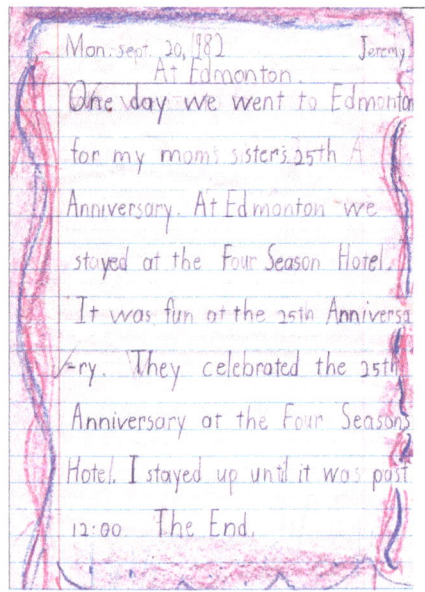

Jeremy, age eight, who accompanied his mother and grandparents on the trip to Edmonton wrote this travel report (September 1982).

A happy family: Wilf and Hedy with their three boys (1982).

Company Trip to a Warmer Climate (1982)

The year 1982 started out well for us since we were blessed having been invited by my company to travel to Jamaica. It was an all-inclusive award trip that included our wives.

Off to Jamaica, January 1982

Vic Miller, my highly appreciated regional
manager, with us in Jamaica, 1982

CHAPTER 8

Success in Career (1983–1986)

At the National Conference in Winnipeg in January 1984, the president of Squibb Pharmaceuticals Canada announced me as the national representative of the year. This is the highest award a representative in pharmaceutical sales could obtain. It included a first-class flight and a "red carpet" weekend for my wife and me in Montreal, plus a cheque. Also included was a portrait taken by Montreal's leading photographer and a letter the company sent to all physicians and pharmacies in my territory announcing this award.

Jacques Boisvert, the president of Squibb Canada, congratulating Wilf as the **National Sales Representative of the Year 1983** at the National Conference in Winnipeg.

Wilf Hein expressing words of thanks during a National Meeting in Winnipeg in January 1984.

Miracle 19: Winning Top Award (1983 and 1984)

Never would I have dreamt that a grade 8 high school dropout without a university degree would receive the highest award in the pharmaceutical industry in Canada twice in a row and be chosen five times as regional representative of the year. All my colleagues had university degrees. It showed me that a university degree is not always necessary to have success in life.

However, being eager to further my *education*, I have taken many courses in my area of interest, which when added up exceed the years of obtaining a university degree. Especially helpful to me were correspondence courses taken through Briercrest Distance Learning, which allowed me to study at my own pace. I have included my alternate educational background in the appendix for those who are interested. Unfortunately, most of these courses are not accredited by universities or colleges.

When I was chosen the national representative of the year, probably the only one without a university degree among at least sixty colleagues, it was a miracle to me, and I thanked God for it. My company sent the following award letter to more than five hundred physicians and all the pharmacies in my Lower Mainland territory.

Contributing Factors to Success

Some people may be wondering what contributed to this success. I must say that I enjoyed my work tremendously, especially the organizing of symposia, planning and executing telephone conferences, and showing video films to groups of doctors in my territory. Usually I asked a specialist, such as a cardiologist, to speak to a group of doctors about a specific topic of interest. The speakers generally were neutral and objective in the evaluation of the various treatment options and did not shy away from also saying negative things about the product I represented. But the audience knew who was sponsoring this meeting. When I arranged symposia in my hometown in Abbotsford, I sometimes asked my wife, Hedy, to play her violin during dessert time. On some other occasions, she brought along our three children, who accompanied her with their violins. One of my doctors said, "Wilf is the only 'rep' who brings some culture into our meetings."

The telephone conferences worked out well, because physicians from my territory could ask specialists specific questions. In one case, I coordinated a telephone conference in three different towns, all at the same time. When my national sales manager found out about this, he called me and said, "Wilf, please send us a tape in which you explain everything in detail as to how you arrange these conferences. Let us also know all the 'pros and cons.'" When I sent him the audiotape, he made copies of it and sent it to all our seven regions in the country. All the representatives across the country had to listen to it.

Award Weekend in Montreal

My wife and I were invited to fly first-class to Montreal for an all-inclusive weekend. Having arrived in our top-notch hotel, we were welcomed with a bottle of champagne and beautiful flowers in our room. A horse and buggy ride through Old Montreal had been arranged for the afternoon. Sitting next to the president during dinner, I enjoyed the best filet mignon I believe I have ever eaten. After dinner, we were invited to attend a delightful entertainment show. The treatment couldn't have been better! An appointment had been arranged with Montreal's best award-winning photographer the following day.

THINGS MY MOTHER TAUGHT ME

The national sales representative award of the year 1983 included a 20" × 24" portrait taken by Montreal's award-winning photographer Laszlo.

When I received the same top award the following year as well, it was my wife's turn to get her portrait taken by Laszlo.

The cheque I had received during the award ceremony was sufficient to cover a two-week holiday to Hawaii including accommodation, food, and entertainment for our whole family.

Our boys enjoyed climbing a Banyan tree in Lahaina, Maui, 1984.

During our first week in Maui, we booked a trip with a tour company to the top of Mount Haleakala (the name means "House of the Sun"). After viewing the deep crater of the dormant volcano, we were given bicycles to bike down the three-thousand-meter-high mountain. Included in our Maui excursion was also a glass-bottom boat tour with a snorkeling experience for the whole family. We spent the following week in Honolulu, where our children enjoyed the zoo, the aquarium, the Polynesian center, and the waterslides. It became a memorable holiday, thanks to the generosity of my company.

This was not the only treat we received from our company. In February 1984, Squibb Pharmaceuticals celebrated its 125th anniversary. All representatives from across Canada were invited to come to Montreal for a national meeting. As usual, we heard many presentations and took part in training sessions. For the anniversary celebration, our company rented the Olympic Stadium in Montreal. Then the contests started, with each region representing a different country, competing against one another. Among the various contesting sports disciplines were water polo, bike races, canoeing, and ball games. The winning teams received their trophies. At the end of the celebration, each employee was given a gold coin embossed with the Squibb logo and the Olympic rings on it.

The 1980s were the best years I have ever experienced in the pharmaceutical industry. All employees appreciated the generosity of our company. We were motivated to work hard and to give our best. The German proverb "Ohne Fleiss, kein Preis," or the saying, "No pain, no gain" also applies at work. In 1983, our western region was chosen the "Region of the Year." The award was an all-inclusive weekend trip to Las Vegas (November 1984) and included our spouses.

In 1985, we were privileged to take part in another company trip, this time to Barbados, which again included our wives.

Lord Sam's Castle in Barbados, where the Squibb
National meeting was held, in January 1985.

During the company banquet, national sales manager, Ross Reid announced Wilf Hein as the national sales representative of the year 1984 (the second time in a row).

Family Life (1983–1986)

As it takes much work to be successful in ones' career, so it also takes work to have a happy and satisfying marriage and family life. We saw a ten-week course on "Creative Parenting," advertised in the newspaper, offered in Mission, British Columbia, and taught by a Christian psychologist. We signed up, not because we had big problems in our marriage or family, but because we wanted to learn more about improving our relationships. I realized that it is easy to become a father, but by far not as easy to be a good husband and father. In a letter written to my favourite aunt Lies, I wrote: "It is amazing to realize how much education is needed before one can succeed in professional life, and how little education one often receives in one of life's most important areas, being a good husband, wife and exemplary parents." This course gave us insight about the complexity in human relationships, values of life, and what our souls yearn after.

It also taught us how to best communicate with our children and equipped us with some problem-solving techniques. It was worth it.

After completing this course, I wrote to my parents: "I cannot wish for any better wife. We suit each other and are happy and thankful for our children and for the Lord's rich blessings." Below are a few more family pictures.

Hein family 1984.
My oldest son, Jeremy, accompanied me on my next trip to Germany.

Jeremy, nine years old (1983)

My brother, Eckart, invited us to a cruise on the Rhine River and accommodated us, at his own expense, in a beautiful hotel in the spa city of Bad Kreuznach, Germany (summer 1983).

Robert, seven years old (1983)

Adrian, four years old (1983)

Our children with their neighbourhood friends.
From Left to right: Barton Thiessen, Adrian, Becky Thiessen, and Jeremy.
Robert is in the center with a paper bag over his head, Halloween 1984.

We moved into our new home in June 1985. Electric heat (no forced
air heating system) markedly improved our oldest son's allergies.

WILFRIED HEIN

Adrian at age seven already showing his talent as a successful future stunt performer (1986).

Oma in Deutschland worried a bit about Adrian's stunt acts, but she wrote, "Adrian, I really miss playing checkers with you ("Mühle and Dame").

My Mother on "Shortcomings"

My mother wrote, "As we get older, it is important that we watch our behaviour and recognize our failures and shortcomings" (1982). The fact that my parents admitted to being far from perfect, despite their mature age, impressed me quite a bit.

My Father on Forgiveness

My father also admitted some inadequacies. This impressed me a lot since I realized that it must have taken quite a bit of humility for a well-educated and accomplished person to do this. My father wrote:

> It is so comforting to know that it is only through God's grace and mercy that we are accepted, be it in life or death. May our heavenly father grant

you and us his grace as we continue to serve him. It is important to be able to forgive each other so that we can live our lives in inner peace and keep on walking toward the goal [of perfection that we will reach in eternity]. When we fail, we don't need to despair, because the Lord's Spirit will help us in our weakness. My father concluded his letter with the words (in 1983):

And we know that in all things God works for the good of those who love him, who have been called according to his purpose. (Rom 8:26)

Health Setbacks

In May 1984, I received news that my father had suffered a stroke and was now in hospital. When I visited him that summer, I noticed that his skin was very dry and pale. Shopping around in health food stores and pharmacies, I asked for a naturally composed rejuvenating cream. After massaging my father's whole body with this expensive balm, he felt like a newborn baby and soon perked up. Since he started feeling so much better, my mother continued these applications after I was gone. She later wrote that this crème had excellent wound-healing properties. Before I said good-bye to my father, I asked him what word he would like to give along to me. He said: "Remain in *Him*—remain in love!" (in German: "Bleibe in der Nachfolge, bleibe in der Liebe").

Three Great Celebrations

We were so grateful that God granted my parents the health and strength to be able to fully enjoy three great celebrations within a relatively short sequence. They were my father's eightieth birthday, Christmas, and their golden wedding.

My Father's Eightieth Birthday—November 30, 1985

While my parents were contemplating how they could celebrate my father's eightieth birthday, a lay preacher friend from nearby Deutschhof came to visit them. He offered my parents the youth center at Deutschhof for the celebration, saying: "You can invite all your friends, and we will take care of everything else." My father wrote: "When I arrived, the room was beautifully decorated with flowers, and many guests from across our province had already arrived. Among them were delegates from Enkenbach, Monsheim and Obersuelzen (my father's former parishes). The Deutschhof trombone ensemble played, followed by a choir from Sembach, who sang a variation of Psalm 23. We had a great time singing together." After several speeches and some poems had been read, my father requested the following song:

In German	Approximate meaning in English
Ja, ich will euch tragen	Yes, I will carry you
bis zum Alter hin,	into your old age
und ihr sollt einst sagen,	and you shall proclaim
dass ich gnädig bin	that I [God] have been gracious.
(Jochen Klepper (1903–1942) [1]	

Christmas 1985—Family Trip to Germany

We wanted to be able to celebrate Christmas and my parents' golden wedding with our whole family. Our wish came true, thanks to the award money from my company and the generous help from my brother, Eckart, who provided me with a car during our stay in Germany. Hedy and our children took their instruments along, to contribute musically to the celebration. My wife prepared the turkey for Christmas dinner, and I read a Christmas poem. We sang and played together and enjoyed our time, creating good memories for all of us.

The Golden Wedding

My brother, Eckart, made all the preparations for my parents' fiftieth wedding anniversary. He booked a beautiful hotel in Bad

---

[1] From the German Gesangbuch # 460, v. 1 (Mennonite red hymnbook).

Bergzabern for Saturday, January 4, 1986, to which he invited about two dozen guests, mainly relatives and close friends.

My mother wrote:

> Both Eckart's and Wilfried's families contributed much to make this event an unforgettable and beautiful celebration for us. When we walked into the hotel meeting room, the guests were all standing, while champagne, coffee or juice were being served. This gave us an opportunity to meet, greet, and talk to the guests. The beautifully decorated tables were marked with namecards, welcoming twenty-five guests. Our four grandchildren were seated on a separate, smaller table and they had their own special children's menu. They all behaved well and enjoyed the meal. After their meal, they could play games. Wilfried opened the celebration, welcoming the guests and announcing the musical introduction performed by our dear daughter-in-law, with her three boys, eleven, nine and six years old. Hedy, Jeremy and Robert played their violins and our youngest grandson Adrian, sitting on a small chair, played his cello. They played pieces from Beethoven and Mozart, everything from memory. Then Eckart, our oldest son presented his Golden Wedding speech [excerpts of his speech can be found in my book *A Witness* ch. 8, p. 216 ff]. We especially appreciated that our son Eckart, who had so many other occupational responsibilities, took the time to plan this celebration so well. His words were spoken to our hearts and made us feel very thankful. Arnt Philipp, Eckart's son, presented a poem and then Wilfried gave a speech about the topic "Faith, Love and Hope."

He thanked us individually for passing on to him these spiritual values, emphasizing that our vertical relationship must first be right, before our horizontal relations can function properly. He quoted some Bible verses, illustrating his points in a hand-drawn chart, also including some humour. Other speeches from relatives and friends enriching our souls followed. We indeed felt honored. Eckart arranged for Papa to have an afternoon nap. Everything was planned into the smallest details. It was a wonderful atmosphere of harmony from the beginning to the end. Our boys wanted to make it special for us and they succeeded, bringing much joy and thankfulness into our hearts.

Hedy with our three boys and their cousin at my parents' golden wedding celebration in Bad Bergzabern, Germany (January 1986). From left to right: Robert, Jeremy, Arnt Philipp, and Adrian with his mom.

My mother kept on writing about this celebration:

> We will never forget this beautiful celebration and we don't take it for granted that we could celebrate our 50th Wedding Anniversary in such a wonderful way. We felt honored and regarded it as a gift from God. We are thankful to our Heavenly Creator and to our dear children. Without Eckart this celebration would never have taken place and without our Canadian children and grandchildren it would not have become the celebration we enjoyed so much. The contributions of our Arnt Philipp, and of Jeremy, 'Robbie' and 'Adrylein' who played beautiful music with their mother, and our Wilfried being a great organizer, all this enriched our hearts and made us very thankful.
>
> The following Sunday—on our official wedding day, we attended the church service in the Mennonite Church in Deutschhof, where we were honored as well. Our son Wilfried read a passage from Colossians 3, and added a few personal words. Our appreciated lay preacher Ernst Andres held the sermon. Then our daughter-in-law with her children played Handel's chorus from *Judas Maccabaeus* (in German: *Tochter Zion freue Dich*). After the service, our children came to our home for 1-2 hours. With this, our harmonious celebration came to an end. Within five weeks we celebrated three major events, Papa's birthday, Christmas and our Golden Wedding. Had it been all at once, then it would definitely have been too much for us.

Six months later, my mother writes: "Your two weeks visit last Christmas and in January was of immeasurable value to us. We are happy that the whole celebration turned out so beautifully and harmoniously.

In German:
> "Von unbezahltem Wert ist es uns, dass Ihr im Dezember/Januar die zwei Wochen hier wart und dass alles ganz schön und ungetrübt war."

Our Golden Wedding celebration was a milestone for all of us and remains in our memories for the last stretch of our lives. May our remaining days be illuminated by these beautiful memories."

My Mother on Coping with Old Age

"We are now old. May God give us the strength to endure and carry our burdens, and may he help us to remain thankful and courageous until the time comes when he calls us to his heavenly kingdom."

"Life rolls on for us! I think maybe Papa's heart is now a bit tired. It has served him well for eighty years."

In German:
> "Das Leben rollt weiter. Weißt Du, ich denke vielleicht ist das Herz jetzt müde. 80 lange Jahre hat es seinen guten Dienst getan."

My father adds: "Getting old is a learning experience which needs to be mastered."

*****

On the importance of *Keeping the Faith*, my mother wrote me this poem (1983):

In German:
> Wie Gott mich führt, so bleib ich treu im Glauben, Hoffen, Leiden.
> Steht er mit seiner Kraft mir bei, was will mich von ihm scheiden?
> Ich fasse in Geduld mich fest; was Gott mir widerfahren lässt muss mir zum Besten dienen.

Wie Gott mich führt, so will ich gehn, es geh durch Dorn und Hecken.
Sein Antlitz lässet Gott nicht sehn, zuletzt wird er's aufdecken,
Wie er nach seinem Vaters Rat mich treu und wohl geführet hat.
Dies' sei mein Glaubensanker.
(Composer: Lambert Gedicke (1683-1736)[2]

Approximate meaning in English

No matter which way God will lead me, I will remain **faithful** and hopeful in Him, even during times of suffering.
Nothing will be able to separate me from Him, He will grant me the daily strength I need.
No matter which way God may will lead me, I will remain patient, since God has the best in store for me.
I will follow the way God directs me, even if it means walking through rough terrain and thorny bushes.
Although we can't see his face right now, he will reveal himself in the end,
To show me how wonderfully he directed my ways according to his divine purpose.
This is the anchor of my faith.

---

[2] Stanzas 5–6 of hymn 373 from the German Mennonite red hymn book.

CHAPTER 9

Some Joys and Sorrows (1987–1990)

The year 1987 started out well for us. We were again privileged to be invited by my company to participate in an all-inclusive trip, this time to Acapulco, Mexico.

Enjoying dinner night in Acapulco during a
national conference in January 1987.

When my school friend from Germany came to visit me in summer 1987, we showed him some parts of beautiful British Columbia and Alberta. Jeremy, our oldest son, accompanied us on our trip through the Okanagan to Banff and Lake Louise.

Jeremy, nearly thirteen, on our tour through
the Okanagan Valley (July 1987).

As a small child, Jeremy had already demonstrated an interest in technical things and problem solving. He could spend hours on his Lego set and often assembled very creative models. Wanting to support our children in their interests, gifts, and talents, I took my boys shopping for a computer. Their main interest was having a PC with a good graphic display and a superior sound quality since they wanted to hook up an electronic piano keyboard. After seeing some demonstrations, we decided to buy an Amiga computer, which in the late

1980s had an edge over others. It turned out to be a good investment since Jeremy soon became the computer whiz of his class. His report card said: "Everyone likes Jeremy because of his quiet and friendly manners. Whenever there are any [computer] problems or anyone else gets stuck, Jeremy is willing to help" (report card, November 1986). He developed a career out of it, and now has his own computer networking business. In retrospect, I can now say that it also was a good investment that benefited me since Jeremy solved some of my computer problems and gave me many good hints that enhanced my computer skills.

Robert got his chance to travel as well when he accompanied his mother to the International Suzuki Music Conference in Berlin in August 1987.

Sumas & Matsqui News — Wednesday, July 22, 1987

Youth/Education

Violinist to attend Berlin conference

An Abbotsford-area violinist has been chosen to attend the eighth Suzuki method international conference in West Berlin, Aug. 10-16.

Robert Hein, 10, will be taking the student course at the gathering, attended by teachers and students from around the world.

His mother, Hedy Hein, a Suzuki violin teacher and the Suzuki co-ordinator at Central Valley Academy of Music (CVAM), will be accompanying him to the conference where she will attend the teachers course.

She said her son was chosen to attend after he sent an audition tape to headquarters of the Suzuki Association of the Americas in the U.S.

Hedy, who taught her son to play violin, continues to give him lessons. She said he began playing the instrument when he was about five.

Robert Hein

Robert was gifted musically in that he could easily play a piece of music on his violin after listening to the music on records or tapes. He also played trombone in the award-winning Razzberry Jam Band of the MEI (more about this in chapter 11). He was a quick learner.

After the Berlin conference, he and his mother visited his grandparents in southwest Germany. My mother wrote to me: "You, my son, have a very beautiful and fine wife and a dear son. Hedy has become even more beautiful." (In German: "Du mein Sohn hast eine ganz schöne, feine Frau und einen lieben Sohn. Hedy ist, wie ich finde, jetzt noch schöner geworden.")

A Manager We Loved

Not all was fun, however. I was deeply saddened when I heard the news that my beloved manager, Vic Miller, of Squibb Pharmaceuticals, was severely ill and was given only a short time to live. We organized a party for him in one of Vancouver's top-ranking hotels.

Vic Miller's retirement party at the Pan Pacific Hotel Vancouver, November 1987. Vic sitting on the right in the wheelchair, next to him his wife, Phyllis. Surrounding him are his "Lucky's Lushes," together with some representatives from our head office in Montreal.

Four weeks later, on December 19, 1987, we met again, but this time it was for his funeral at the Mormon church in North Vancouver. Vic Miller was the best manager I ever had. Some of his qualities were the following: he was very understanding, he listened to what we were saying, and he cared for our concerns and needs.

He was a father figure to all us. For this reason, we named ourselves "Lucky's Lushes."

A year later, I wrote Phyllis Miller (Vic's wife) a Christmas card. She responded:

> You will never know how wonderful your letter made me feel, even though I read it with streaming eyes. It arrived precisely on December 14th, a very tender time and was indeed a marvelous comfort to me to think that even a year later you would take the time to remember in such a beautiful and tangible way. Our oldest son is getting an ancestral file for his computer and so your letter will be included in the history and book of remembrance for his dad. May the true joy of Christmas be around you and your family, and I know it will. Many, many thanks, again.

With loving thoughts, *Phyllis Miller*

During Vic's last year of illness, I had sent him some humorous diagrams periodically, and his wife, Phyllis, mentioned to me that some of these illustrations also made it into Vic's memoirs and ancestral records.

Some More Trips and Family Pictures

Not knowing how long we would have our aging parents, I thought it would be a good idea to visit them again. This time, it was Adrian's turn to accompany his dad in February 1988.

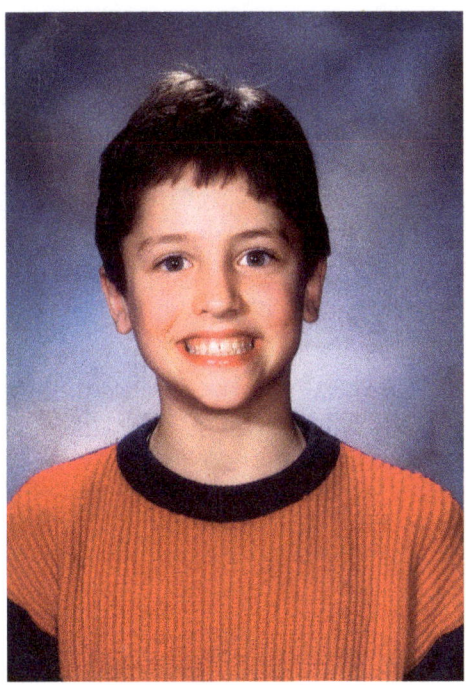

Our youngest son Adrian at age nine. His teacher said: "Adrian can write very creative and illustrative stories!"

In **June 1988**, my wife had the privilege of being part of a choir traveling through the Soviet Union. This tour was sponsored through the Mennonite Central Committee (MCC) who had asked choir director, Rudy Baerg, to assemble a choir. They performed mainly in Mennonite and Baptist churches in the Ukraine and in Siberia, visiting Novosibirsk, Bratsk, Karaganda, Frunze, Alma Ata, Kiev, and Zaporozhe. The last days were spent visiting Leningrad—now St. Petersburg—and Amsterdam.

Since our children missed their mother during her three-week trip to Russia, we promised to take them on a family vacation to Alberta (Edmonton) and Manitoba. The main occasion was our participation in the Wiebe reunion (mother Sawatzky's relatives). The event took place at the Bible school in Winkler, Manitoba.

Adrian on the lawnmower at the Zacharias farm
in Rhineland, Manitoba (fall 1988).

Hein family (picture taken by photographer Andrew Simpson, 1988)

THINGS MY MOTHER TAUGHT ME

Happy Children—Happy Parents

When I sent some of our family pictures to my parents my mother commented:

My Mother on Happiness:

> I am so happy that God gave you your lovely Hedy, your family, a beautiful home, and a work you love. Even though you are far away—the happiness of children makes us parents also happy.
>
> It is a great gift to us to have two sons who faithfully stand by our side. We find this especially valuable now in our old age. This enriches our golden years and we appreciate it every day. We would be very lonely without you. I am praying that God will richly bless each one of you and keep you healthy and safe. I am very happy that you have already experienced God's blessings in your marriage, in your family and at work. May God also keep you healthy and protect you. Our parents and grandparents [from both sides] were praying people.

In German:

> Ein ganz großes Geschenk ist es Papa und mir, zwei Söhne zu haben, die uns so treu zur Seite stehen. Gerade im Alter empfinden wir das als besonders wertvoll, täglich. Unser Alter ist dadurch vergoldet. Wie einsam wären wir ohne Euch. Ich kann nur bitten, dass auf dem Leben jedes Einzelnen von Euch ein großer Gottessegen ruht. Ich freue mich so sehr, dass Ihr jetzt etwas davon erlebt, in Ehe, Familie, Beruf, Gesundheit und bisheriger Bewahrung! Schon unsre Eltern und Großeltern waren Menschen, die gebetet haben.

When I forwarded a newspaper article to my parents, depicting Hedy teaching her students, my mother remarked:

> "I am proud of my loving, competent, beautiful and fine daughter-in-law. I am very happy that I have two hardworking and competent daughters-in-law, I can love. Recently I prayed for you Hedy, that you will continue to be a great blessing to your family."

Oma on LOVE:

Addressing her grandchildren, she wrote: "Be assured, our dear grandchildren, that even when people are very old, their hearts can still be full of love."

Our oldest son, Jeremy, in his McDonald's work uniform. He became one of the chief hamburger flippers (1989).

Jeremy gave me some very good advice about barbecuing. He taught me that the best time to flip the hamburgers is when the top just turns a different color and shows some bubbles. I applied this same principle to other meats as well and became a barbecuing connoisseur.

My mother often wrote separate letters for our children's birthdays. This time, it was a letter to Jeremy. Reflecting on his life, she wrote about Jeremy's visit to his grandparents in 1976 when he was two years old:

"Dear Jeremy: We really loved you as our first grandchild. When you stayed at our place for a week during the time when Robert was born in Bielefeld, you were sleeping in Aba's study. One night you couldn't sleep and wanted something, but I didn't understand what you meant. It sounded like 'kuku'. Later I found out that it was not something you wanted to eat. Then, suddenly I realized that you wanted me to sing a song from the cuckoo (in German: "Kuckuck') songbook, the song your father liked so much when he was a young child. When I sang it to you, you fell asleep!"

Besides loving his "Sparki," Adrian also loved playing his cello (1989).

Our family playing for Grandpa Sawatzky's eightieth birthday in 1990.
From left to right: Robert, Hedy, and Adrian
A family holiday in the beautiful and peaceful Chilcotin
area of British Columbia (summer 1990).

Robert horse riding at the Big Bar Ranch
northwest of Clinton, British Columbia.

THINGS MY MOTHER TAUGHT ME

Our boys having fun fishing at Bridge Lake, southeast of 100 Mile House (summer 1990).

Our family in our newly extended patio area (previously lawn) of our Glenavon home in Abbotsford (1990).

My mother writes: "It is always a day of celebration for us when your letter arrives. After rereading your letter, and sitting down to respond to it, I often feel like I have visited with you!"

"I will never forget the words you said to me when you phoned me on Christmas 1970, the first Christmas you were married. You read me the following verse:

In German[1]	In English
Das ist das Licht der Höhe	This is the light from heaven
Das ist der Jesus Christ	Which is found in Jesus Christ
Der Fels, auf dem ich stehe	The rock on which I stand
Der diamanten ist;	Firm and not wavering like a diamond
Der nimmermehr kann wanken,	is my Saviour and my Redeemer
mein Heiland und mein Hort,	who enlightens my thoughts
die Leuchte der Gedanken,	shining here and there
die leuchtet hier und dort.	

These words come from the song entitled 'I Know Whom I Have Believed.' When I heard you say this verse, I had to cry, since these words meant so much to me."

My parents' FAITH in their divine Creator gave them the daily strength they needed to face the last stretch of their lives.

---

[1] German Mennonite hymnbook no. 257, stanza 4 (red hymnbook). The text was written by Ernst Moritz Arnt (1769–1860) and the music was composed by Heinrich Schuetz (1628).

CHAPTER 10

Faith Makes the Difference (1989–1990)

In her letters, my mother often shared their experiences during past years. What follows are some excerpts from her correspondence, reflecting her ability to remain thankful no matter the difficulties they had to face:

> We are *thankful* for receiving good reports about our children and grandchildren. We are so fortunate that we live in countries where there is no war, and where so many opportunities exist. It is wonderful that you can immerse your children in so many activities. This was not the case, when I, whose husband was gone most of the time during World War II, had to raise my two sons. Time flies—but faith, love and hope remain!" Addressing her growing grandchildren, she mentions: "Even when you get older, you still remain our gold-children. (December 1989)
>
> To this day am *thankful* that the Lord had restored my health and allowed me to remain with my family. When you were born at the hospital in Kaiserslautern, doctors thought that I might not survive. The best prognosis they had for me, was to live the rest of my life in a wheelchair. I

loved my life, and I wanted to stay alive, even if that meant being severely handicapped. During the first few months I was unable to nurse you. But I am so *thankful* that God restored my health without having to spend the rest of my life in a wheelchair. (February 1989)

Nothing was too much for you, Hedy, when you took care of us during our Canada visit. That we could experience so many beautiful things during our visit with you was made possible only through the grace of God. Our wish is that we may be able to experience God's grace also during the last stretch of our lives, even during some dark hours of our lives. Wilfried, I am so happy that you met Hedy, and that she became your wife and mother to your dear children. We are *thankful* that we can love and appreciate our daughters-in-law. We are sure that Hedy will be a great blessing to your children. It is important to encourage each other and be there for each other's needs during our life's journey. Greetings to all five of you. With much love in our hearts. Your very old Mutti and Ama. (March 1989)

We are so *thankful* for our two grown-up sons, who still faithfully stand at our side and love and care for us, even though you are fathers yourselves, and have your own family responsibilities. You are our best friends! (July 1989)

We *thank* God that our soul and spirit are still in good shape, and that we can experience God's grace and mercy every day anew. (August 1989)

You, our sons with your families are our biggest earthly gift from God. This is of immeasurable value to us, especially now in our old age. It makes us very *thankful*. (September 1989)

Our hearts are full of good wishes for you, my dear son, and for your loved ones! May the Lord be gracious and bless you in 1990 with his peace, good health, happiness, courage and wisdom. The latter is by far the most important, even more important than knowledge. May all the experiences and maturity we gained throughout our lifetime help us to be gracious towards others. We feel that God has given us a gift in our old age to love people even more, no matter who they are, or where they come from. It remains important that we free ourselves from negative thinking and that we see positive things in others. We have much reason to *be thankful* for God's infinite grace which he has shown to us in the past, and still reveals to us today. We can depend on this grace from our loving heavenly Father until the very end of our lives. May God pour out his rich blessings upon you, my son, and you, our dear Hedy, and your God-given children, so that you can pass on these blessings to others as well. (December 1989)

In German:
Wie viele gute Wünsche haben wir, Papa und ich für Dich, mein lieber großer Sohn und für Deine Lieben! Für das Jahr 1990 und weiter hinaus, wünschen wir Euch Gottes, unsres Vaters, Frieden, Segen und Gnade im Herzen und im Haus! Gesundheit und Frohsinn—Tapferkeit und Weisheit. Letzteres ist weit mehr als Klugheit. Das Leben mit seinen Erfahrungen, mit seinem Erleben, mit gewordener Reife und Güte zu allen Menschen soll uns prägen. Vielleicht ist's ein Gottesgeschenk, dass uns im Alter die Menschen, jeder in seiner Art, lieb werden, dass wir viel

Gutes sehen, vom negativen Denken frei werden, und erfüllt mit Dankbarkeit für unendlich viel Gnade im vergangenen und heutigen Leben. Mit dieser Gnade unsres lieben Vaters dürfen wir rechnen bis zum Schluss unseres Lebens. Gott "überschütte" Dich, mein Kind, Deine liebe Hedy und Eure drei geschenkten Kinder mit seinem Segen und seiner Fülle.

My Father's Deteriorating Health

My mother writes: "It is already five years since 'Papa' experienced a setback in his health (In German: 'Papa ist schon fünf Jahre lang angeschlagen'). This all takes much strength, energy, patience, and the right loving kindness. He sometimes wants to do more, but I have to 'put on the brakes.'" (August 1989)

Wilf's comments: My father suffered a stroke in 1984 and needed much individual attention. Thanks to her nursing background, my mother was able to give him the best possible care with all kinds of natural treatments, creams, and potions. Sometimes my father felt quite sorry that he couldn't play a larger role anymore, like he used to be. He missed, for example, that people no longer asked him to preach or write articles. But my mother tried to cheer him up by maintaining her positive outlook. When his eyesight deteriorated, she read Bible passages and many biographies to him. She played piano and sang to him. All of this, I am sure, helped to lift his mood.

My Mother on Keeping Mentally Active

"I am reading Papa biographies of well-known, influential people—not only of theologians—but also life stories of leading politicians. We still appreciate visits from old friends, and we participate in our Bible study group ('Hauskreis'). We try to *keep mentally* and spiritually *active* by reading and praying for you, our grandchildren, and many of our friends. We think of you daily with much love, joy and *thankfulness*—this way we don't get bored" (February 1989).

On Faith in God My Parents Write

"Our first ten retirement years were wonderful. Being old needs to be learned and practiced [In German: Alt-Sein will geübt werden]. We have much reason to be *thankful* to God who is compassionate and who will continue to lead us. We *keep on trusting the Lord!* We know that He [the Lord] loves us in life and in dying, and he will make sure everything will turn out well!" (November 1989).

My father often added something to the three or four pages my mother wrote, but due to his stroke and deteriorating eyesight, his writing increasingly became very hard to read. Following are some of his quotes:

My Father on the Importance of Keeping the Faith

"Since we celebrated our 56th engagement anniversary this Sunday, we read once more our own memoirs. Looking at some of the pictures, we noticed that most of those who attended our engagement, are no longer alive. Now we wonder when is it our turn? But we know everything is in the Lord's hands."

"Dietrich [my father's brother in Canada], wrote the following words to me which became very meaningful. I still thank him for these words" (October 21, 1989):

German	English
Ach, mein Herr Jesu, Dein Nahe sein bringt großen Frieden ins Herz hinein.[1]	O, my dear Lord Jesus, your presence brings great peace into my heart.

"An old edition of the *Mennonitischer Gemeinde Kalender* contains my poem based on Matthew's Gospel: 'And surely I am with you always to the very end of the age.' Please read the last verse of my poem to my brother Dietrich on his birthday." (October 21, 1989)

---

[1] These words come from a German hymn book *Feiern und Loben*.

The Last Verse of One of Gerhard Hein's Poems Reads: [2]

German	English
Er ist bei dir; Du darfst nicht bange sein Er wird durch Tag und Nächte dich geleiten Und du wirst endlich Ihm dein Dankeslied weihen."	He is with you, you don't need to be afraid He will be with you throughout the day and the nights And at last, you will sing him your song of praise.

"Considering my old age and illness, I am still doing quite well."
In German:
"Mir geht es 'leidlich' gut. Manchmal etwas leidlich, aber im Ganzen doch erfreulich gut" (September 1989).

"It's good to know, that God is not far from each one of us" (Easter 1989).

Despite my parents' deteriorating health, they kept their positive attitude, remained thankful, and maintained their trust in the Lord to the very end.

Another great event that made most Germans very happy and thankful occurred in the fall of 1989.

Miracle 20: The Fall of the Wall, November 9, 1989

Hardly any German believed that the Berlin Wall would ever come down and that West and East Germany would be reunited. It is worthwhile to mention that this event started after the "Prayer of Peace" was said in the weekly Monday evening church services held at the Nicholas Church (Nikolaikirche) in Leipzig, in East Germany. What started out with a few hundred nonviolent demonstrators grew into tens of thousands of East Germans marching peacefully to the nearby Augustus Platz. They demanded free travel to foreign countries and the

---

[2] Gerhard Hein, *Vertrauen, Freuen, Danken,* Weisenheim am Berg, Germany, Agape Verlag, 1992, 28.

privilege to elect a democratic government. After the evening services on subsequent Mondays, the crowds increased steadily reaching more than three hundred thousand peaceful demonstrators. Eventually peace demonstrations spread into other East German cities as well.

Confusion grew at the border crossings, especially at the Bornholmer Straße in Berlin. Guards could no longer hold back the crowds. They opened their gates on November 9, 1989. West Germans welcomed their East Germans brothers and sisters on their side of the wall with flowers and champagne. They had been cut off from them for decades, being unable to visit them. Some enthusiastic Berliners jumped on the wall and started dancing on top of it. The event moved many to tears.

The fall of the Berlin Wall affected the whole world. The official reunification of the former Soviet-occupied East Germany with free West Germany happened a year later, on October 3, 1990.

The Fall of the Berlin Wall on November 9, 1989
(picture from Wikipedia).

Factors contributing to this event may have been the downturn of the Soviet economy, and years of wise and diplomatic negotiations initiated through German Chancellor Helmut Kohl's government with his communist counterparts.

Having lived in Germany for more than thirty years and in Berlin for several years, I see in this event God's wonderful grace upon the German nation. It was a dream come true for many Germans. I believe that God has forgiven Germany for the atrocities that happened during World War II. He has blessed Germany economically and granted it the reunification in this peaceful way. To many others and me it was a miracle.

My Mother's Reflections

> First it was World War I, then the period of depression followed by World War II. A time of poverty ensued, in which there was very little to eat. Then came the period of economic growth, (the "Wirtschaftswunder"), and now the reunification ("Wiedervereinigung") of Germany. The "DM" (Deutsche Mark) currency has now been introduced also in the East, the border controls are gone, and economic integration is starting to take place.
>
> We have to be very *thankful!* Now in our advanced age we pray that our lives will increasingly reflect Christ's spirit and gratitude. May the Holy Spirit fill and guide our thoughts and speech, our feelings and desires, and what we say and do. May His mercy be with us during our remaining time here on earth. May He be near us during the times of suffering and dying. May His grace which we experienced so often in our lives remain in us and in you my dear, dear children! (July 1990)
>
> **In German:** Wie viel haben wir zu danken! Und nun soll im Alter, das erbitten wir uns so

sehr, unser Leben im Geiste Jesu mehr und mehr reines Danken sein.—Sein guter Geist möchte unser Denken und Reden, Fühlen und Wollen, unser Tun und Lassen bestimmen. [Möge] seine Gnade über unsere letzte Wegstrecke hier auf dieser Erde, im Leiden und Sterben bleiben, wie sie im ganzen Leben spürbar war—bei uns—bei Euch, meine lieben, lieben Kinder!

My Father's End-of-Life Attitude

My mother wrote: "Papa is now nearly blind. He takes his limitations with grace and patience without complaining. He speaks to himself many Bible verses and hymns by memory. In doing this, he finds much peace and consolation" (January 1990).

My father wrote his last letter to me for my fiftieth birthday, six months before his Creator called him home. In it, he spoke about *the Lord being the spring of living water*.[3] He concluded his letter by quoting Psalms 31:15-16: "*You are my God. My times are in your hands . . . Let your face shine on our servant, save me in your unfailing love*" (Feb. 16, 1990)

While my father was thinking much about his end of life, my cousin Ruth Beringer thought about how to celebrate her sixtieth birthday in a meaningful way.

Invitation to a Birthday Party 1990

Ruth Beringer, my mother's niece, invited all her relatives, including Hedy and me, to celebrate her and my mother's birthdays, which fell on the same day, August 29. They planned a barbecue (Gartenfest) in the backyard of their beautiful home in Germany's Odenwald region.

---

[3] He didn't quote a specific Bible verse, but he may have thought of the following Scripture passages: "Whoever drinks the water I give him, will never thirst. Indeed, the water I give him will become in him a spring of water welling up to eternal life" (John 4: 14). Or maybe it was the verse in Revelation 21:6: "To him who is thirsty I will give to drink without cost from the spring of the water of life."

We brought my blind father along in a wheelchair. It turned out to be the last big highlight of his life, in which he could once more meet with all our relatives. My wife had brought her violin along and played some musical pieces. We sang several songs and enjoyed a delicious barbecue and the company of one another.

My Father on Imperfection

Before our departure, my father said to me in a somewhat sad-sounding comment "Das Leben ist nur Stueckwerk," meaning, "Our life's accomplishments are only partial" (or bits and pieces). Perhaps he thought of the Apostles Paul's words to the Corinthians: "For we know in part and we prophesy in part, but when perfection comes, the imperfect disappears" (1 Cor 13:9–10). Then he requested that speakers at his funeral talk about God's grace. He chose 1 Corinthians 13 (Paul's love chapter) and King David's beautiful Psalm of praise, Psalm 34, as possible Bible passages.[4] As a congregational hymn, he requested the praise song "Sollt ich meinem Gott nicht singen."

After our return to Canada, my mother wrote:

"I am so glad that I could take care of Papa for six and a half years. I am also *thankful* that God gave me the necessary strength up to now in my advanced age. All of this is made possible through God's wonderful grace. May our last stretch of life be a rich and blessed time together. May God grant us to hear and understand his word and give us the ability to live by it. I wish you, my dear children, together with your family, that you may be able to experience the same divine grace that has become so real to us. It was and is a gift from heaven. My additional wish to you and your family is that you may become a blessing to others, as you continue to serve the Lord" (August 1990).

---

[4] On my Germany visit the following year (in August 1991), I included this Bible passage in my thank-you speech to the Deutschhof congregation (see next chapter).

In German

"Ich bin so froh, dass ich Papa für 6 ½ Jahre besorgen konnte. Ich bin auch so dankbar, dass Gott mir in meinem hohen Alter bisher die nötige Kraft dazu gegeben hat. Es ist nur Gnade, Gottes Gnade! Mög' die letzte Lebenszeit für Papa und mich noch eine ganz reiche, beglückende Zeit werden, durch Wesentliches Hören aus seinem Wort, durch Erfassen, und auch durch Ausleben. Ich wünsche Euch, meine lieben Kinder mit Euren Kindern auch diese spürbare, sichtbare Gottesgnade, ein Geschenk des Himmels! Ich wünsche Euch, dass Ihr in Familie und Beruf zum Segen für Andre werden dürft und mit Freude das Eure tun könnt."

On October 7, 1990, a telephone call came from my mother, saying: "Papa has stepped into a *new life*." (In German: "Papa hat die Schwelle übertreten.")

It was only five weeks ago since we last met at that enjoyable birthday party with our relatives. Now I had to get ready again to travel to Germany, this time to attend my father's funeral.

My Mother After My Father's Passing Away

In passing from life to death and to *eternal life,* we noticed Papa's very peaceful facial expression. May God grant also me, and you my dear sons, my daughters-in-law and my grandchildren such a peaceful end stage of life. (In German: "Gott schenke auch mir und meinen, unsern lieben Söhnen und Schwiegertöchtern und Enkelchen solchen Frieden im Leben and Sterben ("Danke Büchlein", October 1990).

Our old age was beautiful, rich and very happy, despite some health setbacks. I am writing these words with much love, a love that connects us and flows to our heavenly Father, to whom we want to *give our thanks.* We want to continue putting our trust and confidence in Him. May *He* continue to guide us into the future.

Excerpts from My Brother's Letter to My Mother

Dear Mother and Wilfried, October 9th, 1990

We three have much reason to remain calm and thankful for having had such a good father. He will always remain in our thoughts with much appreciation. My wish to you mother is that you may continue to be happy and thankful, and that your faith will remain anchored in the One who gave us our lives. You cared sacrificially for Papa as best as you could, without concern about your own health. You helped Papa to grow closer to his Maker and prepared him for eternity. We, your sons and especially I, who lives not very far away from you, will remain standing close to your side. We all want to stay closely together. Mother, I promise you that I will assist you to the best of my ability. Please remain strong and try to live a healthy lifestyle by getting enough sleep and eating well balanced meals. Let us remain thankful in beautiful memories to our dear "Papa". May the Lord help us enjoy our lives together for many more years.

*****

Some Excerpts from Wilf's Letter to His Mother

Dear Mother,

Now I won't be able to address my letters with "dear parents" anymore, since our beloved "Papa" is in a different world, the heavenly kingdom. It is a new period for your life now, difficult days for you dear "Mutti", since you are all alone now. But your heavenly Father, and we your children, will continue to stand close to your side. Quietness and meditation are necessary and beneficial now. With it comes a period of mourning, which is a natural process.

In your last letter before our heavenly Father called Papa to his eternal home, you wrote about God's grace. My wish to you now is, that God may comfort you with His grace in a new way, especially in the days and months to come. (October 24, 1990)

Dear Mutti, I just would like to say that you had been the best mother I could wish for. Growing up during the wartime, with Papa gone for five years, it often must have been very difficult for you. Opportunities during and after the war were limited, and so was your strength. To me it is a miracle that you could cope with the situation, despite various health issues. God granted you a long life and you have been a blessing to me and us. Hopefully, we two sons were and still can be a blessing to you as well. (November 12, 1990).

CHAPTER 11

Some Setbacks (1991–1992)

We all experience peaks and valleys at different stages of our lives, but life goes on and problems need to be mastered.

Major structural changes happened in the company I worked for since it merged with a larger pharmaceutical corporation. Many employees had lost their jobs, but the sales force was largely kept in place. Restructuring, however, resulted in many changes affecting us on the field as well, and this included the way we promoted our products to the medical profession. Previously, one representative was assigned to promote two to three products to physicians in his or her own territory. Now all this was going to change in that two and sometimes three representatives copromoted the same products to the same physicians in the same territory. This meant that medical doctors heard the same message from different representatives. The idea was that repeated "hits" would generate increased sales. The result of these new marketing tactics often had the opposite effect since many physicians refused to see pharmaceutical representatives at all.

During a company sales meeting (in Kananaskis in 1991), we were told that "teamwork" will always supersede individual efforts in terms of sales. To illustrate this, we heard an animal story about Canadian geese flying in formation in the wind shadows of the lead goose, thus reaching longer distances. The message was to follow the "leader" without asking questions. This story motivated me to compose another animal anecdote demonstrating the opposite effect. In my fable, several animals where called to participate in a contest, but their roles were changed. The squirrel who previously was an excellent climber was assigned to be a swimmer. The rabbit who was a great runner before was supposed to participate in a flying contest. I included a few more animals whose natural roles were changed, demonstrating the unfavourable outcome. At our next regional meeting, when I presented my somewhat funny story and handed out copies to some of my colleagues, it did not go over very well with our management. Had it not been for some influential people, who interceded for me, I would have lost my job.

In the end, I had to cope with the new company policies, working with two other representatives, copromoting the same products to the same physicians in the same territory. It was not easy for me to adjust to these changes. In many instances, it also resulted in a decreased sales performance.

Several times I poured out my heart to my mother about these difficulties. As usual, she tried to encourage me. Since we all face some adversities throughout different stages of our lives and many of us can learn from some good advice, I am including extracts of what my mother wrote me.

Motherly Advice When Facing Job Problems

> It seems to me that switching to a totally new career, now at your age of fifty-two, is no longer possible. I think it would be good for you to try to stay in your field of expertise, and focus on your continued education. (January 1992)
>
> Please refuse to let negative thoughts enter your mind, since they only drag a person down. Try starting every day with happiness, utilizing the God-given time in a positive way, make the best use of the opportunities coming your way. Continue to do your best in all the tasks to be managed. My wish for you is that all the cloudiness and unhappiness that weigh so heavily on

your mind, may disappear and that the Lord's peace may flood your soul. (February 1992)

Try to focus your mind on the LORD, who is still alive and in His great love understands us, and can help us solve any problems. Think of good and positive things and let your mind be filled with love towards others, including your boss and your colleagues. (December 1991).

She concluded her letter with the following poem (birthday letter 1992):

In German	In English
Er ist ein Fels, ein sichrer Hort,	He is a rock and a safe refuge
Und Wunder sollen schauen,	Those who trust in his true
Die sich auf sein wahrhaftig' Wort	word will see wonders
Verlassen und Ihm trauen.	He said it, and for this reason I
Er hat's gesagt	dare to remain happy and fearless
Und darauf wagt,	Without letting my
Mein Herz ist froh und unverzagt	heart be terrified
Und lässt sich gar nicht grauen.	
(Spitta)	

A Bible verse reinforcing this truth is found in 1 John 5:14:

> "*This is the confidence we have in approaching God: That if we ask anything according to His will, He hears us*" (from a letter dated February 1990).

Family Matters (1991–92)

Our boys showed their appreciation toward their mom by writing the following notes to her on Mother's Day 1991:

THINGS MY MOTHER TAUGHT ME

May 12/91

I love you, mom because:

You cook dinner, mostly make my lunch, wash my clothing, bought me a cello so I can become good and earn my money. You let me vacuum the house for a money earning job. You let me eat when ever I want, before 5:00. I love you mom because you are pleasant to me, you buy me nice clothing, and you let me watch late t.V shows Occasionally if its good; you most of the time let my friends over when your not home. You let me go to german school. We'll you and dad drive me to gymnastics. Thanks for paying for my grips and letting me go to provincial

Love ADRIAN

Adrian at age twelve wrote the above words
of appreciation to his mother (1991).

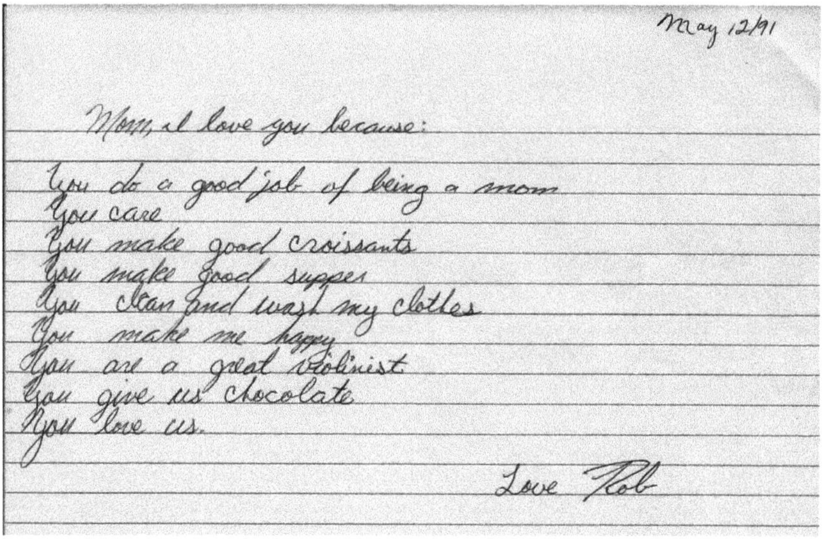

> May 12/91
>
> Mom, I love you because:
> You do a good job of being a mom
> You care
> You make good croissants
> You make good suppers
> You clean and wash my clothes
> You make me happy
> You are a great violinist
> You give us chocolate
> You love us.
>
> Love Rob

Robert not only credits his mom for playing violin well but received credit himself for being an excellent trombone player. Larry Nickel, the instructor of the MEI *Razzberry Jam band*, thought that his band reached their peak in the years when Robert played the bass trombone. At high school band competitions of the Canadian and Western United States, the MEI band won first prize. This qualified them to participate at the international high school band competitions in Banff in May 1992.

Award-winning Razzberry Jam band of MEI (Mennonite Educational Institute) at the Banff International High School Band Competitions in May 1992. Robert played bass trombone, backrow right. To the extreme right of him is accomplished instructor Larry Nickel.

At Banff, forty high school bands competed. The two top bands, among them the MEI *Razzberry Jam* and a band from Saskatchewan, were chosen to participate at the International Association of Jazz Educators in Texas the following year.

In January 1993, the MEI band travelled to San Antonio, Texas, where they heard the world's best jazz musicians perform. Again, they won first prize. Those who would like to hear the *Razzberry Jam* play on YouTube can google "Razzberry Jam, Surrey, Jazz Festival, 1993" or type the link given below into the search engine.[1]

---

[1] https://www.youtube.com/watch?v=7TqHpRnllJk&sns=em

Jeremy graduated from Yale secondary high school in Abbotsford, British, Columbia, in May 1992.

Before our boys started developing too much independence, we decided to take them on some family adventures.

Our three boys (front and second row) enjoying river rafting at Adams River, near Shuswap Lake (July 1991).

From left to right: Adrian, Jeremy, and Robert holidaying at a timeshare resort in Leavenworth, Washington (Aug. 1992).

Adrian on his thirteenth birthday, April 1992. Excelling in gymnastics, Adrian had his picture drawn, jumping on the trampoline.

Invitation

My brother, Eckart, had invited our youngest son Adrian (about the same age as his German cousin) to spend a holiday with their family on the island of Sylt on the northeastern coast of Germany. We arranged for our son Adrian (twelve years old) to fly to Frankfurt, where my brother picked him up at the airport. I followed ten days later to meet them at the holiday resort.

A few months earlier, we had invited my mother to come to visit us, but she was not quite sure whether she, at her advanced age of eighty-three, could still risk going on a long flight to Canada. When we suggested that she could travel with us on our return flight, she changed her mind and wrote:

"Regarding your suggestion to come for a visit to Canada, I will be thinking about it, and may even consider it" (June 1991).

"It is so nice to hear, that you are looking forward to the visit of your old mother. It is very kind of you, to assure me that it won't be too much [work] for you. Being alone at this old age, one doesn't take things for granted. I am so thankful for all the love and kindness people show me… To this day, I still appreciate that you, Hedy, brought along your violin and played it when Papa was still alive" (July 1991).

In German:

> "Wie lieb von Euch beiden, dass Ihr Euch auf das geplante Kommen der altgewordenen Mutter freuen könnt! Wie lieb, dass Ihr mir versichert, dass es Euch nicht zu viel werden soll. Ist man allein—und im hohen Alter, dann nimmt man nichts selbstverständlich hin und wird dankbarer für alle Liebe…Heute noch freue ich mich, dass Du zu Lebzeiten von Papa—kurz vor seinem Heimgang—noch Deine Geige mitbrachtest und Du uns so einiges spieltest."

"Now I am starting to look forward to visiting with you soon. Thank you for your faithful prayers. It seems to me as if my heavenly Father has already given me the spirit of peace, joy, love and thankfulness. May His Divine Spirit supersede my imperfect human spirit.

'*He must increase, but I must decrease*' (John 3:30). This is a lesson we must learn until we die."

In German:

"Aber jetzt kommt die Freude im Herzen auf! Danke für Euer treues Beten! Mir ist's, als hätte mein lieber Vater mir schon den Geist des Friedens, der Freude, der Liebe und Dankbarkeit geschenkt. Mög Er seinen guten Geist erhalten und vermehren, und meinen nicht guten menschlichen Geist wegnehmen. 'Er muss wachsen, ich aber muss abnehmen.' Eine Lehre bis zum Tode! Für uns alle!"

Adrian at the Rheinfels castle near St. Goar in Germany, enroute to his grandmother (August 1991).

While visiting my mother in Bad Bergzabern, I was asked to say a few words at the Mennonite Church in the Deutschhof community, where my father often preached. I still have a few notes of what I said at that church service, nearly one year after my father passed away. Following are some excerpts of my August 1991 speech.

> Dear Deutschhof congregation,
>
> Before my father passed away, he had mentioned to me two of his favourite Bible passages, which I would like to read to you. The first passage comes from 1 Corinthians 13:1-3, where we read:
>
> "If I speak in the tongues of men and of angels, but have not love, I am only a resounding gong or a clanging cymbal. If I have the gift of prophecy and can fathom all mysteries and all knowledge, and if I have a faith that can move mountains, but have not love, I am nothing. If I give all I possess to the poor and surrender my body to the flames, but have not love, I gain nothing."
>
> These words reflect the kind of love and care that you have given to my parents before and during my father's illness, and to my mother, after my dear father passed away. On behalf of my mother and my brother, I would like to thank you once more for all your love you have shown to us. You have visited my mother and helped her so much during my father's illness and assisted her after the Lord called him home. You also helped organize my father's beautiful celebration of life, which we will never forget.
>
> Towards the end of his life, my father once said: "All our human knowledge and our actions are only piecemeal" (**In German:** *"Alles Wissen*

and Tun ist nur Stückwerk"). He expressed this in a somewhat regretful tone, perhaps realizing that life is far from being perfect. The fact that these words came from my well-educated father, who had achieved so much during his lifetime, surprised me. It takes a degree of humility to be able to admit this. My father's words encouraged me not to despair when I see so much imperfection in my own life. It is good to know that we can try to work towards the goal of perfection, even though our accomplishments may not be perfect. It is wonderful that believers don't have to despair because of any shortcomings, and that we can build on the divine promises given to us through God's inspired word. This brings me to my father's second favourite Bible verse he passed on to me.

"The Lord redeems his servants; no one will be condemned who takes refuge in him." (Ps 34:22)

This assurance of salvation can fill our hearts with a joy and hope promised to those who put their faith and trust in the Lord. They reflect that the Lord forgives our sins and shortcomings. All this is made possible through the grace of God, indeed a reason to be thankful.

I believe that my father would agree that I convey to my dear mother the following Bible verse coming from the same psalm:

"I will extol the LORD at all times; his praise will always be on my lips." (Ps 34:1)

*****

Burdens Lifted Through Four Dreams

During my stay in Germany, my mother shared with me some things weighing heavily on her mind. She blamed herself for not having done enough for my father during his last days of life. I mentioned to her that she did what she could and that her long-term care of him had taken a toll on her health and strength. A few days later, she shared with me four of her dreams, which she said lifted her guilt feelings.

Dream 1:

Yesterday afternoon, (June 25th, 1991) when I took a nap on our living room couch, the Lord gave me a dream. I heard "Papa" call "Mutti", the way he always used to call me. It sounded like his real voice. I went to his office, even though I knew that he now is in heaven. At first, I longed for him, but then I knew that he is still alive, and that he is now together with his Lord and Saviour. This experience brought peace to my mind and made me feel very happy and thankful.

We as His children, can indeed trust the Lord in everything. He directs the path of His children in better ways than we ever can expect. For this reason, we want to accept God's wonderful plan for the rest of our lives.

In German (last three sentences):

Wir dürfen wirklich—in allem—ganz kindlich vertrauen. Über Erwarten lenkt er alles im Leben seiner Kinder—jedenfalls so, wie es gut ist. So wollen wir auch den weiteren Verlauf Gottes großen Planes für uns hinnehmen.

Dream 2:

In my second dream, I saw "Papa" in heaven, sitting together with his mother. I said to his mother: "Yes, he was one of a kind and a very loving person!" (**In German**: "Ja, er war einmalig"). Then I stroked his left cheek with my right hand and woke up. I was so happy that I could express my thanks to Papa once more. This dream freed me from my guilt feelings. I regarded it as a gift from God and said: Thank You!

Dream 3:

In this dream, I heard "Papa" sing in a large auditorium in a supernatural, heavenly and beautiful voice. He just sang three words "*Jesus my Lord*" (Jesus mein Herr) in the pitches of F, E-flat, C and A. This dream appeared so real to me, that I went straight to the piano and played the tunes the way I heard them. Now, I knew that Papa is in the presence of his Lord and Saviour. (June 28, 1991)

Dream 4:

In this dream, Papa was sitting (half-way reclining) in a corner of a room. He stretched out his arms and I approached him, and could touch him once more. But his hands were cold. Now I knew that he is in his new eternal body.

She concluded saying: "I regarded these four dreams as a gift from God. They imparted peace to my mind and lifted my burdens."

*****

It was on August 30, 1991 that we three (my mother, Adrian, and I) embarked on our trip to Canada. My mother stayed with us in our Glenavon home for almost a month. Our boys at that time were seventeen, fifteen, and twelve, and it was good for them to meet their "Ama" once more.

My mother, age eighty-three, visiting us at
our Glenavon home in Abbotsford
with our dog, Sparky (September 1991).

On my mother's return to Germany, my brother picked her up at the airport. After her safe arrival at home again, she wrote: "I am so blessed to have such dear sons!"

Some Excerpts from Wilf's Letter After My Mother's Return

>Dear mother,
>
>Thank you so much, dear Mutti, that you risked this long journey to come and visit us here in Canada. We are so thankful for having been able to spend such a blessed time together with you. Beautiful memories of your visit remain, and will be especially valuable for our children.

We will continue to stay in contact through letters, phone calls, thoughts and prayers. My wish to you is expressed in the well-known Bible passage:

"Do not be anxious about anything, but in everything, by prayer and petition, with thanksgiving, present your requests to God. And the peace of God, which transcends all understanding, will guard your hearts and your minds in Christ Jesus." (Phil 4:6-7)

We will pray that God may grant you this peace of mind and fill your heart with His spirit of love, thankfulness and joy in your advanced age. We feel richly blessed through your motherly love, knowing that you will keep on praying for us.

In love,
Your five Canadians

*****

Loneliness

Having been married for fifty-four years, and now left alone, my mother felt increasingly lonely. I admired her for the following reasons:

Her trust in the Lord

She wrote:

"I have to think very much of our dear 'Aba,' but I know him to be in God's glorious kingdom—as is promised to all those who put their *trust in the LORD*."

In German:
> "Ich muss sehr viel an unsern lieben Aba denken
> und suche ihn immer in der Herrlichkeit Gottes,
> die uns verheißen ist."

"What matters now is to remain calm and *trust that the LORD* that he will continue to be gracious to me. Our first ten years here in Bad

Bergzabern were wonderful. Even afterwards we still experienced many happy hours and days. Getting old, however, needs to be coped with."
In German:
> "Unsre ersten 10 Jahre hier waren wunderschoen! Aber auch danach gab's noch manch reiche, gute, und schöne Stunden und Tage. Das 'Alt-Sein' allerdings muss neu verkraftet werden" (May 1991).

"Our Heavenly Father will know what will be best for my future. I wonder whether he will give me more strength or whether he has some other ideas. I am sure that His thoughts will be thoughts of peace" (January 1991).

Her remaining thankful: "I have to get used to my 'loneliness' without 'Papa.' But I am happy in my apartment. Being alone now is part of the reality of life . . . . When I look at Papa's picture, it sometimes causes me heartaches, but I *want to be thankful to God* that he allowed me these many good years together with him.

"Old age is here and *I am thankful* that I still can manage" (May 1992).

Her remaining active: "I continue to read, write and be patient. I hope and pray that the Lord may give me some small task besides periodically reading to an old lady. He knows us and is aware of everything."
In German:
> "Jetzt will ich wieder lesen und schreiben und warte, dass mein Vater mir vielleicht—außer dem Vorlesen einer Dame—mir noch eine kleine Aufgabe vor die Füße legt. Er kennt uns, er weiß um Alles."

"I am planning to attend again a women's conference between Christmas and New Year."

Health Challenges

I admired my mother for keeping her positive attitude despite having to face some health challenges. She remained thankful and continued putting her trust in the Lord. Following are some excerpts from her letters:

"Everything seems to deteriorate, my eyesight, my hearing, and my walking. My memory doesn't want to function as well as usual, probably due to a decreased blood circulation."

In German:
>Das 'Ober Stübchen' funktioniert auch nicht mehr so gut, wahrscheinlich durch die nachlassende Durchblutung.

Hopefully I will not end up getting Alzheimer's disease. I pray that God may spare me from a future like this, and that he would call me home, before something like this would happen" (June 91).

Seeing Things in a Positive Light:
"Each stage of life, even getting older, has its own characteristics and is interesting and enjoyable."

In German:
>Eine jede Lebenszeit hat ihr eignes Gepräge— und jede ist in ihrer Art interessant und schön, sogar das 'Älter-Werden.'

Her Prayer Request: "May God, my Heavenly Father, whose child I am privileged to be, be gracious unto me during the last little stretch of my life."

In German:
>Möge Gott, mein lieber Vater, dessen Kind ich sein darf, mir im letzten Stücklein meines Weges weiter gnädig sein!" (February 1991).

Her Thankfulness and Wishes for Her Children: After my generous brother paid for a two-week holiday for my mother in the beginning of January 1991, she wrote these beautiful words:

"It is a great gift in old age to have two loving sons. This can't be taken for granted. Being able to still sense the love and acceptance of my children, despite my old age, is a great help. Thank you also to you, Hedy my dear daughter-in-law, for your kind attitude towards me and your loving, sincere invitation. You know, when one suddenly is left alone in old age, after so many years of married life, one sometimes doesn't feel as secure anymore. It was so good to live together with a loving and caring husband. Without being consciously aware of it, our 'togetherness' was a great help. God knew what he was doing, when he created husband and wife and the institution of marriage."

"God granted me nearly 55 years with my dear Papa. For this I *want to be very thankful.* I wish both of you a "growing together" in love and understanding. May your relationship towards each other get better, the longer you live together. May you experience growth and maturing in your innermost being. No one will see the Lord without sanctification. We need to let the Holy Spirit work in our lives, and try to live lives that honour God. This is my petition and prayer for the last stretch of my life."

In German:

> Wenn man zwei liebende Söhne hat, dann ist das im Alter geradezu ein Geschenk! Man nimmt das gar nicht selbstverständlich hin. Man fühlt, dass man eben alt ist und dass man dann noch die Liebe geschenkt bekommt und ‚voll' genommen wird, ist eine große Hilfe! Auch Dir meine liebe Hedy, als Schwiegertochter vielen herzlichen Dank für Deine Haltung zu mir und Deine liebe Einladung. Wisst Ihr, wenn man im Alter plötzlich nach vielen Ehejahren—allein ist, fühlt man sich manchmal gar nicht mehr so sicher. An der Seite eines liebenden Mannes ist es so schön. Ohne dass man es bewusst merkt,

ist diese "Zweisamkeit "eben doch eine Stütze im Leben. Dass ich die nahezu 55 Jahre erleben durfte mit unserem lieben guten Papa, will ich immer wieder bedenken und dafür danken. Ich wünsche Euch beiden—je länger, umso mehr—ein Zusammenwachsen in Liebe und Verstehn. Dass wir selbst innerlich wachsen ist dabei eine große Hilfe. ("Ohne Heiligung wird niemand den Herrn sehn"). Wir wollen seinen guten Geist in uns wirken lassen und unserm Gott keine Unehre bringen! Das ist meine Bitte für die letzte Wegstrecke.

About my brother Eckart, she writes:

"I am very thankful that Eckart calls me every day and visits me every few weeks. He is always willing to help, whenever help is needed. He did this, despite the many responsibilities in his work" (October 1992, documented in her "Danke Büchlein").

Thinking about her end of life, my mother writes:
"Often I think about my last stretch of life and the privilege of transitioning into the promised new world. May God grant that this may be a peaceful experience" (March 1992).
In German:
"Wie oft denke auch ich an die letzte Wegstrecke— und an das "Hinüber-Gehen-Dürfen" in die uns verheißene neue Welt. Möge es im Frieden geschehen."

"In a few days, it will two years, since Papa fell asleep. I am so happy that I can know him to be with our Heavenly Father in his eternal home. My prayer is that God may grant me a similar peaceful "transition" into eternity" (September 1992) [Wilf's comment: Her Heavenly Father granted her four and a half more years].

In German:
"In wenigen Tagen sind es zwei Jahre, dass Papa einschlief . . . Ich bin so froh, dass ich ihn in der "Herrlichkeit" suchen kann und muss immer wieder bitten, dass auch mir solch ein friedvolles "Hinübergehen" geschenkt wird."

What always amazed me about my mother was that despite her loneliness and some health challenges, she always tried to find reasons to be thankful.

CHAPTER 12

An Attitude of Gratitude (1993–1994)

My mother was a person people felt drawn to. It was fun to be in her company. Part of the reason was her positive attitude and her *grateful* nature. This chapter is dedicated to her uplifting character as the following excerpts from her letters will demonstrate.

Birthday Wishes

> Dear Wilfried,
> My birthday wish to you is that your heart may be filled with *thanksgiving* and that you will be able to enter the new year with much confidence as you keep on trusting the Lord. My prayer is that our gracious Lord will continue to bless you and your family and in your work. May He also grant you wisdom in communicating with other people. It remains important that we let ourselves be guided by the Holy Spirit who can fill our hearts with love and understanding towards others. I often think of the Bible passage that exhorts us to be the temple of Christ, and I pray that God will help me to live up to this expectation.

[**Wilf's comment:** Checking my concordance, since my mother did not include the specific verse, I believe she was referring to the following Scripture passage found in 1 Corinthians 6:19–20, where we read:

> *"Do you not know that your body is a temple of the Holy Spirit, who is in you, whom you have received from God? You are not your own; you were bought at a price. Therefore, honour God with your body."*

My mother continued:

These words are difficult to comprehend! I also would like to pass on to you the Bible verse appearing in my *Losungsbuch* (daily devotions) on your birthday:

> *"Do not be anxious about anything, but in everything, by prayer and petition, with thanksgiving, present your requests to God"* (Phil 4:6).

My wish to you, dear Wilfried, is that God may grant you these special blessings!" (February 1993)

In German:

"Von Herzen wünsche ich Dir mit den Deinen einen dankbar schönen Tag, ein zuversichtliches Hineingehen ins neue Lebensjahr—und dann auch ein Jahr unter der Güte Gottes für Dich persönlich nach Geist, Leib und Seele, in der Familie, im Beruf, im Umgang mit allen Menschen, die Dir begegnen. Wie wichtig, dass wir selbst vom guten Geist geleitet—von Liebe und Verstehen—die Verbindung mit den Unsern und Allen, die uns begegnen—aufrecht halten sollen und dürfen. Ich muss für mich immer wieder an das große Wort denken und in Ehrfurcht bitten, dass unser Leib ein Tempel des Heiligen Geistes werde. Kaum fassbar! Darf ich Dir ein

Wort vom 28.2. aus unserem Losungsbuch weitergeben: '*Macht euch um nichts Sorgen. In euren Gebeten sollt ihr Gott um das bitten, was ihr braucht. Betet immer mit dankbarem Herzen*' (Gute Nachricht: Phil 4:6). Wie sehr wünsche ich, dass du diesen Gottes Segen spürbar erleben darfst, mein lieber Wilfried."

My mother's Birthday Letter to Hedy
"I am always very happy to have you as our dear daughter-in-law. Right from the beginning [when we met], there was a good inner connection between us that became increasingly better as time went on. I am happy to know that you are Wilfried's wife and the mother of our three splendid grandchildren" (Feb. 1993).
In German:
"Immer wieder freue ich mich, Dich als "unsere", nun als meine Schwiegertochter zu haben. Es ist solch eine gute innere Verbindung mit Dir gewesen von Anfang an und die ist immer herzlicher geworden. Dich als Wilfried's Frau und als Mutter unsrer drei prächtigen Enkelsöhne zu wissen, ist wunderbar."

"Since staying with you for a few weeks, I now feel even more closely connected with you."

"Sometimes I almost feel like weeping in my loneliness, because I am so thankful for the love I can experience."
In German:
"Beinahe muss ich in meinem Alleinsein weinen
vor Dankbarkeit und Liebe."

Celebrating My Mother's Eighty-Fifth Birthday in Germany (1993)
My wife and I flew to Germany to be part of my mother's eighty-fifth birthday celebration on August 29, 1993. When my brother, Eckart, asked Mutti whom we should invite for her birthday party, her response was: "Rather than people honouring me, I would

like to invite my closest friends and honour them." Eighteen close friends and relatives came together at the beautiful Petronella Hotel in Bad Bergzabern to celebrate this milestone of my mother's life. My generous brother, Eckart, who organized everything, took care of the bill as well. My brother and I both spoke, and Hedy played a violin solo. Since I had kept my birthday speech, I am including it in these memoirs as well.

My Speech for My Mother's Eighty-Fifth Birthday

Dear relatives, dear friends and dear Mutti:

As the junior of the family I would like to say a few words of thanks to you, our dear guests, and to my dear mother on her 85th birthday. Mutti requested that you, our valued guests, be the focus of this celebration. For this reason, we would like to express our *gratitude* and recognition to you today. We would like to *thank you* for the many great and small deeds of love you have shown to our dear mother in the past. You cared for her during times of joy and especially during the times of sorrow and suffering. You visited my parents when they were ill, and when my father lay on his deathbed. You helped write letters and assisted in mailing the funeral announcements after my father passed away. You offered rides to my mother, phoned her, and sent flowers and gifts. We appreciate and will never forget all these kind deeds.

We are thinking in *gratitude* also of my mother's four sisters and her two brothers-in-law, who can't be with us today. They are:

- Aunt Martha with Uncle Heinrich
- Aunt Trudel with Uncle Paul
- Aunt Lies
- and Aunt Lene

Even though, you Mutti did not want to be the focus of attention, you won't get away from being recognized today on your 85th birthday. It is the same day Ruth Bahner, your niece, celebrates her birthday as well. We extend our congratulations and best wishes to both of you.

If I had to express in three words what you meant and still mean to me as my mother, then it will be these keywords:

1. LOVE
2. FORGIVENESS
3. *GRATITUDE*

We, your sons, together with our families, would like to *thank you* especially for your LOVE, your prayers and your understanding. You are and remain an example to me in the way you accept others who hold different opinions or diverse religious views. You listen to them, without criticizing or judging others, and you try to value their opinions. We see qualities in you, which remind me of the Bible verse written on the dining room wall of the Menno home in Berlin:

"A new command I give you: Love one another as I have loved you, so you must love one another. By this all men will know that you are my disciples, if you love one another." (John 13:34–35)

We thank our Heavenly Father especially for His great love and His promise for eternal life, which He shows to all those who believe in Him. (Mark 16:16)

True LOVE includes also FORGIVENESS. Thank you Mutti for not holding grudges against others and for being able to forgive quickly. We know that no one is perfect and that we all need forgiveness. Jesus, for this reason, included this sentence in the Lord's Prayer: *"Forgive us our debts, as we also have forgiven our debtors."* (Matt 6:12)

Where there is LOVE and true FORGIVENESS, there is also *THANKFULNESS.*

Mutti, in your letters to me, you often mentioned how *thankful* you are. Even when your eyesight got worse, making it very difficult for you to read, you said: 'When I started *thanking* God for the remaining eyesight, it became easier to carry this burden. From this we recognize, that *thankfulness* can give strength and energy to face the daily challenges.

Like water utilized to generate heat and light, so our spiritual resources can help us live a more productive life and to accomplish our daily tasks.

Some examples illustrating these resources are reflected in the following words Jesus spoke:

> *Whoever believes in me, as the Scripture has said, streams of living water will flow from within him.* (John 7:38-39)

> *To him who is thirsty I will give to drink without cost from the spring of the water of life.* (Rev 21:6)

> *Whoever drinks the water I give him will never thirst. Indeed, the water I give him, will become in him a spring of water, welling up to eternal life.*
> (John 4:14)

> *I am the light of the world. Whoever follows me will never walk in darkness, but will have the light of life.* (John 8:12)

> *You are the light of the world.* (Matt 5:14)

As increasing air pollution can harm our health and may lead to inefficiencies when nothing is done about it, so it is also in our spiritual realm. We should not shy away from saying 'I am sorry!' God calls us to confess our sins. Jesus wants to forgive our sins and grant us freedom from guilt. But this now is enough of preaching!

Finally, I would like to also express my *thanks* to my brother Eckart, who made it possible for us to celebrate this occasion with you, our dear guests, in this beautiful setting. In his generous way, he not only helped finance our trip, but also supplied a nice car for us to use during this time of our Germany stay.

Our wish to you Mutti is, that God may continue to grant you a long life filled with love, forgiveness and *thankfulness*. Our prayer is, that God may keep on blessing you and filling you with his perfect peace. The same wish is also extended to all of you, our dear guests.

Thank you!

PS: We concluded the celebration by singing together two stanzas of the song *"Now Thank We All Our God."*

*****

Some Excerpts from My Mother's Letters

"You have enriched my birthday through your presence. I appreciated your kind words dear Wilfried, and your beautiful violin solo, dear Hedy. You have made this day special and enriching for me, bringing much joy and *thanksgiving* into my heart" (September 1993).

In German:
> "Ihr habt durch Euer Dasein, durch Deine Worte, lieber Wilfried, durch Dein Geigen-Solo, liebe Hedy, unsere Feier verschönert und bereichert und mir Freude und Dank ins Herz gesprochen und gespielt!"

"*Thank you* for your telephone call. *Thanks* for your encouraging and kind words, which you spoke to me in your uplifting and cheerful voice! The fact that you understand me means very much to me! Now it feels that some burdens are lifted from my heart, and I can feel happy again. My advanced age, the loneliness and all that comes along with it, need to be mastered. It is good to know that our Lord Jesus is near me! I appreciate that you and Eckart are so kind and good to me! You, Wilfried, have always been a dear child and loving son to me. I am so glad that you have your loving family, a beautiful home, your work, the church-community, and very loving and kind relatives. May God continue to bless you visibly in body, soul and spirit. With much love, I remain your now very old mother" (September 1993).

In German:
> "Wie erleichtert und dankbar bin ich nach dem Telefongespräch! Dank für Deine guten, mir wohltuenden Worte und Deine frische, liebe Stimme! Dass Du mich verstanden hast, ist mir so viel wert! Mir ist, als könnte ich nun wieder froh sein. Das hohe Alter, das Alleinsein, muss verkraftet werden—mit all dem, was sich einstellt… Wie gut, dass unser Herr Jesus da ist! Wie schön, dass Du und Eckart lieb und gut zu mir seid! Du warst mir immer ein liebes Kind, ein lieber Sohn, mein Wilfried. Ich bin sehr froh, dass Du die liebe Familie hast und das schöne Heim, Deine Arbeit, die Gemeinde und die liebe Groß-Familie. Möge unsres Gottes spürbarer Segen weiterhin auf Euch ruhen—nach Leib, Seele und Geist. In herzlicher Liebe bleibe ich Deine altgewordene Mutter."

"My dear Wilfried! I read your kind letter once more. *Thank you* again for your good and encouraging words. *Thank you* also for all the love, the understanding and loyalty you have shown me, especially now in my advanced age. I am so *thankful* I can remain calm in the assurance my dear Lord Jesus is near me and walks with me. His love and His words are my strength. They live in me. We can be comforted, knowing that he will take care of our daily needs and that everything will turn out well" (November 1993).

In German:
> "Mein lieber, guter Wiwi! Nochmal las ich Deinen lieben, lieben Brief. Lass Dir nochmal danken! Du hast so gute Worte gefunden. Weißt Du, als Mutter, möchte auch ich Dir, mein lieber Sohn von Herzen für alle Liebe und alles Gute danken!… Danke für Dein Verständnis, Deine Liebe und Treue zu mir auch jetzt im hohen Alter. Ich bin so dankbar, dass ich innerlich still und gelas-

sen sein kann, dass ich wissen darf, mein Herr Jesu ist mir nahe—er geht mit. Ich halte mich an Seine Liebe, an seine Worte. Sie leben in mir. Wir dürfen getrost sein—er wird's wohl machen."

Keeping a Positive Attitude in Old Age

Despite her deteriorating health and physical limitations, my mother maintains her positive attitude and keeps on trusting the Lord. She concluded her letter (in December 1993) with the following poem:

In German	In English
Weil denn alle meine Tage Gnade waren, Nichts als Gnad' bis zu diesem Augenblick, So wird auch das letzte Stück, Wenn nicht voller Sonnenschein, So doch voller Gnade sein. U. von Bülow	Since all my days have been under God's grace Nothing but **grace**, to this very moment, So, I trust that my remaining time Even if it is not full of sunshine May be filled with God's wonderful grace.

Birthday Wishes to Hedy

"It is natural that I think much of you and earnestly pray for the health of both of you. The children's well-being is essential for a mother to be happy. Dear Hedy, you are such a lovely daughter-in-law to me. Our relationship could not be better. May the Lord continue to bless you and grant you his peace. This is my heart's desire" (February 1994).

In German:

> "Menschlich natürlich ist, dass ich an Deine Gesundheit denke und diese Sache immer wieder unserm Herrn Jesu ernstlich anbefehle. Das Glück der Mutter ist eben das gute Befinden der Kinder. Du, liebe Hedy, bist mir eine so liebe, nahestehende Schwiegertochter, wie es innerlich nicht schöner sein könnte. Ich wünsche Dir, dass

Du weiterhin die "Sonne der Familie" sein kannst und dass Du zum Segen aller wirst. Möge Dein Leib und Deine Seele neu den Gottesfrieden und Segen erfahren. Das wünsche ich Dir von Herzen."

On Expressing Appreciation and Being Thankful

"I listened once more to the cassette-tapes you sent us during the time when Papa was still alive. Hearing you and your children's voices again, nearly made me cry, because they brought back such good memories. Thanks again for sending us these tapes."

"Your telephone calls and letters mean much to me. They are a great gift to me in my loneliness and old age."

"In my old age, I want to remain *thankful* for all the good things I still can experience. Being *thankful* is and remains a great help. Being unhappy is neither beneficial for my own well-being, nor pleasing for other people" (April 1994).

In German:
> "Für alles Gute möchte ich in meinem hohen Alter sehr dankbar sein. Die Dankbarkeit ist eine große Hilfe. Unglücklich sein ist für einen selbst nicht gut—und für andere Menschen unangenehm."

"Reflecting on my life, I have much reason to be *thankful* for so many good things God has allowed me to experience. I am *thankful* for having had Papa at my side throughout most of my life, and for my two sons, and much more! If the heart is filled with gratitude, if it remains open for God's word, then it is much easier to accept old age and being alone" (November 1994).

In German:
> "Rückblickend muss ich immer wieder sehr dankbar sein für unendlich viel Gutes—dass ich mit Papa durchs Leben gehen durfte, dass Ihr zwei Söhne uns geschenkt wurdet und vieles mehr! Wenn das Herz voll Dankbarkeit ist, wenn

es offen ist, die guten Jesu-Worte aufzunehmen, dann ist alles im Alter, im Alleinsein, viel leichter hinzunehmen."

*****

Family Events (1994)

After completing his YWAM (Youth with a Mission) discipleship training course (DTS) in Montana, Jeremy left for a mission assignment to Africa (Kenya) in March 1994.

Family and friends saying farewell to Jeremy at Seattle Sea Tac Airport. Jeremy in the teal shirt next to Adrian (white shirt), his youngest brother, and his mother and friends (March 1994).

Robert, MEI graduate (1994)

Participating in provincial gymnastic competitions at the British Columbia Winter Games, Adrian won the gold champion award in his age category.

Adrian, BC Champion in gymnastics, Smithers,
British Columbia (winter **1994**).

THINGS MY MOTHER TAUGHT ME

Wilf Hein family, 1994, by photographer Andrew
Simpson, Abbotsford, British Columbia.

CHAPTER 13

Transition to a New Life (1995–1997)

Health Declining

When my mother's health deteriorated, we visited her in September 1995 and then again in May 1996 since we did not know how much longer we would have her.

Hedy and I visiting my mother in Bad Bergzabern,
Germany, (at her condo entrance).
To the right, my brother, Eckart, and his wife, Helga (September 1995).

My mother now speaks much about her *transition to a new life*. What follows are some excerpts of her last letters, reflecting her faith, love, and hope:

"Now I feel more and more the symptoms of my old age [she is 86 years old now]. May God be near me to the end of my earthly life, and may he prepare me for the *transition to eternal life*. We do not know when this will happen. I commit all five of you, into the LORD's caring hands, asking him to protect and guide you. I will remain connected with you through the inner bond of *love*. Greetings, Mutti and Ama!" (January 1995).

In German:
"Ich merke jetzt sehr mein hohes Alter (86). Gott schenke ein gutes Weiter-Leben und Hinübergehen. Wann, wissen wir nicht! Euch meine lieben Fünf lege ich immer wieder in die gute Hand Gottes und bleibe in Liebe, in innerer Verbundenheit Eure Mutti and Ama."

"Since my eyesight is getting worse, writing becomes very difficult. It is distressing. But the inner connection with my Lord remains. I will keep on *trusting* Him" (May 1995).

In German:
"Meine Augen werden immer schlechter. Das Schreiben geht nur sehr schwer. Es ist schmerzlich, aber die innere Verbindung mit meinem Herrn bleibt. So, will ich weiterhin vertrauen."

Computer technology made it possible to write my letters in larger fonts so that my mother could read them more easily. Just as my father during his last stage of life grew closer to the Lord, so it was also with my mother, who experienced the reality of God's grace.

Feeding Mind and Soul with the Good News

I always admired her urge for wanting to learn more. When reading became impossible, she listened regularly to God's word on audiotapes. She also ordered tapes about great men like Albert Schweitzer and listened to their interpretations of New Testament passages and remarked: "This lifts my spirits" (January 1996).

Some more of my mother's comments:

"Listening to the beautiful music of Bach and Haendel is a great help, now that I have trouble reading. It contributes to my physical and spiritual well-being" (May 1996).

In German:
"Das Hören von Bach und Haendel Musik ist für mich da die Augen schlechter werden, eine große Hilfe für den Verlauf des Alltags."

"The fact that Eckart calls me daily and that you Wilfried phone me every Sunday, brings joy to my heart and helps a lot" (February 1995).

In German:
"Dass Eckart täglich und Du Wilfried mich jeden Sonntag anrufst, ist mir im Alleinsein eine große Freude und Hilfe."

She concludes her letter with the following poem:

In German	In English
"Mein Leib, mein Seel, mein Leben ist Gott dem Herrn ergeben er mach's wie's Ihm gefällt!" (A spiritual Song from: *Die kleine geistliche Harfe der Kinder Zions*)	"I submit my body, soul and spirit into your hands oh Lord. May you lead and direct me according to your holy will!"

"Jesus' words are always a great comfort to me, giving me the daily strength I need. When people sometimes question, whether the transmission of God's Word is still valid for us today after such a long time, then I must say, that I can sense God's unique Spirit pervading His word. I am always happy reading the gospel of John, especially since he says that he has seen and experienced what he is writing about, and that he tells the truth. I would not want to live without this faith. Jesus said to his disciples before he died, that it remains important to keep on trusting the Lord in all aspects of our lives, be they small or larger. In Jesus' view, not believing and not trusting in him, is the greatest sin" (January 1996).

In German:

> "Ich halte mich immer wieder so gern an Jesu Worte. Und wenn manche Menschen fragen, ob denn die Überlieferung nach so langer Zeit stimmt, dann spüre ich doch den einmaligen Geist unseres Herrn Jesu der alles durchzieht. Über Johannes freue ich mich immer wieder, wenn er sagt er habe es erlebt, er sage die Wahrheit. Ohne diesen Glauben möchte ich nicht leben. Dass das Vertrauen im Kleinen und im Großen so wichtig ist, sagt Jesu vor seinem Tod zu seinen Jüngern. Das "Nicht-Vertrauen" meint er, sei die größte Sünde."

My Mother Writes About LOVE

My mother was an example to me for what it means to be a person who lives a life of Faith and Love. She wrote:

"The well-known Bible verse came to my mind and spoke to my heart in a new way:

> *'Love the Lord your God with all your heart and with all your soul and with all your mind and with all your strength.' The second is this: 'Love your neighbour as yourself.' There is no commandment greater than these"* (Mark 12:30–31).

She also added the following words:

"We should let our whole body be indwelled by God's love. We are also called to love ourselves—as we are. Then we should extend this love especially to those who the Lord brings into our path".

Recently my wife mentioned that we should never forget the Bible verse from 1 Peter 4:8, which says, *"Above all, love each other deeply, because love covers over a multitude of sins."* These were the words by which my mother lived, and it seems to me that where faith and love exist, there exists also a joyful hope.

Birthday Wishes

"May you keep a positive attitude of life, towards your work and towards other people. It springs from an understanding of God's grace in our lives and an inner gratitude for what God has done for us. He keeps his promise: *'Surely I am with you always, to the very end of the age"* (Matthew 28:19–20).

"May the words 'I am with you always' guide you and give you strength and comfort in your new year of life. May they give you strength and fill your heart with joy and thankfulness, as you keep on trusting the Lord. Please pass on my greetings of love to Hedy and your dear children, your and my dear big boys. With love, Mutti" (February 1996).

In German:

> "Ich bin bei Dir all Tage". . . soll mit Dir durchs ganze Jahr hindurchgehen—Dich halten, Dich getrost machen, Dir Freude und Dankbarkeit und starke Zuversicht ins Herz schenken. Mit Deiner (und unserer) lieben Hedy, und Euren—meinen lieben großen Jungens—seist Du mein lieber, guter Wilfried in Liebe und Verbundenheit gegrüßt! Deine Mutti."

THINGS MY MOTHER TAUGHT ME

My Mother's Last Letter to Me

My mother wrote her last letter to me on May 26, 1996, when she was eighty-seven years old. At that time, she said that she was unable to reread her letters due to her deteriorating eyesight. I was always amazed at my mother's very beautiful handwriting, her excellent grammar, her inspired composition, her kind and unique expressions and the gratitude reflected in her letters. She retained this ability to her very last one, written seven months before the Lord called her home. Below is the first page of her last letter.

Following Are Some Excerpts from My Mother's Last Letter:

"During the time when you still lived in Germany, you experienced God's wonderful guidance and protection in many ways. In this connection, I am thinking of your rescue as a child, when you nearly drowned. Then the amazing meeting with Hedy, an answer to many years of our prayers. And how many more things lay in between? All this was made possible through our Heavenly Father's wonderful *grace*, His continued protection and His divine guidance. We need to be thankful as it says in Psalm 50:23: '*Whoever offers thanks as a sacrifice honors me. I will let everyone who continues in my way see the salvation that comes from God*' (God's Word Translation). I also have much reason to be thankful. To me, in my advanced age, it is a great gift to know that you and your family are in the hands of our gracious God!"

In German:

> "Du durftest wirklich in jener "Deutschland -Zeit" wunderbare Führungen und Fügungen Gottes erleben! Und als Kind jene Errettung! Dann das schöne, erbetene Treffen mit Hedy! Und was lag alles dazwischen? Gnade, immer wieder Bewahrung und gnädige Fügung! Wir haben zu danken! Und "Dank ist der Weg, dass ich ihm zeige das Heil Gottes" (Psalm 50:23) . . . Auch ich habe unendlich viel zu danken. Für mich im hohen Alter ist es ein großes Geschenk, Dich mit Hedy und den Söhnen glücklich und in der Gnade Gottes zu wissen."

My Last Letter to Mutti

Following are some excerpts of my last letter to my mother, written on August 17, 1996, five months before the Lord called her home.

"Dear Mutti,

I am glad that I could visit you this spring and that we could have a happy and blessed time together. In case we don't meet again, I would like to thank you once more for being such a *loving mother*. You have been a *great blessing* to us. You modelled how important it is to *remain friendly* and retain a *positive attitude,* even when others hold different opinions. You continued to be *courageous* and *thankful* even when having to face health challenges. Our thoughts and prayers are with you, especially now during your time in hospital. Should things turn worse with your health, then I will come and visit you again. May God, who holds our lives in his hands, continue to be near you and comfort you. Please keep on praying for us and our children that God may continue to bless us and remain gracious to us. With much love from your "Kleiner" (little one). Greetings also from Hedy and our dear children, in whom we already sense God's blessings as well. With much love, Your Wilfried."

*****

After Christmas 1996, I received a phone call from my brother that my mother was nearing the end of her life. I went to see her once more (my second trip to Germany that year). When I asked my mother what her last wish was, she said:

"I don't want to ask for anything, I only want to remain *thankful,* and trust that He will take care of me."

In German:

"Ich möchte mir nichts erbitten, nur danken, dass Er's wohlmachen wird!"

The Year My Mother Died (1997)

It was in January that my mother was hospitalized in Landau, their neighbouring city, where I visited her twice a day. In the first week she was still alert, but during the second week, she was no longer able to speak and seemed unresponsive due to the high morphine doses. Standing beside her deathbed, I suddenly felt compelled to say:

"Your word is a lamp to my feet"

These words from Psalm 119:105 came out of my mouth without thinking. I then sensed from her emotions, that this was what she needed to hear. When I reviewed all my mother's letters (more than six hundred), I discovered that she had written the same words to me eight years earlier, prior to my father's passing away. Then, while still in Germany, I received a phone call in the afternoon of January 13, telling me that my dear mother had left this earthly life.

My parents' gravesite at the Deutschhof, near Bad Bergzabern, Germany.

No one in our family anticipated that my mother would survive my father by eight years, reaching the blessed age of eighty-eight. Several times in her young married life, she nearly died giving birth to her children. Then came a few health challenges. In the early sixties (1962), she thought her end was near and wrote to me: "May I be able to conclude my life in happiness." [1] Due to her nursing background and her interest and knowledge in alternative (herbal) medicine, she always knew how to take care of herself, and I believe that this helped her reach a long life.

Cleaning up her desk, I found a note my mother left behind. It said: "With this expression of *hope and faith,* I would like to leave you, my dear sons!"

In German	In English
Der Tod ist Durchgang zu Gott ist Heimkehr in Gottes Verborgenheit ist Aufnahme in seine Herrlichkeit" (Hans Kueng, well-known German Catholic theologian)	Death is a breakthrough to God It is a homecoming into God's sanctuary And a reception into his glorious kingdom

Of special comfort to me after losing my dear mother were the following words written to us by a friend:

In German	In English
Der Tod eines geliebten Menschen ist das Zurückgeben einer Kostbarkeit, die Gott uns geliehen hat. (by Margarete Seemann)	The death of a loved one is the returning of a treasure that God has lent to us.

Family Events and Celebrations

Like my mother, we were also thankful, especially when we could celebrate our silver wedding with many relatives and friends in 1995.

---

[1] An excerpt from a spiritual song by Christian Fuerchtegott Gellert, a German poet, 1715–1769.

The year 1995 also marked the thirty-fifth anniversary of my wife's graduation from MEI (Mennonite Educational Institute). Some of her friends commemorated this event by going on a Caribbean cruise. We joined them for this fun trip to St. Martin and other Caribbean islands.

Departing from Miami on the Norway cruise ship
we sailed to St. Martin (July 1995).

THINGS MY MOTHER TAUGHT ME

Our son Adrian ready for a skydive (summer 1995).

Adrian with his mother at his high school graduation, (May 1997).

Adrian's School Essay

Adrian's school essay was published in the Abbotsford News on November 7, 1996.

Yale student shares thoughts: Why we're here

Adrian Hein, a Grade 12 student at Abbotsford's Yale Secondary, was recently asked to write an essay on the topic Why are we here?.

This was his response:

I believe we are on earth for one main reason which is to follow God all of our lives. God created the earth and everything in it. He created humans in his own image to love one another and to live in fellowship.

The problem is that people don't understand God's love for them. It's sad because most people view God as an angry God who hates those who don't have a perfect life.

The fact is that everyone is sinful, even the Christians, but God loves us anyway because he created us.

When most people hear the word Christianity, they associate it with religion. "Real Christians" are not religious.

In Christianity, each person has a personal relationship with God. The fact is that most non-Christians are more religious than most Christians because some non-Christians believe that you have to earn God's love to get to heaven.

With this belief, no wonder so many people don't want to have anything to do with God. They think that they have screwed up too much for God to love them, which is totally a lie.

God will forgive anyone who asks. God sacrificed his son Jesus Christ to die on the cross for the world's sin. Three days later Jesus rose from the dead and was united to become one with his father.

In every religion I know of, their God is dead. But My God is not dead, he is loving, caring and alive.

"For God so loved the world that he gave his one and only Son, that whoever believes in him shall not perish but have eternal life."

(Remark by teacher: "Adrian, I admire your faith.")

We also experienced God's love and care as a family when he provided us with a lovely daughter-in-law for our middle son Robert, who was the first to marry.

CHAPTER 14

Some Gains and Losses (1998-2004)

Robert and Jennyfer's Wedding

We gained a *beautiful daughter-in-*law when Robert married Jennyfer Phelps-Poulette on June 15, 2002. The wedding was held at Bakerview MB Church in Abbotsford, British Columbia, and the reception took place at Cascade Community Church in Abbotsford.

Robert and Jennyfer on their wedding day, June 15, 2002, Gardner Park in Abbotsford.

For their honeymoon, the young couple chose an Alaskan cruise. We loved Jennyfer from the first moment we met and since then increasingly more.

The Hein family with Jennyfer, the beautiful bride, June 2002.

Robert and Jennyfer with their first son, Matthew.
November 2004 (our first grandchild).

Job Loss

    Not all life is smooth sailing, and that is what I experienced after a company merger and a restructuring process. Tough economic times led to company downsizing, and several territories were eliminated. After pointing out some inefficiencies to management, I was put on probation, and this after having worked for the company for more than twenty years. In February 2002, I was told that my services were no longer needed. When my manager asked whether I would like to say something, I replied: "Thank you for all the good times which I could experience with the company." Overall, I had enjoyed my work, and the company had treated me very well, even giving me a satisfactory retirement settlement.

    Now the time had come to do what I always wanted to do, namely, to further my education, especially in fields that interested me. Reviewing some university and college calendars, I tried to establish which courses would interest me most. Almost all of them were in the fields of theology and history. I then decided to take them as correspondence courses since this approach allowed me to study at my own pace. This worked very well for me (see appendix: "Wilf's Educational Background").

    Not quite ready to fully retire at age sixty-two, I decided to work as a consultant for a smaller pharmaceutical company on a part-time basis for four more years.

    Besides experiencing a job loss in 2002, we suffered another loss, when my much- appreciated father-in-law passed away in December of the same year.

    Coming from Germany, I was so glad to have married into a family in which my parents-in-law accepted me like their own son. Father Sawatzky was a good storyteller. On at least one occasion he mentioned to me that he had always wanted to write a book about his experiences but regretted that he did not have enough educational opportunities during his younger years. Young people and often children, who came from Russia as immigrants, needed to help and work so that their families could survive in those early days. Since the Sawatzkys were a very close-knit family and since they affected my life so much, I would like to pay my personal tribute to them and include at least one of Father Sawatzky's interesting stories in my memoirs.

Jake Sawatzky

Jake J. Sawatzky, who died on December 19, 2002 at age ninety-two.[1]

Jake Sawatzky was a humble, practical, and hardworking man with a great entrepreneurial spirit. He had a good business sense and knew how to trade and how to fix things. We appreciated his humour and admired him for his good memory and ability to tell interesting stories.

Some of Jake Sawatzky's stories found such great interest that Dueck Production in Winnipeg included him as one of the storytellers in their award-winning docu-drama video entitled ***and When They Shall Ask***. The DVD deals with the exodus of Mennonites from Russia in the 1920's.[2]

---

[1] Picture from video *and When They Shall Ask,* Dueck Film Production, Winnipeg.

[2] Dueck, David Dueck Film Production, *and When They Shall Ask, A Doku-Drama of the Russian Mennonite Experience*, DVD (Winnipeg, MB, Mennonite Media Society, 2010).

In the main part of the video, Jake tells how his father (Pa, Jakob Sr.) survived the horrible times of the Bolshevik Revolution in the Ukraine. One night someone banged against the front door. Machno gang members accused Pa of setting a fire to signal the enemies. They were ready to get him and shoot him for this. All the children immediately surrounded him and yelled, "He did not do it. He is innocent!" The communist soldiers were unable to push him through the door since the children and their mother clung so firmly to their father. Suddenly a gunshot could be heard from the outside. The commander shouted, "Retreat!" The soldiers left, and Pa Sawatzky survived.[3]

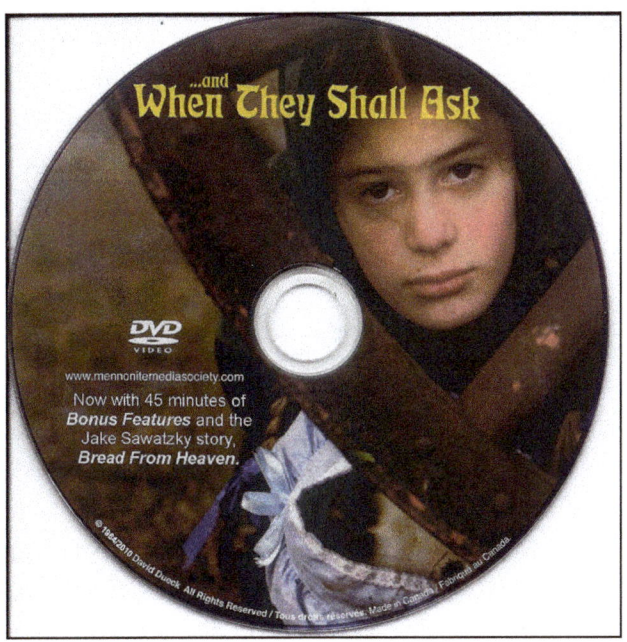

Jake Sawatzky's most moving story is the anecdote of how his family survived starvation during the famine in the Ukraine. It is included in the same DVD as an addendum appearing under the separate title **Bread from Heaven**, in a seven-minute presentation.

---

[3] Elsa Redekopp, *Two Worlds for Jash*, (Winnipeg, MB: Windflower Communications, 1991), 20

The best way is to listen to the eyewitness story as told by Jake Sawatzky on the DVD. But since some readers may not have it, I will try to relate it as I remember father Sawatzky telling it.

The Bread from Heaven Story
As told by Jake Sawatzky (in Wilf's words)

Prologue

The Sawatzky family lived in Rosenthal in the Chortitza colony of the Ukraine.[4] The events took place in the year 1922, after the Russian Revolution, but civil war was still raging. Rebels and anarchists stole everything they could lay their hands on. They often ransacked Mennonite farms in the Ukraine, murdered fathers and family members, or sent them to forced labour camps in Siberia. In the fall of 1921, there was famine in the land. The communists had confiscated the crops of farmers. By February 1922, the Sawatzky family had consumed the last potato peels. Now they just had to live on hot water only.

The Story

Since we had nothing to eat, my father decided to go to his parents who lived in Nieder-Chortitza, about sixteen kilometers south of our town (Rosenthal), to check whether they had some food. It was the last week of February in 1922. The roads were full of ice and snow. Pa hitched his skinny horses to the sleigh, and off he went. The trip took him several hours. When he arrived at his parents' home, he found out that they also had nothing to eat. They were starving too. My father then stayed there overnight. The next day, a warm Chinook wind swept through the area and the snow started melting. He knew he had to leave right away. Regretting to have to return empty-handed, he headed toward home.

---

[4] A very good map of the Chortitza Colony can be found in the *WIEBE SCRAPBOOK* composed by Erica Suderman in honour of Philipp Wiebe and Anna Bestvater, Abbotsford, British Columbia, July 2003, which is also available as a CD.

Travelling along the snow-covered gravel road, they reached a crossroad, when suddenly the horses stopped and snorted. Pa climbed down from the sleigh, trying to find out why the horses unexpectedly stopped. Looking around, he saw a big black hump sticking out from under the snow. He went to see what it was, because he knew there were no rocks in the rich soil of this area. It was a big, round Russian rye bread. Lifting it up, he thought it must weigh nearly twenty to twenty-five pounds. He couldn't believe it! How did it get there? Overjoyed and thankful for this unexpected provision, he could hardly wait to get home. He tried to make the horses walk a pace faster, but they couldn't, since they were too weak from not having had enough to eat.

When he finally arrived at home, he saw the children looking out from over the top of the Dutch door. They called, "Pa, did you bring some bread?" Full of emotion, Pa could not say a word; he only nodded. Since the children did not have any shoes, they were not allowed to go outside into the mud and snow. For the children to wait until Pa had unhitched the horses and bringing them to the barn, until he came in, seemed like an eternity. Pa entered with his big heavy frozen loaf of bread. He sliced it. Then they all bowed their heads and prayed: "Come, Lord Jesus, be our guest, and let this food to us be blessed. Amen!" Each child received a slice about the size of mother's palm, and about half an inch thick. Since the bread was still frozen, Ma warmed it in the pan on the stove and admonished the children to eat it slowly. Every day at eleven o'clock sharp, each child got their portion.

This, however, is not the end of the story. We kept on wondering, how did this loaf get there? One Sunday afternoon, several years after we had arrived in the small village of Gnadenthal in southern Manitoba, my dad invited our local minister, Mr. Bueckert. As they were reminiscing, my father related his bread story and how they had survived the famine in Russia. The pastor perked up his ears when he heard this. "What? When? Where did this happen?" Mr. Bueckert then told his story:

"I was among three people who had to pick up bread in a bakery in Alexandrovsk and deliver it to the headquarters of the Red

Army. On the crossroad our wagon tipped over, because of the deep ruts in the road. We re-loaded our wagon and noticed that there was one loaf missing. We searched everywhere, since we knew that we had to account for every single loaf. We also knew that our lives were at risk, if something was missing. But we could not find it. When we arrived at our destination, our commander accused us of stealing. We feared for our lives. But because there were three of us, they did not shoot us and let us go."

To us, this loaf of bread remained the *bread from heaven*. It fed us for a whole month from mid-February to mid-March 1922 and kept us alive just long enough until the first food supplies arrived from caring North Americans. Then the Mennonite Central Committee (MCC) established soup kitchens in the Ukraine and made sure that the food donations reached the starving people, especially the malnourished children.

Epilogue

The major reason the Sawatzky family emigrated from Russia was because their horses were stolen. Without horses, their livelihood was gone. Pa Sawatzky often said: "If I would ever meet that thief who stole our horses, I would reach out my hand to him and thank him from the bottom of my heart. This helped us make the decision to immigrate to Canada. What seemed to be a tragedy at that time, turned out to be a blessing for us." Jake initially hated the thief who stole his favourite horse, but when Pa repeatedly told how he now felt, Jake eventually could forgive that thief as well.

Jake Sawatzky always wished that he could leave some of his interesting memories and experiences with his descendants. His wish became fulfilled through the above-mentioned DVD, which was released eight years after his death. In addition, his sister Elsa Redekopp wrote a novel based on Jake's adventurous life, immigration, and settlement in Canada in 1923.[5]

---

[5] Elsa Redekopp, *Two Worlds for Jash* (Winnipeg, MB: Windflower Communications, 1991), 161–165.

THINGS MY MOTHER TAUGHT ME

Since some readers might be interested in reading Jake Sawatzky's obituary (August 23, 1910–December 19, 2002), I have enclosed it in the appendix.

*****

Tina Sawatzky

Less than two years later, God called Tina Sawatzky, Jake's beloved wife, into his heavenly kingdom. I learned to know my mother-in-law as a hardworking mother, who kept her family of eight children well fed to accomplish great things. One great gift she passed on to her children was the love of music. She often sang German hymns and folksongs while her children were young, and they keep on singing the same songs to this day.

Tina Sawatzky (Wiebe)
January 15, 1914–September 13, **2004**
(picture taken at their golden wedding in 1985)

Growing up in Germany in a home that loved classical music, where my father often sang Schubert songs and Bach arias accompanied on the piano by my mother, I valued marrying into this music loving family. Music was in the veins of the Wiebe descendants. Three of Tina's daughters chose a musical career, Hedy became a violin and cello teacher, Herta and Ingrid became voice teachers. At a youth choir reunion in Winkler, Manitoba, in September 2002, the idea was born to commemorate this musical heritage by composing a CD containing many German hymns and songs they had learned from their parents.

In the following year in May 2003, about fifty Philipp Wiebe descendants (children, grandchildren, and cousins) met at the recording studios of CMU (Canadian Mennonite University) in Winnipeg. The outcome was the production of thirty-eight favourite hymns and folk songs, most of them sung in German. The CD is entitled *Stimmt an* ("Let's Sing") and has become one of my favourites since the songs bring back memories from my homeland and impart a great sense of peace.

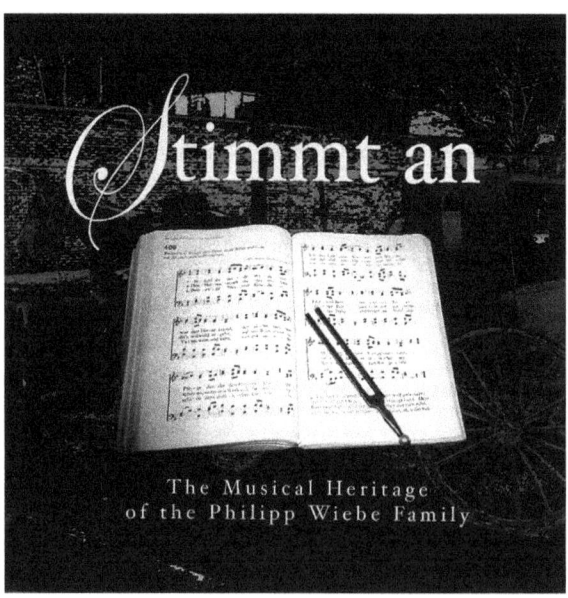

The Executive producer of this CD was Phil Ens; the conductor who put the program together was George Wiebe. The CD was produced at the recording studios of CMU (Canadian Mennonite University) facilities in Winnipeg in 2003.

My wife's parents may now sing in the heavenly choirs. If they would know (perhaps they do) that their stories and musical heritage lives on, they would be proud and very pleased about it.

What impressed me about Tina Sawatzky was her positive attitude and her deep trust in the Lord. Her motto in life, reaching even to her deathbed, was:

*"**What I cannot change, I will accept patiently.**"*

In German: "Was ich nicht ändern kann, nehm ich geduldig an!"

More about Tina Sawatzky's memories, including her life in Russia, her immigration, and her family in Canada can be found in the *Legacy book* of the Philipp Wiebe family.[6] Another book, the *Wiebe Scrapbook* was composed by Erica Suderman. It contains many pictures of relatives and a tribute to Tina, written by Hedy Hein, including many pictures of Tina's children and their families.[7] Tina's obituary is included in the appendix of this book for those who are interested reading it.

*****

Some of Life's Rewards (1998–2004)

We have experienced how the Lord had blessed our parents (on both sides of our families) and how he rewarded their faith. We are also aware from scriptural promises that believers will receive their rewards in heaven some day as well. One of the Bible verses promising such a reward is found in Colossians 3:23–24, where we read:

---

[6] The legacy book contains the story of the descendants of the Philipp and Anna Wiebe family. It was compiled by Alfred Schellenberg from Winnipeg in July 1998 and includes Tina Wiebe-Sawatzky's memoirs, written by Hedy Hein.

[7] Erica Suderman, *Wiebe Scrapbook,* Abbotsford, British Columbia, 2003, 181 ff. Most of the Phillip Wiebe descendants have a copy of this coiled memoir containing their rich heritage.

"Whatever you do, work at it with all your heart, as working for the Lord, not for men, since you know that you will receive an inheritance from the Lord as a reward.
It is the Lord Christ you are serving.[8]*"*

But it is also wonderful to be able to experience some rewards while still living, through trips, vacations, and through meeting with our family and relatives. Some of our choicest memories are reflected in the following pictures.

Wilf and Hedy at a time-share hotel in Cabo San Lucas, Mexico, March 1998.

Move to New Home in 1999

We enjoyed our new home that had enough room for a spacious music studio, accessible from the outside. Our moving day was March 12, 1999.

---

[8] Some other similar Bible verses are found in: 1 Sam 26:23, Matt 16:27, Eph 6:7-8, Heb 11:6, and Rev 22:12.

Our new home at Amberpoint Place in Abbotsford.

My brother, Eckart, and his wife, Helga, invited us to Helga's sixtieth birthday celebration in a first-class hotel in Germany's Black Forest area. All expenses were paid, including a three-day stay in a beautiful hotel in Baden-Baden afterward.

My brother, Eckart, with his wife, Helga, and their son, Arnt Philipp, at her sixtieth birthday party in Tonbach near Baiersbronn, Germany (April 1999).

My lovely princess, Hedy (picture taken in 2000)

Chichen Itza Temple in Yucatan, Mexico (August 2003)

The name Chichen Itza means "at the mount of the well of Itza." These Mayan ruins date back to the years AD 750–1200. The twenty-four-meter-high Kukulkan Pyramid, also known as El Castillo (the castle), has 365 steps on each of its four sides. Chichen Itza is located about 125 kilometers west of Cancun.

Coffee break at Chateau Lake Louise on our return
trip from a 55 Plus retreat in Banff, Oct. 2003

When my brother, Eckart, and his wife, Helga, visited us in June 2004, we traveled to Jasper, Lake Louise, and Banff with them.

At Columbia Icefields, June 2004

The Central Valley Academy (CVAM) of Music celebrated its twentieth anniversary in summer 2004. As a cofounder of the academy and having served as the head of the Suzuki program, Hedy was honored at this occasion, just before she retired. She had taught violin there for twenty years and later also cello. The picture below shows Hedy with her cello students playing during the anniversary.

Cello concert at the twentieth anniversary of CVAM, summer 2004. Hedy with Elisa Woo, Rita Green, and Karen Brown.

Other enjoyable and very educational memories came from some international trips in the following years.

CHAPTER 15

Ruins Speak Volumes (2005–2006)

A tour to the Holy Land, Turkey, and Greece opened a new field of interest for me, as I learned much about the rich history linked to some historical sites in Europe and the Middle East. In summer 2005, we took part in a guided tour sponsored by the Christian broadcasting organization *100 Huntley Street.* Besides local guides, we had some expert theologians and historians in our group who explained the historical significance of many places. Our tour entitled *In the Footsteps of St. Paul* started in Turkey, the country in which the Apostle Paul grew up. We followed Paul's missionary routes through Turkey and Greece, concluding our sightseeing tour in the Holy Land. This experience inspired me to take some correspondence courses on the history of Christianity. Since I found this subject fascinating, I have included pictures and examples of some of the interesting sites we have seen.

Turkey

In Turkey, we visited the ancient city of Antioch near the Syrian border, whose modern name is Antakya. This was the place where Christ's disciples were first called "Christians" (Acts 11:26). In ancient times, Antioch was the capital of Syria. With a population of about five hundred thousand, it was one of the largest cities in the Roman Empire. In 1939, the city was returned to Turkey. Among other places we visited in Turkey were Tarsus, the town where

Paul was born and spent his childhood; Cappadocia, the picturesque region in central Turkey with its many "fairy chimneys" and underground caves, which early Christians used as hiding places during times of severe persecution; the thermal resort of Hierapolis; and the cities of Ephesus, Pergamum, Troy, and Istanbul.

Shown in the above mentioned picture is the partially reconstructed façade of the Celsus Library in Ephesus, Turkey. It was built by Gaius Julius Aquila in honour of his father, Roman Senator Julius Celsus. Construction was completed in about AD 120. The library's main purpose was to store twelve thousand scrolls. It also served as a mausoleum for Celsus, the builder's father. The Ephesus library was the third largest library in ancient times, next to Alexandria and Pergamum. The statues in the niches between the columns are replicas of the originals. They represent wisdom (Sophia), knowledge (Episteme), intelligence (Ennoia) and excellence (Arete) (May 2005).

Istanbul's famous Haggia Sophia (the name means holy wisdom) was the largest Christian church of the sixth century. Throughout the centuries, however, it went through many changes. After Istanbul fell to the Ottomans in 1453, it became a mosque and its gold-leaf frescoes were whitewashed over. When Kemal Atatürk came to power in 1923, declaring Turkey a Republic, Haggia Sophia was turned into a museum. Since the early 1930s, many of the original iconographic mosaics with Christian motives have been uncovered, and restorers have tried to attain a balance of maintaining mosaics of both Christian and Islamic cultures.

The Haggia Sophia Church in Istanbul was built by Justinian I in AD 530. The impressive dome, measuring thirty-three meters in diameter, made it one of the largest domes in the world at that time. (May 2005).

At the opening ceremony, Emperor Justinian was so overwhelmed by the beauty of his church that he shouted: *"Solomon, I have surpassed you!"*

Greece

Traveling through Greece from the north to the south, we visited the cities Philippi, Thessalonica, Athens, and Corinth.

The Parthenon in Athens was built in the fifth century BC under the auspices of Pericles in honor of Athena, the patron goddess and guardian of the city (May 2005).

Mars Hill in Athens, near the Parthenon, where Pastor Dale Lang from Calgary read to us the Scripture from Acts 17:22–34.

Mars Hill, sometimes called Aeropagus, used to be the meeting place of the city council during the early centuries. It was here where the Apostle Paul addressed the Athenians very diplomatically by saying:

"Men of Athens! I see that in every way you are very religious. For as I walked around and looked carefully at your objects of worship, I even found an altar with this inscription: TO AN UNKNOWN GOD. Now what you worship as something unknown, I am going to proclaim to you" (Acts 17:22–23).

Israel

God, who remains unknown to many even in our modern days, has been written about more than two thousand years ago, not only by biblical writers, but also by the Essenes, who hid their scrolls in caves of the dry desert near Qumran, some fifty kilometers east of

Jerusalem. The famous American archaeologist Dr. W. F. Albright announced in 1948, "The finding of the Dead Sea Scrolls (DSS) is the greatest archaeological discovery of the twentieth century." They were discovered accidently by a young Bedouin goat herder in 1947. When he threw a stone into a cave, he heard a clinking sound, and upon checking, discovered many scrolls hidden in clay jars. After archeologists and historians examined them, they discovered that these were ancient scrolls of irreplaceable value, some of them dating back more than two thousand years.

Most Dead Sea Scrolls, among them the oldest, were found in Qumran Cave number 4. This cave contained seven hundred scrolls in about sixteen thousand fragments. (Picture taken by Wilf Hein, 2005)

The significance of the DSS is that they predate the earliest Masoretic text (MT) by more than one thousand years. They correlate closely with the contemporary Septuagint (LXX). The DSS have been dated by paleography, carbon dating and infrared photography to about 250 BC to AD 70. They constitute another extra-biblical source confirming the accuracy of the Old Testament (OT) written mostly in Hebrew and Aramaic. Dr. Peter W. Flint, director of the Dead Sea Scroll Institute, says, "The DSS confirm that our Bibles are 99 percent accurate." It is interesting to note that most of the DSS discovered come from the books of Psalms, Deuteronomy, and Isaiah, which incidentally the New Testament refers to most often.

In his presentation, Dr. Flint mentioned that in some instances the DSS reveal omissions found in other texts and clarify some biblical passages, not well understood. He gave the example of Psalm 22:16 where the Hebrew reading of the traditional Masoretic text says:

"For dogs have surrounded me: the assembly of the wicked have encompassed me: *like a lion* are my hands and my feet," while the DSS give a more accurate rendering: "For dogs are [all around me]; a gang of evil[doers] encircles me. *They have pierced* my hands and my feet." [1]

When questions in interpretation existed, some Bible translators have included a clarifying text coming from the DSS in modern translations.

The best-preserved scroll is the seven-meter long Isaiah Scroll, of which a copy is displayed in the center part of the Shrine of the Book Museum in Jerusalem. The roof of the museum resembles the lid of a clay jar, in which most scrolls were found. The scrolls are displayed in the basement of this unique building, where it is easier to maintain a constant temperature, essential for the longevity of the scrolls, fragments, and artifacts.

---

[1] Soucre: Handout from a lecture *The Dead Sea Scrolls and the reliability of Bibles Used Today*, held by Peter W. Flint on October 16, 2004, at United Church, Aldergrove, British Columbia.

The Shrine of the Book Museum in Jerusalem contains many valuable DSS. But the most treasured DSS are stored at the Rockefeller Museum in East Jerusalem, where only certified researches can have access to them (photo by Wilf Hein, 2005).

The famous Western Wall in Jerusalem, the site for Jewish prayers and pilgrimage. Jews put their prayer requests into the cracks between the stones in the wall. I left a booklet of the *Four Spiritual Laws* on a book display table, for someone else to pick up (photo Wilf Hein).

The Western Wall is the most holy accessible Jewish site in Jerusalem, since it is the only remaining part of King Herod's temple. The massive stones on the bottom of the wall date to the Herodian period, while the smaller stones on top originate from the time of the Muslim conquest between 1536 to 1539. More than one half of the wall is underground. Israel regained the Western Wall, previously controlled by Jordan, during the Six-Day War in June 1967.

Not far from the Western Wall, one can find the seven-branched golden menorah displayed at the Jerusalem's Temple Institute. It was reconstructed in keeping with Old Testament specifications given in Exodus 25:31–40 and is an accurate representation of the lampstand used in Moses tabernacle and in future temples. The menorah has been a symbol of Judaism along with the Star of David and is an emblem of the state of Israel.

Reconstructed golden Menorah, weighing forty-two kilograms.
Photo: Wilf Hein, 2005

Pure olive oil was used to keep the lampstand burning. The light generated correlates to the Word of God in the Old Testament: "*Your word is a lamp to my feet and a light for my path*" (Ps 119:105) and "*The unfolding of your words gives light; it gives understanding to the simple.*" (Ps 119:130).[2] Jesus refers to himself as the light of the world, when he said: "*I am the light of the world. Whoever follows me will never walk in darkness, but will have the light of life*" (John 8:12).

Jewish tradition says that the coming Messiah is going to enter through the Eastern Gate. The Golden Gate on the eastern wall of Jerusalem is the oldest of the existing eight gates and the only double-arched one. It is believed to have been built around AD 640.[3]

The Golden Gate on the eastern side of the Jerusalem wall.
(Photo: Wilf Hein, 2005)

---

[2] A similar association is reflected in Proverbs 6:23.

[3] An alternate date could have been AD 520, during Justinian's I time.

When Muslims conquered Jerusalem in the sixteenth century, the sultan of the Ottoman Empire, Suleiman the Magnificent, rebuilt the wall and the Golden Gate. The Muslims sealed this eastern gate to prevent the Messiah from passing through it. Most Christians believe that the intentions of the Creator of heaven and earth will likely not be thwarted by any human effort. In this context, it is worthwhile to remember the words of the Messiah, who said,

"I am the First and the Last" (Rev 1:8, 17; 22:13) and
"I am the Gate, whoever enters through me will be saved" (John 10:9).

Family Celebrations and Trips

We were thankful to God for our health, a wonderful family, and opportunities to see many beautiful parts of the world. The year 2005 started out well when my dear wife organized a wonderful sixty-fifth birthday party for me to which she invited some relatives, friends, and former colleagues.

Hedy, Adrian, and Robert playing Mozart's *Eine Kleine Nachtmusik* for my sixty-fifth birthday (2005).

Alice, Hedy's sister, composed a humourous song, which she and her sisters sang to us, to the melody of the German folksong *"Heut kommt der Hans zu mir, freut sich die Lies."* Hedy and her sisters sang the first stanza in the original German, followed by the remaining five stanzas (see below).

In German	In English
Refrain: Heut kommt mein Schatz zu mir, das ist gewiss, Ob er aber über Oberammergau Oder ob er über Unterammergau Oder ob er überhaupt nicht kommt, ist nicht gewiss (Peter Wackel)	Today my darling comes, that is for sure, Whether he comes from Oberammergau Or whether he comes from Unterammergau Or whether he comes not at all, Remains uncertain

Five stanzas
1. In 1969, to Germany Hedy as a UBC student hosted seniors at a Christian resort The Senior Hein's' there, gave a good report, of their son, Wilf!
2. His name was Wilfried Hein their second son. of bearing true and kind Oh, what a super find, This Canadian Fräulein fein, Wilf was not blind
3. With pharmaceuticals Wilf was a whiz. Betablockers, Bristol Myers Squibb, Earned him recognition, gifts and trips But his love for faith and family Still took the prize!

4.	First son was Jeremy, who thrilled his heart. Robert next was born in Germany, Active Adrian made the trio true, Gorgeous Jenn then joined the family, now young Matthew.
5.	Congratulations, Wilf, now 65 Yet aspires to strive for knowledge, truth and right, Organizing skills, computer's his delight, God, grant you many, many more, Wonderful years!

Oma singing songs to our first grandchild Matthew (November 2005).

Five beautiful sisters on an outing. From left to right: Ingrid Suderman, Hedy Hein, Alice Willms, Erica Suderman, Herta Thiessen (Summer 2005).

Enjoying Warmer Climates

In 2006, I retired from a part-time job as pharmaceutical specialty representative with a smaller pharmaceutical company. How wonderful it was to be free of any obligations during retirement and to be able to do what we enjoy! We invited our family to an all-inclusive holiday in Puerta Vallarta, Mexico.

Family holiday in Mexico, Puerto Vallarta, March 2006

Oma with our first grandson relaxing on the
beach, Puerto Vallarta, March 2006

Celebrating Erin's birthday, December 2006

More celebrations soon followed!

CHAPTER 16

Two Weddings within Two Weeks (2007–2008)

Jeremy and Kalina (Smith) on their wedding day March 16, 2007 at the Rowena Inn on the River. Congratulations Jeremy for finding such a lovely young lady.

The beautiful bride in an appropriate classy
setting, Rowena Inn, March 2007

Picture taking: Rowena's Inn;
Church service: Bakerview MB Church in Abbotsford;
Reception: Heritage Valley Restaurant in Abbotsford;
Honeymoon: Mayan Riviera

Jeremy's wedding, March 2007

Two weeks later, on March 31, 2007, Adrian and Erin Wiens from Montana got married.

Beautiful Erin, the bride with our son Adrian.
Place of wedding: Free Reformed Church, Chilliwack.
Reception and picture taking: Minter Gardens.
Honeymoon: Costa Rica (March 31, 2007)

Adrian and Erin with Wilf and Hedy at Minter Gardens, March 2007

Where Is Adrian?

The church was packed with guests waiting for the groom to appear. Adrian was nowhere in sight. One of the groomsmen asked, "*Where is Adrian?*" Taking his cellphone, the groomsman phones Adrian. At this point, the video starts:

The groom is in deep sleep. The alarm rings! Shocked to see that it already is 11:00 a.m., Adrian runs in his boxers, almost tripping, into the shower. Shaken by the cold water and bleeding from a razor cut, he is dressed in less than two minutes. Rushing out for a free run, he leaps on his motorbike, not caring about any speed limits. He ignores the blue and red lights flashing behind him, gets a grip on the back of a passing pickup truck, and slides on his shoes along the wet street en route to the church. At this very moment, the front door of the sanctuary opens, and in walks the groom, calm and collected.

The congregation applauds! (Comment by his father: A well-done film clip of a successful stunt actor in the movie industry).

THINGS MY MOTHER TAUGHT ME

Hedy's 2007 Christmas letter

Jeremy and Kalina   Adrian and Erin

Dear Family and Friends,   December 2007

What a special year this has been! Two sons married in the same month! But what weddings they were—even in March!

Both boys got engaged in December, and both have interesting stories to tell about how that happened.

On March 16, our eldest son, Jeremy, married Kalina Smith, a grade 7 teacher who grew up in this area, and on March 31, our youngest son, Adrian, married Erin Wiens, a recent Trinity Western graduate, who comes from Montana.

Our second son, Robert, has been married to Jennyfer for five and a half years. They have two beautiful little boys, ages three and eighteen months, and are now expecting their third in January. What a delight those two little boys are! Both were born with very dark hair, and now both are quite blond. We're pleased that Jennyfer can be a stay-at-home mom, something that can't be taken for granted anymore.

Wilf still spends lots of time in his study: studying Christian history and putting together a timeline of major events and historical characters. He finds it fascinating!

I have joined Fraser Valley Symphony again and find it very stimulating. I am so grateful that I can manage it. It seems the regular strength exercises I do for my arms have helped so that I can play violin at length again and not find it too stressful.

In April, Wilf and I got a cheap flight to Wendover, Nevada, right on the Utah border. This small gambling town had nothing much to offer us, but it gave us the opportunity to rent a car and visit Salt Lake City. We really enjoyed the two days there: the Rockies, the beautiful tulips, and Temple Square, hearing the Mormon Tabernacle Choir, in rehearsal, a noon-hour organ concert in the tabernacle, and the ballet "Giselle." Plus, our hotel was right downtown within walking distance of these venues. We also drove out south of the city to see the largest open pit copper mine in the world, apparently visible from space.

In August, we spent time in Alberta, at sister Herta and Ron's fiftieth anniversary celebration. What a wonderful weekend that was! Then we visited the Drumheller area, friends from Wilf's Berlin days in Stettler, and back to British Columbia via Radium and the Kootenays.

Now we're in the Christmas season with its wonderful church services and concerts.

THINGS MY MOTHER TAUGHT ME

Thanks be to God that we have something very wonderful to celebrate!

Blessings to you and yours in this Christmas season!

Hedy

Attending a rehearsal of the Mormon Tabernacle Choir in Salt Lake City, Utah (April 2007)

Fraser Valley Symphony Orchestra with conductor Lindsay Mellor
Violinist Hedy third in second left row

Family Growth

We gained two new members

Five-month-old Jadelynn was born in January 2008

THINGS MY MOTHER TAUGHT ME

Nathan, born July 2008

Vacations and Other News

Family holiday, Puerto Vallarta, Mexico, March 2008

Three happy brothers enjoying the beach
near the Royal de Cameron hotel,
Puerta Vallarta, Mexico. From left to right:
Robert, Adrian, Jeremy, March 2008)

Hedy with three of her sisters at the Newlands Golf and
Country Club. From left to right: Erica Suderman, Hedy Hein,
Ingrid Suderman, and Alice Willms (Summer 2008)."

Erica, Hedy's second oldest sister, passed away a year after this picture was taken, in June 2009. She, as a former school librarian, has done much voluntary work for the Mennonite Historical Society, especially in the computerized compilation of ancestral records. The obituaries of Erica and Albert Willms (Alice's husband, who passed away in 2012) are included in the appendix, for those interested in reading it.

CHAPTER 17

South America and Europe (2009–2010)

Peru, Brazil, and Paraguay

An opportunity arose to be part of a tour to South America. We joined several people from our church wanting to attend the Mennonite World Conference in Asuncion, Paraguay. Our three-week tour included stops in Peru (Cusco, Machu Picchu, and Lima), as well as in Brazil (Rio de Janeiro, Curitiba, and the world-famous Iguassu waterfalls).

Machu Picchu is the famous Inca settlement in the Andes of Peru. It is also called the secret city of the Incas since the Spanish never knew about it. The American Professor Bingham discovered it in 1911. Machu Picchu, which dates to the fifteenth and sixteenth century remains South America's most spectacular archaeological site (July 2009).

The famous Christ the Redeemer Statue in Rio de Janeiro located on top of the 710-meter-high Corcovado Mountain. It belongs to the New Seven Wonders of the World. The statue is 38 meters high and 30 meters wide. Construction began in 1922 and was completed in 1931 (July 2009).

View to Rio and its famous Copacabana Beach from Sugarloaf Mountain.

The Iguassu waterfalls, a UNESCO World Heritage site at the Brazilian and Argentine border. They are the world's widest waterfalls, consisting of 274 individual falls and spanning nearly four kilometers in width. They plunge down about 90 meters (July 2009)

More than six thousand delegates from many countries congregated at the 15th Mennonite World conference in Asuncion, Paraguay. The concluding service included a reconciliation ceremony (see picture below), in which Helmut Isaac shakes hands with the chief of the Ayoreo tribe who killed his missionary brother Kornelius in 1958 with the same spear he holds in his hand. Helmut Isaac said to him: "More than fifty years ago, your clan and tribe were resisting us, but now we aren't enemies anymore, but brothers in Christ." In those days, the Moros, as they were then called, hunted white men they thought were a threat to them.

The final service and reconciliation ceremony at the *Centro Familiar de Adoracion* at the Mennonite World Conference in Asuncion, held in July 2009.

During our time in Paraguay, we also had an opportunity to travel to the Mennonite settlements in the Chaco, often referred to as "Green Hell," since there was nothing but green jungle when the Mennonites arrived from the Red Hell (Communist Russia). The accomplishments of Mennonites in Paraguay impressed me very much. Through generous donations of many North American fellow believers and the Mennonite Central Committee (MCC), they built their own homes, schools, and even a 450-kilometer-long highway, connecting their villages in the Chaco with the capital of Asuncion.

In 1951, the Paraguayan Mennonites built their own hospital, the *Mennonite Hospital Kilometer 81*, so called, since it is located 81 kilometer southeast of Asuncion. Initially it was built for leprosy patients, but later it expanded into treating other diseases like tuberculosis as well. It had its own factory making custom-made prostheses for patients who had to have their legs amputated. Paraguay was the first country to introduce outpatient and mobile treatment for leprosy patients on a national level.

On our way to Asuncion, we visited the *Lactoland* Dairy Factory in Sommerfeld. This plant, run by Mennonites, produces 85 percent of all dairy products in Paraguay. Considering that Mennonites constitute less than 0.5 percent of Paraguay's population, this achievement is quite remarkable.[1]

*****

Germany and Czech Republic (2010)

Wanting to do some more traveling while still healthy, we embarked on a trip to Europe to see some places where we had not been before. On our agenda was a visit to the Czech Republic and some historic places in former East Germany. Before traveling to Prague, we attended the famous Passion Play in Oberammergau, performed only once every ten years. More than two thousand actors, singers, instrumentalists, and stage technicians, all inhabitants of this small town in South Germany are involved. The newly renovated theater with its open-air stage holds more than five thousand spectators. It was an awe-inspiring performance and a memorable experience.

Not far from Oberammergau is the well known, Rococo-style *Wieskirche* in southern Bavaria, a site recorded in the Unesco World Heritage list.

---

[1] More information about Mennonites in Paraguay is given in my book *A Witness in Times of War and Peace,* pp 200–206 and 321–323.

The *Wieskirche* in southern Germany, built in the 1750s (September 2010).

THINGS MY MOTHER TAUGHT ME

Prague, Czech Republic

Hedy at the *Moldava* River with the Prague castle and St. Vitus Cathedral in the background (September 2010).

The Prague castle is the largest ancient castle in the world. Its construction began AD 870 and was completed in 1929. It underwent its greatest expansion during the reign of Charles IV (1346–1378), when Prague became the seat of the Holy Roman Emperor. Now it is the official residence of the president of the Czech Republic. The center of attraction within the huge castle complex is the gothic St. Vitus Cathedral which had its beginnings in the eleventh century.

The city's architecture reflects the different styles that prevailed throughout these centuries. A monument in the middle of the Prague Old Town Square is that of the famous martyr John Hus, who was burned at the stake in 1415, for what he believed. The Czech inscription at the base are the words Hus spoke just before his martyrdom: "*The Truth Shall Prevail.*"

The John Hus monument was unveiled in 1915 to commemorate
the five hundredth anniversary of his martyrdom.

John Hus (1369–1415) can be regarded as a forerunner of the
Reformation who preached key reformation themes a century before
Luther posted his ninety-five theses on the door of the Castle Church
in Wittenberg. Hus proclaimed the Bible as the final authority for
the church. He disapproved of the practice of indulgences of the
Roman Catholic Church and preached the Gospel in his vernacular
language, which was regarded as a crime in the eyes of the Roman
Catholic Church at that time. Declared a heretic, he was excommunicated, imprisoned, and burned at the stake. Before his death as a
martyr, Hus cried out: "Fire does not consume truth."

Traveling north into former East Germany, we visited the historic cities of Dresden, Meissen, Weimar, and Leipzig. In Leipzig,
we heard the world-famous *Thomaner Boys Choir* perform in the
Thomaskirche where J. S. Bach had spent a major portion of his life.
We also toured the well-*known Gewandhaus Orchestra Hall* where

Felix Mendelssohn was a conductor and composer. After one hundred years, he brought the music of Bach to the forefront again.

Our next major point of interest was the Luther city of Wittenberg.

Luther City Wittenberg, Germany

It was here, at the door of the Castle Church (*Schlosskirche*) in Wittenberg, where Martin Luther is said to have posted his ninety-five theses in 1517 (September 2010).

Luther's purpose for posting his theses was to discuss these issues with the hierarchy of the Roman Catholic Church. His intention was not to split the church. Thanks to the development of the printing press, their quick distribution was made possible, eventually triggering the Reformation. His theses dealt primarily with indulgences, penance, and purgatory. Some of his key points were the following:

> "Every Christian who feels sincere repentance, has perfect remission of punishment and guilt even without an indulgence" (Thesis 36).

> "The true treasure of the Church is the most Holy Gospel of the glory and grace of God" (Thesis 62).

Berlin

Not very far from Wittenberg is Germany's capital city Berlin, where we participated in a guided walking tour through its restored center core, the former East Berlin. This part of the city was inaccessible for West Berliners during the time of the Berlin Wall (from 1961 to 1989). We also visited the beautifully restored Reichstag building which houses the German Parliament, only one block north of the Brandenburg Gate.

The well-known symbol of Berlin, the neoclassical Brandenburg Gate, was commissioned by King Frederick William II of Prussia and built during the years of 1788–1791.

The year 2010 was also the year of our fortieth anniversary, which we celebrated in Victoria, British, Columbia, in May.

Family Update

After bearing with me for forty years, Hedy opened her anniversary gift at breakfast and was surprised to find a new ring in a big box!

A lady who loved her tulips but hated the weeds (spring 2009). She also hated when deer came in stealthily and ate up tulip and rose buds in our backyard, their former territory.

A buck in our backyard, a frequent visitor in the early morning hours.

The cow wonders what Nathan is up to (June 2009).

A hike at *Camp Squeah*, British Columbia, during an Anabaptist conference (September 2009).

Our family, summer 2010

Opa and Oma with their grandchildren, 2010

Hein family escalating in numbers.
(Summer 2010)

From left to right: Jadelynn, Nathan, and Malakai, summer 2010.

Jennyfer, Jadelynn, Mali, Matty, and Robert, summer 2010.

Nathan at age two (summer 2010).

CHAPTER 18

Enjoying Family and Traveling (2011–2013)

As a teenager, I often walked past ancient buildings, churches, and monuments, some of them more than one thousand years old, without paying much attention to their historical significance. This changed after I retired when I became interested in the history of Christianity.

Since we never know how much longer we will be granted good health, we wanted to travel to more European countries for the specific purpose of seeing the more interesting historic sites, especially cathedrals, museums, castles, and other points of interest. Of the many impressions, I would like to include a few highlights of our trips since some readers might be interested in visiting some of these places as well.

In September 2011, we embarked on a trip to **Ireland, Scotland, and England**.

A. Ireland

One of the greatest tourist attractions in Dublin is the **Book of Kells exhibit** at the Trinity College Library. The Book of Kells contains the four gospels written in Latin in beautifully designed ornate letters by Celtic monks. It is regarded as a masterwork of Western calligraphy. Irish monks wrote it about AD 800 at a monastery on the Island of Iona, on the northwest coast of Scotland. This monastery was founded in the sixth century (563) by Columba, an Irish missionary to the Scots. Below are some examples of this great artwork.

Some pictures from the Book of Kells (from a postcard)

We had prebooked a guided bus roundtrip through Ireland that led us through the Connemara National Park area to Galway on the Irish west coast. Some of our stops were Kylemore Abbey; Killary

Harbour; Cliffs of Moher; Killarney; Ring of Kerry; Muckross House, which is a Victorian mansion built in 1843; Blarney castle; the Crystal factory in Waterford; and the Glendalough Celtic monastery with its medieval chapel founded by St. Kevin's in the sixth century.

Beautiful serene natural setting in the Connemara area of Ireland (August 2011).

Kylemore Abbey, a former Benedictine monastery
located in the beautiful Connemara area.

B. Scotland

Edinburgh Castle was the place where Mary Queen of Scots gave birth to her only son, who became the future King James VI of Scotland, and King James I of England, and who authorized the King James version of the Bible, published in 1611 (picture taken September 2011).

In walking distance from this castle is **St. Giles Cathedral**, the mother church of Presbyterianism, where the famous Scottish reformer John Knox (1560) preached. He was a key figure in the formation of modern Scotland. In the Treaty of Berwick (1560), the English and French agreed to leave Scotland, assuring the future of Protestantism in Scotland.

Strolling along the High Street (also called the Royal Mile), we visited the **Palace of the Holyrood House** ("rood" meaning cross), which is located on the opposite end of Edinburgh Castle. It was the residence of Mary Queen of Scots and the place where she got married. It is also the place where the queen resides when she comes to Edinburgh.

While in Scotland, we toured Glamis Castle that began as a hunting lodge in the eleventh century. It became the beautiful childhood home of Queen Elisabeth's mother and the place where Princess Margaret was born. Not far from Glamis Castle is the idyllic town of Perth with its St. John's Cathedral, the church where John Knox preached.

Another place we found worthwhile visiting was the **Traquair house,** a former hunting lodge for kings and queens. It is located about fifty kilometers south of Edinburgh and is the oldest continuously inhabited house in Scotland, dating back to 1107. It used to be a refuge for Catholic priests during times of religious persecutions. Now it is a museum attracting many tourists. Among other interesting exhibits one can find a rare copy of a Koberger Bible written in Latin and printed in 1479 in Nuremberg, Germany.

C. England

Westminster Abbey in London was built over a period of eight hundred years. It was founded in 1052 and completed in the 1860s. Having been the nation's coronation church since 1066, many kings and queens, including Queen Elisabeth II, have been crowned here. It is also the resting place of famous monarchs, poets, and scientists. George Friedrich Handel, composer of the oratorio Messiah, is also buried here. Above the outside entrance of the west portal are ten statues. Among these are Dietrich Bonhoeffer and Martin Luther King.

West Portal of **Westminster Abbey**. The fourth statue from the right above the portal is Dietrich Bonhoeffer, holding up his Bible (September 2011).

Among the most impressive cathedrals we have ever seen is **St. Paul's Cathedral** in London. It was constructed by Christopher Wren between 1675 and 1710. Here Churchill's funeral took place and in 1981 the marriage of Prince Charles and Lady Diana Spencer. Buried here, among other scientists, poets, monarchs, and statesmen, is Isaac Newton (1687) who said: "Gravity explains the motion of the planets, but it cannot explain who set the planets in motion." We also had the great pleasure of being ushered into the "quire" section for the Vesper service and hearing their wonderful boys' choir sing from up close.

Places we toured were **London Tower** containing the crown jewels and where Henry VIII had his second and fifth wife beheaded, and **Hampton Court Palace**, the home of King Henry VIII, where in 1604 the Hampton Court Conference took place, in which King James I announced the new translation of the Bible which became the King James Bible.

Renting a car, we visited the following places: **Canterbury Cathedral** which had it beginnings in AD 597, and where Archbishop Thomas Becket was murdered in 1170; **Cambridge** with its thirty-one colleges founded in 1209; **York**, which was England's second most important city during the years from 1100–1500; **Stratford upon Avon**, Shakespeare's birthplace with a statue near his home inscribed with the words: "*The fool does think he is wise, but the wise man knows himself to be a fool*"; **Oxford** University, the oldest institution of higher learning in the English-speaking world, established in 1170 and now having thirty-six colleges; and **Bath**, England's first spa resort with hot springs. We also visited with two of Hedy's cousins who have made England their home.

Two years later, in September 2013, we traveled to France and Switzerland.

A. France

After spending three days in **Paris** and seeing its major tourist attractions, including **Versailles** and the world's largest museum, the **Louvre**, we rented a car to visit the following places:

Rouen, where Joan of Arc was burned at the stake in 1431; **Mt. St. Michel**, the Benedictine monastery founded in 708 which is declared a UNESCO World Heritage Site; **Nantes**, the city where Henry IV signed the Edict of Nantes in 1598. Traveling up the beautiful **Loire Valley**, we stopped in **Tours** and **Amboise**, where Leonardo da Vinci is buried. From **Orleans**, heading in an easterly direction, we visited the oldest surviving Cistercian monastery of France, the **Abbey of Fontenay**, founded by St. Bernard de Clairvaux in 1118. One of the most powerful monastic foundations in Europe was the **Cluny Abbey** founded in 910 by Duke William of Aquitaine. Worthwhile to visit was the famous *Isenheimer Altar* at the Unterlinden Museum in **Colmar**. It is considered one of the world's most treasured works of ecclesiastical art and holds the world famous *Isenheimer Altarpiece* carved by Nikolaus Hagenauer in 1505 and painted by Matthias Grunewald in 1515. **Riquewihr**, a small romantic village on the Route du Vin in Alsace, also belongs to our delightful experiences. Before returning from Paris, we admired the grandiose cathedral in **Reims** whose construction began in the thirteenth century. Here France's first king, King Clovis I (496), is buried. He was the founder of France, who introduced Christianity to France and made Paris its capital.

Reims Cathedral. French kings have been crowned here since medieval times until the early nineteenth century (photo by Wilf Hein, September 2013).

B. Switzerland

Those interested in Reformation history and Switzerland may like to stop in **Geneva** to see the ninety-one-meter-long *Reformation Wall* built in 1917, depicting the four reformers, Farel, Calvin, Beza, and Knox. These are surrounded by two massive concrete blocks of Luther and Zwingli.

From left to right: William Farel, John Calvin, Theodore Beza, and John Knox (photo by Wilf Hein, September 2013).

After a stop in **Bern**, the area to which many Anabaptists fled during the sixteenth century persecution, we visited **Zurich**, the city of the Swiss Reformation. **Ulrich Zwingli** (1484–1531), leader of the Swiss Reformation, like Luther a Catholic priest, opposed many practices of the Roman Catholic Church. Among them were the following:

- The exaggerated role of relics and saints and the frequently associated promises of miraculous cures.
- The indulgences.
- Celibacy (Zwingli was secretly married).
- The format by which the Eucharist was celebrated. He opposed the dogma of transubstantiation. Instead he wanted to celebrate the Lord's Supper as a symbolic memorial and thanksgiving.

Zwingli presented sixty-seven theses, which became known as the "First Disputation." He resigned from the priesthood and kept on preaching at Zurich's Grossmuenster Church.

The Grossmuenster Church in Zurich, where Zwingli preached (photo by Wilf Hein, September 2013).

Unfortunately, Zwingli was opposed to the Anabaptists, resulting in many of them having to die a martyr's death. A memorial plaque honouring Anabaptists, who according to some scholars were the first who stood for separation of church and state, can be found nearby, about three hundred meters on the northwest side of the Limmat River.

Memorial plaque of first Anabaptists martyrs displayed on the Limmat River bank in Zurich (photo by Wilf Hein, September 2013)

The inscription says: "Here, Felix Manz and five other Anabaptists were drowned from a platform in the middle of the Limmat River during the Reformation years between 1527 and 1532. The last Anabaptist executed was Hans Landis in 1614."

When war broke out between the Catholic and Protestant cantons, Zwingli was killed at the young age of forty-seven.

Before our return flight, we enjoyed a visit with my cousin Jochen Schowalter and his wife, Hanni, in Bennhausen, Germany.

Visiting my cousin Jochen Schowalter in Germany, September, 2013.

Family Matters

Realizing how much our forefathers had to suffer for what they believed, we appreciate even more the freedom we are granted in this beautiful country. More relaxing than travelling long distances to Europe was gardening and activities with our grandchildren.

A garden lady who enjoys planting and pulling out the weeds (July 2011).

Oma taking her grandchildren to Aldergrove Zoo, May 2011.

Jeremy and Kalina's Katelynn seven months old (February 2011).

Hedy's Seventieth Surprise Birthday Party (2012)

From a video clip composed by my cousin Hildegarde Baerg.

We had the privilege of two top musicians entertaining us: Lorin Friesen playing the violin and Mel Bowker accompanying on the piano. What a great time we had with our close friends!

"Downsizing" Yet Upsizing in Terms of Floor Area

Getting tired of the weeds and the yard work, we decided to move into a townhouse. Our home on Amberpoint finally sold after being on the market for six months. We moved into our new place in August 2012. It turned out that the floor area of our townhome, which was built in the early 1990s, was even larger than our previous home. We love the quiet, central, and beautiful location.

Our townhome at the Lakepoint Villas Complex in Abbotsford (August 2012)

Our townhome, view from the south side

Christmas dinner in our new townhome, 2012

Celebrating New Year's Eve with family in Hawaii (Oahu)

We feel blessed with our children, our beautiful daughters-in law, and our grandchildren (Hawaii, winter, 2012–13)

Our three sons from left to right: Adrian, Jeremy, and Robert at the Townline farm home (March 2013).

CHAPTER 19

Golden Years (2014–2017)

If I were asked what makes the "golden years" golden, I would probably say, freedom from work obligations and being able to choose how to invest the remaining time the Lord grants me. Even before I retired, I decided that continued education would be on the top of my list. I reevaluated my interests by checking various calendars of colleges and universities. Almost all courses which caught my attention were in the field of theology and history. Since I had experienced difficulties studying in a class setting, I decided to take the courses I was interested in by correspondence. This worked out very well for me. Studying at my own pace allowed me to dig deeper in finding additional answers to many questions. And this method helped me to obtain much better grades.[1] It is wonderful that some institutions, like Briercrest Distance Learning, offer students these options. So far, I have obtained a *Certificate of the Bible Exploration Series* from Briercrest College and Seminary and am planning to take a few more courses in the future.

Another great advantage of retirement is having time to reflect more deeply on the many experiences the Lord had granted us. We are so thankful for our family and the values our parents passed on to us, that we also wanted to be able to transmit something of lasting value to our children and grandchildren. I then considered translat-

---

[1] Of the eight courses taken so far, I received four As and four A+s.

ing my father's memoirs since our boys had only limited exposure to their grandparents in Germany. My father had given me his typewritten memoir, some 140 pages contained in two volumes. In it, he tells the story of his upbringing and schooling in Russia, his emigration, his studies in Germany, how he met his future wife, his wartime story, his ministry as pastor, editor, researcher, and writer, his family, world trips, and his retirement. Since his memoir contained much historical information, we donated a copy to the *Mennonitische Forschungstelle* Library (Mennonite Research Institute) at the Weierhof, in southwest Germany. Those interested in reading it in the original German can find it there under the title *Ein Russland-Deutscher erlebt Ost und West* (author Gerhard Hein). His original memoir, however, contains many handwritten and sometimes hard to decipher corrections. Due to some health setbacks, my father could no longer rewrite it, as he had initially planned. I decided to translate it and improve upon it, by giving it a more attractive title, a better graphical layout, and include more pictures, documents, letters, maps, tables, sketches, foreword, introduction, and afterword, and by adding some explanatory comments. The appendix contains additional information, giving some examples of my father's publications and lectures, showing also the recognition he received, his family tree, and his entire bibliography. Included in the appendix is also a Christmas message he delivered in the Ukraine during World War II (winter 1943) to his officers and colleagues. More than one-third of this 330-page book (the English version of my father's memoir) is additional material not found in the original text. It was published under the title: *A Witness in Times of War and Peace* in October 2015 by *FriesenPress* in Victoria, British Columbia.[2]

    Now that I had written a book to honour my father, I also wanted to pay tribute to my mother, who has meant so much to me. Retirement life gave me this opportunity.

    Next to family life, I really appreciate being part of a church fellowship, where Christ-centered messages are being delivered and where one feels accepted and cared for. I found what I was searching

---

[2]   Book reviews are given at the end of the appendix

for especially in various Mennonite Brethren churches we attended over the years. What impresses me most about Mennonites is that they are people one generally can trust, and they try to practice what they preach. I have found that many Mennonites are very generous and willing to donate to those in need. They also often serve voluntarily in organizations like Mennonite Central Committee (MCC), the well-known international humanitarian aid agency, which sends food, clothing donations to needy throughout the world, irrespective of their faith affiliations. I admire people who sacrificed their lives to serve through this organization. Among them were C. F. Klassen with his wife, Mary, Peter and Elfrieda Dyck and the Pax boys who built homes for refugees, and many others. Many Mennonite refugees who came from Russia, among them my parents-in-law, owe their survival to MCC and the people associated with this organization. MCC also alleviates need through its subsidiaries Mennonite Voluntary Service (MVS) and Mennonite Disaster Service (MDS).

Most of the various Mennonite denominations are connected through MCC and the Mennonite World Conference (MWC) which takes place in different countries every six years. My wife and I had the opportunity to be part of the MWC and meet with our worldwide faith family in the summer of 2015.

Mennonite World Conference, Pennsylvania 2015

About 8,400 delegates from eighty countries, gathered in Harrisburg, Pennsylvania at the sixteenth Mennonite World Conference in July 2015. Fifteen hundred attendees came from outside North America.[3] It was a unique experience to be part of such a big event in which thousands of fellow believers met to worship and serve Christ.

---

[3] https://www.mwc-cmm.org/sites/default/files/website_files/mwc_pa2015_statistics_8.5x14.pdf

Mennonite World Conference at the Farm Show Complex in Harrisburg, Pennsylvania, July 2015

Even though there were many different Mennonite denominations represented, many of them coming from various ethnic backgrounds whose worship styles were different, we felt closely connected through our common denominator (Jesus Christ) and our rich Anabaptist heritage. It was not only words presented by international speakers and the music and songs that impressed us but also the active participation in various workshops. An example of this was the construction of two prefab homes destined for families who had lost their homes in a natural disaster. One of the beneficiary families was from Nebraska and the other from Maryland. A thirty-year-old volunteer who participated in the construction of one of the homes said, "I don't have talent with my mouth and my tongue, but I have talent in my hands." More than 160 other volunteers worked during this conference, for example, in a mobile MCC canner, canning beans, labeling and packing them. Some of this food was immediately donated to the local food bank. Volunteers also helped sewing quilts designated for refugee camps and orphanages.

MWC attendees had the option to participate in tours offered during free afternoons. We decided to take part in a tour to Lancaster County where the first Mennonites had arrived in 1710. Especially interesting to us was the Lancaster Mennonite Historical Society with its display of various Martyr's Mirrors in its library. Among them were copies from Dordrecht (1660), Amsterdam (1685), Ephrata (1748), and Pirmasens (1790).

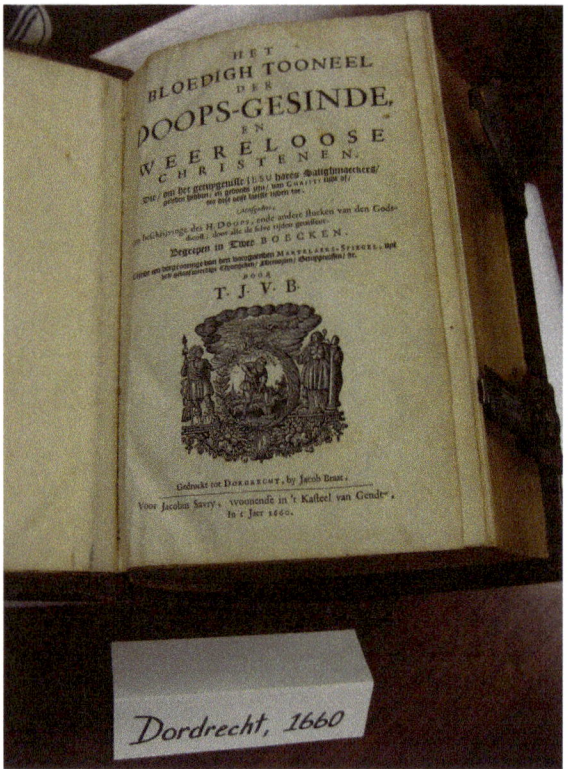

The first page of the Dordrecht Martyr's Mirror dated 1660. Displayed at the Lancaster Mennonite Historical Society (photo by Wilf Hein, July 2015).

Other points of interest were seeing the recreated Old Testament tabernacle, adjacent to the Mennonite Museum, and visiting the Cloister in Ephrata.

At the previous Mennonite World Conference held 2009 in Asuncion, Paraguay, we heard Catholics and Lutherans ask for forgiveness for acts of violence committed to Anabaptists in the past. In a workshop on the Muenster rebellion and on Aryanism at the Harrisburg conference, I heard for the first time that Mennonites needed to ask for forgiveness as well.

A few years ago, my wife had mentioned that she would like to travel through the Eastern United States sometime. In Pennsylvania now, we decided to extend our holiday for another two weeks and tour some of the notable places of early American history.

Traveling Through the Eastern United States, July–August 2015

For those perhaps interested in a similar trip, I am including some of the places we visited. Among them were the following: The richly ornamented **Harrisburg Capitol** and the famous Hershey's Chocolate factory. It was a delight traveling through **Amish country** and seeing the Amish ride in their horse and buggies to and from their Sunday morning services. Our next destination was **Philadelphia,** the city founded by Quaker William Penn in 1682, followed by a sightseeing tour through **Washington, DC**. Especially interesting was a visit to the recreated museum of the first settlers in **Jamestown, Virginia**. The early settlers from England arrived here in 1607. Most of those who survived the harsh conditions moved to nearby **Williamsburg** in 1699. Heading north, we paid a visit to George Washington's estate in **Mt. Vernon**, where he was sworn in as President in 1789. In New York City, we enjoyed the view from the top of the 104 storey, 541-meter-high *One World Trade Center*, completed in November 2014. Another highlight while staying in this great city was attending a concert at the Avery Fisher Hall of the Lincoln Center.

Traveling through Connecticut, we enjoyed a visit with Hedy's brother John Sawatsky and his wife, Karen. John, the author of five books and the director of Talent Development at the ESPN headquarters in Bristol, took us on a company tour through the ESPN headquarters in Bristol and to a visit to the Mark Twain House and Museum in Hartford.

John Sawatsky with his wife Karen on the right at the Mark Twain Museum in Hartford, Connecticut, August 2015.

We continued our trip via **Cape Cod** to **Plymouth**, Massachusetts, where the Mayflower Compact was signed by the Puritans, who had arrived from England in 1620.

Our final stop was **Boston**, USA's oldest and most historic city. We enjoyed strolling the campus of Harvard University founded in 1636. A good way of seeing the major points of interest within only a few hours are the guided city tours with the hop-on, hop-off bus. A Boston harbour cruise brought our New England trip to a satisfying conclusion.

Belgium, Hungary, and Germany, September 2015

One of the main reasons for going on another big trip this year was to attend a conference in Germany which interested me. We first wanted to see some places we had not yet visited and then conclude our planned roundtrip with the Muenster conference. Among points of interest were the two historic Belgian cities **Ghent** and **Bruges**, which played an important role in medieval trade. We admired the architecture of the historic guild houses dating back to the twelfth and thirteenth centuries. These two cities were some of the few places not damaged during the two World Wars. In the Middle Ages, Ghent was, after Paris, the biggest city in Europe north of the Alps.

Market Place, Ghent, Belgium, September 2015

Since it was not too far from the Bruges to the North Sea, we drove the extra kilometers to see the famous Belgian summer resort of Ostend. Here we spent an afternoon and then continued our trip in a southeasterly direction to **Aachen**, the city which Charlemagne had made the capital of the Holy Roman Empire for twenty years. We arrived in time to attend an evensong in the renowned *Pfalzkapelle* (or Palatine Chapel) built between AD 792 and 805. It is the only remaining part of Charlemagne's great palace.

Continuing our trip in a southeasterly direction brought us to **Ulm**, the city of the world's tallest church. Its gothic-style Muenster, constructed during the years 1377 to 1545, is 161 meters high. My cousin Klaus Beringer and his wife, Lara, led us on a walking tour of the city.

A delightful visit at my cousin's place in Ulm, Germany. From left to right: Lara Beringer, Hedy, and my cousins, Liselotte and Klaus Beringer, September 2015.

A visit to **Passau**, the old, romantic city near the Austrian border is also highly recommended. The baroque-style St. Stephen's Cathedral contains the world's largest organ consisting of five individual organs, which can be played from one keyboard. We enjoyed a wonderful noon-hour concert there.

Organ in St. Stephen Cathedral in Passau, Germany. It has nearly eighteen thousand pipes and more than 230 registers (September 2015).

We found it interesting that the three cities, Passau and Vienna and Budapest, all had a famous St. Stephen's Cathedral in which we could hear a concert. **Vienna** was noteworthy for the many beautiful well-preserved buildings, especially along the Ringstrasse, the boulevard surrounding the oldest part of the city center, which has been declared a UNESCO World Heritage Site.

Our furthest destination was **Budapest** in Hungary, indeed a very impressive city. Many of its historic buildings have been renovated and preserved in their original architectural style. Examples of this are the Royal Palace located on the hilly Buda side on the Danube's western bank and the Parliament building on the eastern "Pest" side of the Danube River. During our three-day stay, we viewed the major tourist attractions, which also included a cruise along the Danube.

The attractive Hungarian Parliament Building was designed by Hungarian architect Imre Steindl. When it opened in 1902, it was the largest parliament building in the world (photo by Wilf Hein, September 2015).

Heading back into Germany, we stopped in **Nuremberg**, where the famous painter Albrecht Durer (1471–1528) was born and died and whose museum we visited. This year, we didn't want to miss visiting the Gutenberg Museum in **Mainz**, where Johannes Gutenberg, the inventor of the printing press, produced his first printed Bible in 1456. The Gutenberg Bible is a two-volume copy of Jerome's Latin Vulgate, also known as the Mazarin Bible. We concluded our Europe roundtrip with a visit to **Muenster**, the place where the Peace of Westphalia was signed (1648). Here we spent our last three days attending a conference sponsored by the Mennonite Historical Society of Germany (*Mennonitischer Geschichtsverein*).

In spring 2016, we had the privilege of visiting our sponsored child in the **Dominican Republic.**

THINGS MY MOTHER TAUGHT ME

A visit to meet with our sponsored child, fourteen-year-old Yeremi, in Punta Cana, Dominican Republic. To the right of Hedy is Yeremi's mother, Miled, and Soraya, a staff member from Compassion Canada, and Alcedo, our interpreter (April 2016).

The Latest on the Family

Grandchildren growing up and parents getting older, Thanksgiving 2014.

Hedy's part-time teaching includes giving free lessons to her grandchildren.

Nathan, Jadelyn, and Mali playing with Oma, Christmas 2014.

My brother, Eckart, and his family came to visit us in summer 2015.

From left to right: Arnt-Philipp (my nephew)
with Andrea and Felipe Daniel,
Helga and Eckart (Mill Lake Park, Abbotsford,
British Columbia, August 2015).

My nephew, Arnt Philipp, with his wife, Andrea, and his son, Felipe Daniel (picture taken 2012).

A birthday party with two of my Canadian cousins:

Wilf with his cousins Hildegarde Baerg and Art Hein, February 2016

Adrian and Erin's children: left Charis, December 2014, and right Simyon holding Rayna, March 2016.

Jeremy and Kalina's Andrew 2015

Family Christmas celebration in our *Lakepoint Villa* Clubhouse, December 30, 2016

Jeremy and Kalina with family, from left to right: Nathan, Andrew, Katelyn, and Annika, Christmas 2016

Robert and Jennyfer with family, from left to right:
Malakai, Jadelynn, and Matthew, Christmas 2015

Adrian and Erin with family, from left to right,
Simyon, Rayna, and Charis, Christmas 2016

Opa and Oma with their ten grandchildren, Christmas 2016

THINGS MY MOTHER TAUGHT ME

I would like to conclude this last chapter with a poem my mother sent me. It expresses what I have experienced in my life and what I trust my future will hold.

In German
Schau nun zurück und sieh' die Wunder an,
Die immer neu der Herr an Dir getan.
Dann jubilieren täglich Herz und Mund,
Der treu Dich trug bis heut' zu dieser Stund.
Der bleibt Dir auch bei jedem neuen Schritt
Durch Licht und Dunkel gehet Jesus mit,
Ob auf die Höh' –ob talwärts— Er allein
weiß, welcher Weg der richtige muss sein.
Geh' nur getrost und ohne bange Sorgen!
Sein sind das Gestern, Heute und auch Morgen
(Author unknown)

In English
Reflect on your life and see the **miracles**
The Lord has done for you again and again.
Then you will rejoice daily with your heart and mouth,
Because He carried you faithfully to this very hour.
Jesus will guide you in every new step you take;
He will accompany you through periods of light and darkness
Whether climbing heights or walking through valleys,
He alone knows which way is the right one to go.
Keep trusting and be not anxious,
To Him belong yesterday, today and tomorrow.

*****

AFTERWORD

While my first book *A Witness in Times of War and Peace* was written to honour my father, the main purpose of writing this biography was to acknowledge the positive influence my mother had on my life. She did this by teaching me Christian values that shaped me and helped me experience God's wonderful direction in my life.

My parents: Gerhard & Lydia Hein (picture taken 1967)[1]

---

[1] A short version of my father's biography can be viewed through the following link: http://gameo.org/index.php?title=Hein,_Gerhard_(1905%E2%80%93 1990).

What I Learned by Writing My Memoirs

Writing this memoir now in my retirement years helped me to reflect on my life and learn some things I was not aware of previously. By researching my ancestral history, I have learned to appreciate in a new way my rich Mennonite heritage. This helped me gain a new sense of identity.

My maternal ancestors can be traced to the Swiss Anabaptists, who accepted the theology of the great reformers but wanted to expand the Reformation to be more reflective of the early first century Christian church. This included among other things, separation of church and state, freedom of conscience, freedom to choose their own elders and preachers, nonresistance, no swearing of oath, and adult baptism. All these are theological values I identify with. The great reformers, however, regarded Anabaptists as dissidents and heretics, who deserved nothing less than the martyr's death. It is estimated that four thousand to five thousand Anabaptists were executed in the sixteenth century for what they believed was right.[2] This means that about twice as many Christians died a martyr's death during the Reformation period compared to those executed during the Roman persecution in the first three centuries.[3] Tragically, Anabaptists were persecuted by all reformers of the state churches, Catholics, Lutherans, Calvinists and the Reformed Church alike. My maternal Hege ancestors of the seventeenth and eighteenth centuries were among those Anabaptists.[4]

My paternal ancestors also experienced persecution, mistreatment, and death. They originally came from Holland, then settled

---

[2] Susanne Willms Thielman, and Philip-Sherwood, *Susanne Remembers*, A Mennonnite childhood in revolutionary Russia (Abbotsford, British Columbia: Judson Lake House, 2009), 160.

[3] Harry Loewen, Elisabeth L. Wiens, Elke and Peter Foth. *Warum ich mennonitisch bin*. (Hamburg, Germany: Kuempers Verlag, 1996), Vorwort III. Some other sources, however, state that the number of Christians martyred during the Diocletion period alone may have ranged between 3,000 to 3,500 (https://en.wikipedia.org/wiki/List_of_Christians_martyred_during_the_reign_of_Diocletian).

[4] See appendix, my essay entitled *Additional Historic Information about the Hege Families*.

in Prussia, and after Catherine the Great promised the Mennonites freedom of religion, they were among those who moved to the Mennonite settlement Alexandertal (also called Altsamara) in Russia in 1864.[5] During the Bolshevik Revolution, they again were persecuted. Most of them lost their properties and almost everything they owned. Many of them were imprisoned, sent to forced labour camps, or shot because they were hated as Christians, Germans, and Kulaks.[6]

To this day I appreciate that my ancestors were willing to die so that future generations could enjoy freedom of religion and conscience. Historian and author Bruce Shelley credits the Anabaptists with being the first religious group who stood for religious liberty.[7]

History teaches us that it took decades and even centuries of war to settle ideological differences within Christianity. May we all learn from mistakes committed in the past. It seems to me that freedom of religion and the establishment of democratic values in a society are the prerequisite for establishing peace among world religions. May we be able to be peace builders throughout the world, by drawing strength from the Prince of Peace, who said:

> *"Peace I leave with you; my peace I give you. I do not give to you as the world gives. Do not let your hearts be troubled and do not be afraid"* (John 14:27).

My Mother Taught Me

1. To keep on learning.
2. To be more understanding and loving toward other people.
3. To be more tolerant towards views coming from people of different religious backgrounds and denominations.

---

[5] My father's great-grandfather Dietrich Hamm who came from Fuerstenwerder in West Prussia was elected the first elder in Alexandertal and his son-in-law Jacob Hein was the cofounder of the Mennonite Brethren Church in the Samara region. (Source: Bernhard Harder, *Alexandertal*, 72, 76)

[6] More about the fate of my father's family in Russia is described in detail in my book *A Witness* (chapter 1, especially on p. 44).

[7] Bruce L. Shelley, *Church History in Plain Language*, Dallas, Texas, Word Publishing, 1995.

4. To maintain a positive attitude, even when facing difficult situations.
5. To express my appreciation more often, rather than being too critical.
6. To see my own inadequacies, to ask for forgiveness, and to be forgiving toward others. I want to ask especially my children to forgive me for sometimes being impatient and not loving enough and for having lost my temper at times. Deep down, I love my family, and this was one of the reasons why I wrote the two books for my family as an inheritance.
7. To be thankful.

Thinking about what I can be thankful for, the following points come to mind:

- God's grace, his wonderful guidance and provision throughout my life.
- My parents for laying the spiritual foundation of LOVE, FAITH, AND HOPE (1 Cor 13:13).
- The prayers, love, and understanding they showed me.
- My forefathers and the rich heritage they left behind.
- For God blessing me, because I honoured my parents (Exod 20:12)
- God letting me experience many miraculous events, especially for finding my wonderful wife, who has become a loving mother and grandmother to our three boys and grandchildren.
- Our three sons with our beautiful daughters-in-law and ten grandchildren.
- A job which I liked and the success I experienced despite the lack of a university degree.
- An opportunity to take courses of my choice, including correspondence courses and the wide choice of good literature available for self-education.
- Material blessings, including our home.

- Being able to live in a country where we can enjoy peace and many opportunities.
- Many worldwide travels that created a new field of interest. I had the opportunity to travel to thirty-five different countries, visiting many of them several times (see Travelog in appendix).[8]
- God-given health, energy, and persistence to write two books in honour of my parents and dedicated to our descendants.
- Being able to trust in the promises of God, knowing that He will be with me to the end of my life.

My Future Wishes

May God be gracious and bless and protect our three sons with their families. May he also lead and direct me throughout the last stage of my life. May he grant me His peace and enable me to accept the setbacks that come with old age, frailty, and its finality.

I would like to conclude my memoir with the prayer of the American theologian Reinhard Niebuhr (1892-1971):

God grant me the **Serenity** to accept the things I cannot change,
Courage to change the things I can,
and **Wisdom** to know the difference.

---

[8] I am especially thankful that I could visit Germany, my native country, twenty-one times since I immigrated and spend nine vacations in Hawaii and the same number of holidays in Mexico.

Appendix

Abbreviations

CH-1	Chronik der Familie Hege, Heft 1, Christian Hege, Frankfurt a.M. 1937
CH-2	Chronik der Family Hege, Christian Hege, Frankfurt a.M., Karlsruhe 1970
DSS	Dead Sea Scrolls
HHzG	Hans Hege, 2. Februar 1885 – 2. Januar 1983, zum Gedächtnis
MCC	Mennonite Central Committee
MDS	Mennonite Disaster Service
MEI	Mennonite Educational Institute, Abbotsford, British Columbia
MVS	Mennonite Voluntary Service
ML	Mennonitisches Lexikon
MWC	Mennonite World Conference

Additional Historical Information about the Hege (Hegi, Hegy, Hagey) Families

Persecution of Anabaptists in Switzerland and Germany

The Anabaptists were severely persecuted during the 16th and 17th centuries for what they believed was right.[1] There were also Hegi families among the Anabaptists in the Swiss Aargau canton. When three women refused to join the Reformed Church in 1609, they were tortured. One of these women died due to severe mistreatment (CH-1, 5).

In fall 1639, a Rudolph Haegi, from Urzlikon near Zurich, together with his wife and oldest son, were arrested and imprisoned in Oetenbach near Zurich. He was held in prison for one year and seven months. After their release, their family was banned and had to leave their home and country. Departing their homestead without being allowed to sell their properties, was not an easy decision.[2]

Rudolf, probably the son to the Rudolph Haegi mentioned above, left Switzerland in 1656 and settled in Duehren, near Sinsheim, in the present-day province of Baden-Wuerttemberg in Germany. The situation in Germany was not much better for the Anabaptists. When Rudolf took part in a Mennonite evening service in Steinsfurt near Sinsheim on March 2, 1661, he along with fifty-three other Anabaptists, were arrested by Palatinate officials. During their interrogation, they mentioned that they had arrived five or six years ago, from Bern in Switzerland.[3] Meetings among fellow believers were outlawed at that time (CH-2, 44). For anyone who missed attending a sermon in state churches, the government issued fines (CH-1, 6-7).

---

[1] See my essay entitled *Anabaptists and Mennonites* in my book *A Witness*, p. 266 ff.

[2] This information comes from CH-1, 5 and a single leaflet printed in the antique German "Frakturschrift," found in Gerhard Hein's historic library. No source is given. An additional five-page handwritten letter (no date given and in possession of the author), also mentions this Rudolf Haegi. The letter is entitled *Der Sippe Hege bisher unbekannte Namenstraeger Hege, Hegi, Haegi, Haegy*, and was written by Otto Schowalter, 6749 Kaplaneihof, Germany.

[3] MQR, Vol. XXXIV, July 1960, 204

A legislation issued on July 7, 1603 threatened violators with imprisonment, possible expulsion and withdrawal of food (CH-1, 6). The government also wanted to control the growth of Mennonite families in Germany. They were not to exceed 200 families and they needed to report the size of their families.[4] For centuries Mennonites were limited to work only as farmers on leased property. Later, after the French Revolution, Mennonites could choose different professions. Among them were engineers, theologians, medical doctors and government employees (CH-2, 22).

Improvement of Conditions After the Thirty-Year War

After the Thirty-Year War, the land was devastated, and the government needed expert farmers. Authorities knew that Mennonites were hard working and successful agriculturists. Since they did not agree with their religion, they conducted opinion polls. A government ordered report dated June 16, 1763, says this about Mennonites:

"Even though we detest this sect which should be eradicated, we found that no better and more industrious people can be found among other religions. They are eager to work day and night and are a model for others to follow. We did not hear them swearing, neither did we see any wrong-doing among them. They are not involved in any lawsuits, while those who claim to be perfect, are often found among criminals who need to be disciplined" (CH-1, 40).

Despite improvements, many Mennonites looked for an environment of greater freedom, and immigrated to the United States.

Immigration to Pennsylvania

Government pressures, persecution and loss of personal freedom made many Mennonites immigrate to the United States. Some Mennonites from Krefeld settled in Pennsylvania already in 1683 (CH-1, 36). In 1717 about three hundred Mennonites from the Palatinate immigrated to Pennsylvania, through the help of their Dutch fellow believers. The first emigrant of the Hege family was **Hans Hege** from the Zweibrücken area, who was accompanied by fif-

---

[4] CH-2, 45; CH-1, 39

ty-one other families. They arrived in Philadelphia in 1727.[5] Several of Hans' descendants became preachers and served in Mennonite churches (CH-2, 45). Within five years, more than 3,000 Swiss-Palatinate Mennonites arrived in the Colonies.[6]

One of the better known Hege immigrants was a **Daniel Hege** who came from the Gruenstadt area. He arrived in the United States in 1851. Daniel received formal training in theological leadership in Switzerland and later also in Missouri. He became a preacher at the General Mennonite Church in Summerfield, Illinois in 1859, and served as the first Mennonite traveling evangelist for the Conference, and as a missionary to the Indians. He was the co-founder of the General Conference of Mennonites in North America and became its secretary. Daniel was instrumental in the establishment of Mennonite schools, among them the Mennonite high school at Wadsworth, Ohio.[7]

Jacob Hege (1844- 1926) arrived in America with his family in 1893 (CH-2, 48). He lived in Nebraska and Idaho and died in Paso Robles in California. He was regarded as a talented preacher in his Mennonite community (CH-2,31). In 1897, he published *Christliche Gemeindezucht.*

Many of the Hege families anglicized their name after their arrival in the United States to Hegy, Hagey or some other similar sounding surnames.

Immigration to Ontario

The first Hagey's arriving in Canada came from Lancaster and Montgomery County in Pennsylvania. They settled in Waterloo County, near Preston Ontario in 1801. In 1822 another Hagey family arrived from the same area in Pennsylvania. Their two sons, Jacob, a deacon from 1832-1893 and Joseph, who served as a bishop from 1851-1876, started a church, named after their family name.

---

[5] From a photocopy of a single leaflet entitled *Hans Hege, Immigrant II* (no source given).
[6] MQR, Vol. XXXIV, July 1960, 204
[7] MQR, Vol. XXXIV, July 1960, 204-205; CH-1, 13; CH-2, 45

The *Hagey Church* was built in 1842 and is now called "Preston Mennonite Church." It is located near Cambridge, Ontario (ML 231-232), about 1½ kilometers north of Preston.

Some of My Better-Known Hege Relatives in Germany

Ulrich Hege (1808-1872), the great-grandfather of my mother was married to Magdalena Glück. They had 14 children. Ulrich successfully managed the Oberbiegelhof estate, the place where my mother was later born.[8] He had been ordained as a preacher in 1838, and became one of the leading elders of the Mennonites in Baden in 1843. His grandson Hans Hege writes that one could call him a bishop, a leader like the Apostle Paul was to the early church. (CH-2, 25).

Ulrich's oldest son **Daniel** (1836-1900) was married to Magdalena Schmutz, and lived in Munich, where he helped organize a Mennonite Church. One of Daniel's sons was **Christian**, who became well-known throughout Germany and beyond its borders (see below).

Christian Hege (1869-1943), the grandson to Ulrich and cousin to my grandfather, was the founder of the *Mennonitischer Geschichtsverein* (Mennonite Historical Society) and the editor of the *Mennonitisches Lexikon* (Mennonite Encyclopedia), and the *Mennonitische Geschichtsblaetter*. He also was the financial editor of the esteemed Frankfurter Nachrichten newspaper. One of his outstanding contributions was his historical essay *Die Täufer in der Kurpfalz* (The Anabaptists in the Palatinate). He organized the first Hege reunion at the Thomashof, near Karlsruhe in 1936.[9]

Ulrich's second son **Christian** (1840-1907), who was married to Magdalena Becker, managed the Breitenau estate.[10] He developed a special plow that was patented by a manufacturing plant. He also built his own hydraulic irrigation system. Wanting to be up-to date

---

[8] The Oberbiegelhof is located near Hasselbach, or about twelve kilometers east of Sinsheim in South Germany.

[9] More about Christian Hege can be found in my article published in Roots and Branches, Vol.l 20, no. 4, November 2014, 8.

[10] The Breitenauer Hof is located about twenty kilometers southwest of Oehringen in South Germany.

with the newest agricultural equipment, he imported several harvest machines from America. Christian also served as a preacher and elder in his church, and was a member of the Wuerttemberg *Landtag* (provincial government).[11] One of his capable and admirable children was Hans Hege (see below).

Hans Hege (1885-1983), a cousin to my grandfather, was the 12th of 16 children of Christian and Magdalena Hege-Becker, who lived at the Breitenauer-Hof.[12] After the early death of his father, the responsibility to manage the estate fell on 22-year-old Hans. Hans married Julie Barth in 1913. He and his young family moved to Waldenburg in 1919, where he successfully managed the Hohebuch estate. Here he developed an outstanding and widely recognized plant and seed growth cultivation, which earned him multiple awards. His motto was: "**One needs to sow quality before one can reap quality**" (HHzG 12). Hans Hege served as a consultant and chairman in several agricultural organizations. He held chairs of the crop-growing division of the German Agricultural Union and the South German Sugar Beet Association.[13] Dr. Albrecht Hege, his eldest son (born in 1917), who became Prälat (Lutheran bishop) of Baden-Wuerttemberg, mentioned in his eulogy, that Hans at one point held over thirty memberships and was chairman in different organizations. When he refused to join the Nazi Party after Hitler came to power, he lost many positions he had previously held.[14] In November 1940, his dear wife passed away, and his daughter Charlotte (1920-2012), who became well-known as an author, took over the household responsibilities. Two of his sons, Rolf and Joachim lost their lives during World War II. Hans soon took on new responsibilities after the war. One of them was his life-long support for the *Evangelisches Diakoniewerk* (Evangelical Church-Welfare organisation) in Schwäbisch Hall.

---

[11] CH-2, 29–30
[12] Hans Hege's sister Frieda was married to the famous Benjamin H. Unruh. For more on Benjamin Unruh see my article in *Roots and Branches*, Vol 20, no. 4, November 2014, 8.
[13] https://de.wikipedia.org/wiki/Hans_Hege_(Landwirt); HHzG 2.
[14] Albrecht Hege, Trauergottesdients fuer Dr. H.c. Hans Hege, *Ansprache im Beerdignungsgottesdienst am 6.Jan. 1983 in der Stadtkirche Waldenburg.*

In 1949 Hans founded and supported the *Evangelische Heimvolkshochschule* in Hohebuch, and received an honorary doctor degree from the agricultural high school in Hohenheim a year later.[15] He also was awarded with the *Verdienstkreuz* (a national award) of the German government and named honorary citizen of the city of Waldenburg (HHzG 15). Dr. Schnell of the University of Hohenheim spoke of Hans as a spiritual model, and a very humble and helpful person (HHzG 17). Hans loved classical music, and often played the custom-built pipe organ in the living room of his home in Hohebuch (HHzG 10). In his tribute, the mayor of Waldenburg mentioned that Hans was a very creative person with a clear vision, who could distinguish the important from the unimportant. He was an individual with charisma, optimism and tolerance towards others who held different viewpoints. He added that Hans was one of the first persons who helped re-establish Germany's agricultural system and essential economic organizations after the war (HHzG 14).

In his speech at the second Hege reunion on August 31, 1969, Hans Hege asked the question, "How can we remain the 'salt of the earth?'" Referring to the Parable of the Talents in Matthew 25:14-30, he said: "It is not our talent, our ambition, or our desire to be prominent achievers. What counts is to remain faithful, as servants who invested wisely. Faithfulness is the key to success. Whoever remains faithful in small things, will be blessed by God to take care of greater things."

In another talk held at the 25th Anniversary of the Max Planck Institute, Hans said: "In the end, all our achievements are divine gifts, which we receive through God's grace. Where leaders don't realize their responsibilities towards God, danger is looming."

In German:
> "Letztlich ist doch alles Gabe und Gnade. Wo sich der in der Führung stehende Mensch nicht in der Verantwortung vor Gott weiß, da ist Gefahr im Anzug" (HHzG, 2).

---

[15] Laendliche Heimvolkshochschule / Evangelische Bauernschule Hohebuch, *Hans Hege, 2. Februar 1885 – 2. Januar 1983, zum Gedaechtnis,* Hohebuch, (Mai 1983; abbreviated HHzG), 12, 15.

Dr. Albrecht Hege, Hans' eldest son, concluded his tribute to his father with the Apostle Paul's words to the Corinthians: "But by the grace of God I am what I am, and his grace to me was not without effect" (1 Cor 15:10).[16] **In German:** "Von Gottes Gnade, bin ich was ich bin."

Hans Hege based his hope in the living and resurrected Christ. He knew that he, and all those who put their trust in the Lord, are not doomed to spend eternity in the grave, but are promised eternal life in the heavenly kingdom.

When Hedy and I together with her parents toured Germany in 1973, we paid a visit to Uncle Hans estate in Hohebuch. Uncle Hans' youngest son, Hans Ulrich (born in 1928) and his wife Magdalene, had taken over the seed-growing operation at that time. I remember, how impressed father Sawatzky was, when he, as a Canadian raspberry farmer, admired their operation, and Hans Ulrich's proudly showed us his invented and patented special combine (Parzellenmaehdrescher).

Ulrich's third son **Jakob** (1844-1926) who was married to Elisabeth Landes from Ehrstaett, was a very energetic and industrious farmer, and served as a preacher (1874) and elder (1880). He and his family immigrated to America in 1893 (CH-2, 30-31; see also above).

Ulrich's fourth son was **Johannes Hege** (1847-1911), who leased the Oberbiegelhof, was an ordained preacher and later served as an elder of the Hasselbach church.

Ulrich's fifth son was my mother's grandfather **Philipp Hege** (1848 – 1909) who is described in Chapter 2.

*****

---

[16] From a tribute by Bishop Dr. Albrecht Hege, Heilbronn at the Hans Hege's funeral on January 6, 1983, at the Stadtkirche Waldenburg.

WILFRIED HEIN

Family Tree of Lydia Hein

Abbreviations: b=born; p=place; m= married; d=died; sp=spouse

Ulrich Hege
7 Apr 1808
p. Schwetzingen, Germany
d. 8 Nov 1872

Magdalene Glueck
b. 15 June 1815
Berwangen, Germany
d. 18 May 1893

Heinrich Landes
b. 31 July 1818
d. 1 March 1886
p. Limburgerhof, Germany

Christine Frey
b. 18 Dec 1818
d. 31 May 1864
p. Ehrstaedt, Germany

Heinrich Funck
b. 14 Sept 1808
d. 14 Nov 1869
p. Gondelsheim, Germany

Christine Heer
b. 6 March, 1811
d. 12 Dec 1842
p. Bonartshaeuserhof, Ger.

Daniel Bachmann
b. 2 Sept 1802
d. 4 Dec 1868
p. Gondelsheim, Germany

Babette Funck
b. 6 March 1810
d. 9 Dec 1874
p. Gondelsheim, Germany

Philipp Hege sen.
b. 15 Apr 1848
p. Oberbiegelhof, Germany
m. 13 Sept 1873
p. Oberbiegelhof, Germany
d. 1 May 1909
p. Oberbiegelhof, Germany

Magdalene Landes
b. 29 Jan 1853
p. Ehrstaedt, Germany
d. 17 May 1920
p. Mueckenhaeuserhof, Ger.

Christian Funck
b. 10 Oct 1839
p. Gondelsheim, Germany
d. 14 Dec 1892
p. Gondelsheim, Germany

Magdalena Bachmann
b. 17 July 1848
p. Gondelsheim, Germany
d. 13 Dec 1936

Philipp Hege
b. 16 May 1877
p. Oberbiegelhof, Germany
m. 19 May 1904
d. 1 Nov 1941
p. Rheinduerkheim, Germany

Elise Funck
b. 16 July 1881
p. Bonartshaeuserhof, Germ.
d. 27 June 1943
p. Worms, Germany

Lydia Hege
b. 29 Aug 1908
p. Oberbiegelhof, Germany
m. 5 Jan 1936
p. Germany
d. 13 Jan 1997
p. Landau, Germany
sp. Gerhard Hein[17]

---

[17] The wedding of my parents took place at the Mueckenhaeuserhof near Worms (see picture in chapter 2).

Lydia Hein's Siblings

Name	Born	Died	Married to	Children
Martha Beringer	May 11, 1905	July 12, 1978 (age 73)	Heinrich Beringer	Ruth Dieter Lieselotte Klaus
Lydia Hein	Aug. 29, 1908	January 17, 1997 (age 88)	Gerhard Hein	Eckart Wilfried
Helene Hege	Sept. 9, 1910	February 11, 1991 (age 80)	unmarried	-
Liesel Hege	Nov. 22, 1912	October 30, 1986 (almost 73)	unmarried	-
Gertrud Schowalter	Apr. 15, 1915	March 14, 1989 (almost 74)	Paul Schowalter August 24, 1939	Jochen Uli Hartmut Rolf Hildegard

WILFRIED HEIN

Jake Sawatzky's Obituary

August 23, 1910–December 19, 2002

THINGS MY MOTHER TAUGHT ME

Jacob J Sawatzky was born on August 23, 1910 to Jacob J Sawatzky and Margaretha Warkentin in Nieder-Chortitza, and grew up in Rosental, South Russia. Jacob's father was in the transport business in Rosental. After his valuable horses were stolen and his means of livelihood taken away, emigration plans were put into action.

The family left Russia and, travelling by sea on the S. S. Melita, arrived in Southern Manitoba in August 1923. In the following year, they bought a farm in Gnadenthal, MB. Jacob immediately found work on various farms, helping the family to get established in this strange new country.

Young Jacob had an early thirst for learning which continued throughout his life. With his first dollar earned he bought an English dictionary and a pen. Soon he discovered a thirst for Christ. At an evangelistic meeting conducted by Rev. David Nachtigal, seventeen-year-old Jacob accepted the Lord as his saviour. This marked a great change in Jacob's life. For the first time in his young life he experienced self-esteem. He never doubted his salvation and often spoke of this important time in his life. He was baptized in Gnadenthal, MB in 1934, and had the privilege of attending Winkler Bible School during the winters of 1933 to 1935.

Jacob married Katharina (Tina) Wiebe, daughter of Philip and Anna (Bestvater) Wiebe, on September 22, 1935 in Gnadenthal, MB. They lived in Neuenburg during the first few years, then moved to Gnadenthal in 1940 and to Winkler in 1946. Jacob had a trucking business and also took up photography and bought Winkler Photo Studio in 1946. From 1950 to 1956 he was in partnership in Winkler Motors. He had an entrepreneurial spirit and seemed undaunted in his many ventures.

Jacob had always wanted to move to British Columbia. In October of 1956 his dream was realized when he moved his family to Clearbrook BC. He owned a photo and music shop, and in 1960 bought an acreage which he developed into a raspberry farm.

Jacob and Tina's extensive travels included visits to China, Africa, Egypt, Israel, Europe, and to many points in the USA. He had a great love for music and poetry, which he continued to recite into his 92nd year. He enjoyed the beauty of nature and was an eternal optimist.

Jacob passed into the presence of his Lord and Saviour in the Menno Hospital on December 19, 2002.

Jacob will be greatly missed by his wife Tina; five daughters: Herta & Ronald Thiessen, Erica & Peter Suderman, Alice & Al Willms, Hedy & Wilfred Hein, Ingrid & Ed Suderman; three sons: Helmut & Erika, John, Carl & Colleen; as well as 22 grandchildren and 9 great grandchildren.

WILFRIED HEIN

Tina Sawatzky's Obituary

January 15, 1914–September 13, 2004

THINGS MY MOTHER TAUGHT ME

Katharina (Tina) Sawatzky was born on January 15, 1914 to Phillip and Anna (Bestvater) Wiebe in Gnadental, Baratov colony, Russia. Tina's mother died when she was only three years of age in January 1917, and her father passed away nearly three years later on December 26, 1919. Grandmother Barbara Wiebe looked after the family for the next few years. Tina's older sister Anna had recently married David Schellenberg, and they took Tina in as their own child. She grew up in this loving family and thrived in that environment. In 1923 the entire orphaned family emigrated to Canada due to the desperate political situation in Russia. After an arduous journey, they arrived and settled in Gnadenthal, MB.

Tina accepted Jesus as her Saviour in 1928 during a revival in southern MB. She never wavered in her commitment to the Lord and grew in her faith and devotion to God. She was baptized in 1934. Tina met her husband Jake Sawatzky who also lived in Gnadenthal during these early years, and a relationship developed. They spent time together in a youth (Jugend) group which they enjoyed. Tina played the guitar and also sang duets and quartets with their friends. This was a major part of their social life. Tina sang well into her later years with a small ensemble serving at funerals or senior's activities. Tina and Jake married September 22, 1935 and lived in and around the Gnadenthal area where Jake was involved in farming and trucking. In 1946 they moved to Winkler, a place she enjoyed very much. Then in 1956 a dream was realized when the family moved to Clearbrook, BC. In 1960 they established a raspberry farm, which became very successful. Tina was always a tireless helpmate for father and they modeled a solid partnership. During these years eight children were born. Tina made sure that all her children made commitments to God and taught them to put God first as she always did. She loved to sing with her children even into her senior years. In their later years, Tina and Jake traveled extensively including places such as Europe, Africa, Israel and China. She loved playing board games such as Chinese checkers, which she usually won. She also enjoyed crocheting and made many doilies and afghans. Tina had a soft, loving demeanor, bur her inner strength surfaced easily. As infirmities developed, her motto was, "What I cannot change, I will accept with patience." Tina passed into the presence of her Lord in the Menno Hospital on Monday morning September 13, 2004. She was predeceased by her husband of 67 years, Jake in December 2002, a great-grandson, as well as siblings Helena Peters, Anna Schellenberg, David Wiebe, Maria Ens, Jacob Wiebe, Phillip Wiebe and their spouses. She will greatly missed by her daughters: Herta & Ron Thiessen, Erica & Peter Suderman, Alice & Al Willms, Hedy & Wilf Hein, Ingrid & Ed Suderman, and sons: Helmut & Erika, John & Karen, Carl & Colleen; 22 grandchildren and 12 great grandchildren; sister-in-law Helene Neufeld, brother-in-law Jay & Marta Armin and many nieces and nephews.

Woodlawn FUNERAL HOME
2310 Clearbrook Road
Abbotsford, B.C.
(604) 853-2643

Please visit Jacob and Tina's online memorial at www.mem.com

Erica Suderman's Obituary

July 14, 1938–June 27, 2009

THINGS MY MOTHER TAUGHT ME

Erica Suderman was born on July 14, 1938 in Winkler Manitoba, the second of eight children of Jacob and Tina Sawatzky. The next eight years of her life were spent in the nearby small village of Gnadenthal, Manitoba. The family moved to Winkler in 1946 where Erica completed her education, graduating from Winkler High School in 1956.

During these years, Erica was very involved in activities with friends and family. She loved music, sang in the girls' church choir, took violin lessons and played in the school orchestra. She also loved to play "scrub" baseball.

Erica always had a devout love for her Lord and Saviour. She accepted Jesus into her heart as a young girl and on that confession of faith was baptized in a small prairie creek by Rev. Jacob Quiring. She became active in the church at Winkler and also later on in the Clearbrook MB Church and as a charter member of Bakerview, where she served as Sunday School teacher, librarian and Pioneer Girls leader.

After completing High School in Winkler, Erica took teacher's training at the Normal School in Winnipeg. In 1957, she moved to B.C. to join her family who had moved there in the fall of 1956. She began her teaching career at Barrowtown in the Abbotsford School District, teaching grades 1 – 3 for several years. Erica then taught in several schools in the Surrey School District, leaving her mark of excellence with each assignment. Working passionately, she always included singing activities with her teaching. When Erica moved back to Abbotsford and began working in the school library, she discovered the importance of having learned the Dewey Decimal System in Normal School. This organizational skill, combined with an innate aptitude for order, led her to all of her amazing work in school libraries, church libraries and of course her tremendous contribution to the Historical Society right here in Abbotsford. This later work, which included archival duties, was all learned after she retired from teaching. This great effort will stand as her lasting legacy.

Erica married Peter Suderman in Clearbrook on April 21, 1962. Their marriage was blessed with two children, Jeff and Jackie. During this time, Erica experienced deep new insights into the Christian Faith and was revitalized in her walk with the Lord through her involvement and leadership in the Neighborhood Christian Women's Bible Studies.

Erica lived the Biblical principle that, "it is better to give than to receive." She was extremely generous, always giving gifts, remembering birthdays and inviting people over for dinners. She was an excellent cook and hostess. Despite her accomplishments, Erica was a very self-effacing and humble person. She possessed an extraordinary mind, logically and quickly getting to the core of the issues at hand and seeing projects through to their rightful conclusion. She lived victoriously through her ongoing struggle with Celiac disease, which often limited her diet and activities. Never complaining, she served others with joy and deeply felt thankfulness which she frequently expressed.

Erica and Peter loved to travel. They took many road trips to Manitoba and into the deep southern states. She always carried a hymn book and reading books in the car, so that they could entertain and enrich themselves as they drove along. Trips to Europe, Hawaii, New York and Connecticut and a California cruise just last year were highlights for them both.

Erica loved her family dearly. She was a loving wife and mother, nurturing her children and grandchildren and instilling in them a love for beauty, learning, and the Christian values that were so important to her. Erica was diagnosed with lung cancer in early spring, dying unexpectedly at 6:30 p.m. on June 27. She passed into the presence of her Lord peacefully and surrounded by her family. Erica is mourned by her loving husband Peter, son Jeffrey and his wife Heidi, daughter Jacqueline Gilmore, and husband Cory, and granddaughters, Talia and Ashlee.

THINGS MY MOTHER TAUGHT ME

Al Willms Obituary

August 21, 1935–January 30, 2012

Albert Jacob Willms passed into the presence of His Lord and Saviour Jesus Christ on Monday, January 30, 2012 with his family at his side. Al was born to Abram and Maria (Unger) Willms on August 21, 1935 on the family farm near Kelstern, Saskatchewan.

Al loved the wide open prairie but after many discouraging crop failures his family decided to move to Surrey BC when Al was 12 years old. He soon became acclimatized to the situation and by the time he graduated from Princess Margaret High School he had been active in all the sports programs. He pursued teaching as a career spending many happy years among young students as a classroom teacher, a band instructor and also as a principal in the Delta School District.

Al married Alice Sawatzky and together they raised their family in Surrey later moving to Abbotsford to spend some time growing raspberries. Al never lost his love to work with young people and so in time he found himself at Trinity Western University working as the Director of Financial awards, developing many wonderful friendships. In his retirement years Al gained a lot of satisfaction and pleasure in interacting with his children and grandchildren, woodworking and singing baritone in the Watchmen Four quartet.

Al loved the Lord and worked in the church in various capacities spending nearly twenty years as a choir conductor at Kennedy Heights Church in Delta while living there and in more recent years with the seniors at Northview. We will miss "Big Al" as he was affectionately known to many. His kind, loving ways, quick wit and easy laughter had an impact on many. We will miss him so much but we cherish the memories and the knowledge that to be 'absent from the body is to be present with the Lord'.

Al is survived by his loving wife, Alice, his children Colin (Melody), Jennifer (Carlton Haak) and Andrew (Dana) along with his seven grandchildren, Nathan and Megan Willms, Jared and Daniel Haak and Eva, Micah and Joshua Willms, three sisters Mary Voth, Olga Willms and Linda Willms, as well as many dear relatives and friends. Al was predeceased by his parents, two brothers, Abe and Henry, and one sister Helen Priebe.

THINGS MY MOTHER TAUGHT ME

Wilf's Educational Background

A. Education in Germany

Institution	Graduation	Time-span	# Years	# months
Elementary School, Sembach, Germany		1946–51	5	
High School, Kaiserslautern, Germany		1951–54	3	
Vocational School, Kaiserslautern		1955–57	2	6
Drogistenfachschule Neuwied (Technical institute)	Pharmaceutical technologist ("Drogist")*	1957–58		6
Academy for World Trade, correspondence course	Certificate for 1st semester	1962		6
Academy for World Trade, correspondence course	Certificate for 2nd semester	1963		6
Educational Institute for the German Pharmaceutical Industry, Starnberg, Germany, plus 1 month product training	Pharmaceutical Sales Rep. (API)[18]*	1968		3
Subtotal			**12**	**3**

B. College and University in Canada

Institution	Time-span	# Years	# months
British Columbia Technical Institute (BCIT) Burnaby	1970		4
Courses at Douglas College, New Westminster	1971–72	1	6
Simon Fraser University (SFU), Burnaby	1972		6
Courses at University of Vancouver (UBC)	1973–74	1	
Subtotal		**3**	**4**

---

[18] Ausbildungsseminar Pharma Industrie, Starnberg, Germany.
* Certificates obtained

C. Professional Certificates Obtained

Correspondence Courses Exams written at University of BC (UBC), Vancouver	Organization	Year taken	Duration of studies In months
Basic Course* for qualification to work as Pharmaceutical Sales Representative in Canada	APMR[19]	1980	6
Postgrad: Cardiovascular Drugs*	APMR	1981	6
Postgrad: Infectious Diseases*	APMR	1983	6
Postgrad: Gastrointestinal Drugs*	APMR	1990	6
Postgrad: Psychiatry*	APMR	1993	6
Postgrad: Health Care Management*	APMR	1999	6
Subtotal			**36 months or 3 years**

D. Other Medical and Health Related Courses Taken:

Courses	Place	Date	# hours
Grief Issues Seminar	Cascade Community Church	October, 2011	3
Spiritual Care Volunteer Training	Fraser Health, Abbotsford	Oct-Nov. 2011	10
Aging Well	Bakerview Seminar, Abbotsford	Oct. 2012	6
Many product specific training sessions during national and regional sales meetings not counted in.			
Subtotal			**19 hrs**

---

[19] APMR stands for: Council for the Accreditation of Pharmaceutical Manufacturers Representatives of Canada.

THINGS MY MOTHER TAUGHT ME

E. Sales and Management Courses:

Course Name	Institution	Year taken	Duration of course	
			Months	Hours
Toastmasters	Toastmasters, Abbotsford, met weekly for 3 hours each.	1984		60
Leadership issues	Steve Paul, Fraser Valley College	1988	1	
Leadership tools	Steve Paul, Fraser Valley College	1988	1	
Management Seminar	Myron Rush, Alliance Church, Abbotsford	4 / 1988		12
Focus of success, strength and self esteem	Shirley Floe, Fraser Valley College, Abbotsford	10 / 1988		12
Speak with style	Tony Rekert, Fraser Valley College	1989		12
Fear of public performance	Larry Green, Fraser Valley College	2 / 1989		3
Financial Planning long-term	Fraser Valley College	3/89		2
Phoenix seminar, Peak performance training*	Brian Tracy, Burnaby	8 / 1989		24
Conflict resolution through mediation	Myron Augsburger, Columbia Bible College, Abbotsford	9 / 1989		4
Time Management Seminar	Harold Taylor, Abbotsford	9 /1989		12
Business Management	Lindsey Brooks, Fraser Valley College	1989	3	36
Speaking effectively	Fraser Valley College	10 / 1989		12
Winning in Business	Bill Gibson, Fraser Valley College	2 / 1990		3
Conflict resolution	F. Brown, Fraser Valley College	1990		12
Leading your group to top performance	Neil Osborne, Fraser Valley College	1 / 1991		12
Stress seminar	Val Giles, Abbotsford	6/ 1991		12
Sales Ability	Bristol Myers Squibb (BMS), Montreal, Quebec	10 / 1991		12
Etiquette and corporate success training session	BMS, Montreal	10 / 1991		6
Writing effective business letters	Cheryl Dahl, Fraser Valley College	1991		6
The future is now	David Bond, UCFV	9 / 1999		12
Toastmasters*	Toastmasters, Abbotsford, met weekly for 3 hours each.	5 / 2002		60
Strategic selling skills	Propharma, Ontario	10 / 2002		24
Many sales and medical training courses during national and regional meetings are not counted in.				
Approximate Subtotal			6 months	

F. Computer Courses:

Course Name	Institution	Year Taken	Duration of Course	
			Months	Hours
Computer literacy	RWG, Computer School, Abbotsford	1985	2	
WordStar and Word Perfect	Fraser Valley College, Abbotsford	11 / 1987		45
Intro to Lotus 1-2-3	Fraser Valley College, Abbotsford	1990	1	
Computer Applications	J. Schoenwetter, Columbia Bible College	4 / 1994		6
The Internet for Health professionals	University of the Fraser Valley (UCFV), Abbotsford	1995		12
Intro to computers, DOS and Windows 1	Leading Edge Computers, Abbotsford	5 /,1995	2	
DOS and Word for Windows 1	Leading Edge Careers	7 / 1995	2	
Excel 1*	Academy of Learning, Abbotsford	12 / 1997	2	
PowerPoint*	Academy of Learning	4 / 1998	2	
Access 2000, level 1*	Academy of Learning	5 / 2002	3	
Savvy Senior's	Mennonite Educational Institute (MEI), Abbotsford	Oct. 2016		6
Total Time of Studies:			14	69

G. Writing Courses:

	Place	Instructor	Date	# Hours
Writing workshop	UFV	Richard Van Camp	Nov. 2007	3
Life writing made easy I	MSA Museum, Abbotsford	Philip Sherwood	May 2015	6
Life writing made easy II	MSA Museum, Abbotsford	Philip Sherwood	May 2015	6
Christian Writer Conference Word Guild	Cascade Community Church, Abbotsford	Various	May 2016	8
The Writer's weekend	UFV, Hope, BC		October 27-29, 2017	14
Subtotal				**37 Hours**

H. Theological Correspondence Courses with Certificate in Bible Exploration*

Course Name	Course Abbrev.	Institution	Year taken	For credit courses taken:	
				Months	Grade
Bible Overview	BT 100	Briercrest Distance Learning (BDL), Caronport, SK	2002	6	A+
Evangelism and Global Mission	IS 101	BDL	2004	6	A+
History of Christianity	HIS 237	BDL	2008	6	A
History of Christianity	HIS 238	BDL	2009	6	A
Hermeneutics	BT 213	BDL	2010	6	A
Bible Origins	BT 325	BDL	2011	6	A+
OT Historical Books	BLST 102	BDL	2012	6	A
OT Literature	BT 111	BDL	2013	6	A+
Subtotal				48 months or 4 Years	

Wilf's Total Education[20]

Number of years	Number of months	Number of hours	Number of certificates
24	3	125	14

---

[20] Unfortunately, most of these courses are not given any credit by universities and colleges.

Wilf's and Hedy's Travelog

Geographical List of International Travels [21]

	Countries visited	Vacations / Years visited
1	Argentina	2009 W&H;
2	Austria	1958 W; 1966 W; 1969 H; 1982 W&H; 2015 W&H;
3	Barbados	1985 W&H;
4	Belgium	1963 W; 2105 W&H;
5	Bermuda	1986 W&H; 1989 W&H;
6	Brazil	2009 W&H;
7	Bulgaria	1973 W&H;
8	Canada	1960 W; 1969 W; 1970 W;
9	China	2017 H;
10	Czech Republic	2010 W&H;
11	Denmark	1961 W;
12	Dominican Rep.	2016 W&H;
13	England	1972 W&H; 1985 w. fam.; 2011 W&H;
14	France	1955 W; 1961 W; 1969 H; 1973 W&H; 2013 W&H; (plus several times from Bad Bergzabern)
15	Hungary	2015 W&H;
16	Germany	1969 H; 1971 W&H; 1973 W&H; 1976-78 W&H; 1980 (fam); 1983 W&J; 1984 W; 1985 fam.; 1987 H and Robert; 1988 W&A; 1989 W; 1990 W&H; 1990 W; 1991 W&A; 1993 W&H; 1995 W&H; 1996 W&H; 1996 W; 1997 W&H; 1999 W&H; 2010 W&H; 2013 W&H; 2015 W&H;
17	Greece	2005 W&H;

---

[21] Since living in Canada, Wilf has visited his home country twenty-one times and enjoyed beautiful holidays in Mexico and Hawaii nine times in each of these warmer climates.

	Hawaii	1970 W&H; 1984 fam.; 1989 W&H; 1994 W&H; 1999 W&H; 2000 H; 2001 W&H; 2004 W&H; 2012 fam; 2014 W&H; 2016 H;
18	Holland	1958 W; 1963 W; 1973 W&H; 1988 H; 1992 W&H
19	Ireland	2011 W&H;
20	Israel	2005 W&H;
21	Italy	1962 W; 1965 W; 1969 H; 1973 W&H;
22	Jamaica	1983 W&H;
23	Liechtenstein	1976 W&H;
24	Mexico	1987 Acap. W&H; 1998 Cabo, W&H; 2000 P.V-W&H; 2003 Canc. W&H; 2006 P.V.-fam.; 2008, P.V-fam; 2011 P.V.-W&H; 2015 Maz-W&H; 2017 P.V.-W;
25	Monaco	1973 W&H;
26	Paraguay	2009 W&H;
27	Peru	2009 W&H;
28	Portugal	1992 W&H;
29	Russia	1969 W; 1988 H;
30	Scotland	2011 W&H;
31	Spain	1967 W; 1977 W&H; 1992 W&H;
32	Sweden	1961 W;
33	Switzerland	1955 W; 1961 W; 1964 W; 1969 H; 1973 W&H; 1977 W&H; 2013 W&H;
34	Turkey	1973 W&H; 2005 W&H;
35	USA mainland,[22] Excluding Hawaii	1959-60 W; 1972 W; 1972 W&H; 1981 fam.; 1984 W&H; 1988 W&H; 1988 fam.; 1991 H w. parents; 1991 fam.; 1992 fam.; 1992 W&H; 1993 W&H; 1994 W&H; 1995 WA-W&H; 1995 FL-W&H; 1996 W&H; 1997 W&H; 1998 W&H; 1999 W&H; 2000 W&H; 2001 W&H; 2004 W&H; 2007 W&H; 2009 W&H; 2012 AZ-W&H; 2012 WA-W&H; 2013 W&H; 2014 W&H; 2015 W&H;
36	Vatican	1973 W&H;

---

[22] Within USA mainland, we spent seven holidays in Leavenworth, Washington.

WILFRIED HEIN

Chronological Outline of International Vacations:

Year	Country visited
1955	France (Alsace); Switzerland (W)
1958	Holland (Friesland, youth retreat, W)
1958	Austria, Vienna (MVS Camp, W)
1959	USA (Aug. 5, 1959 – Oct. 1960, W; PA, and FL)
1960	USA (IL, CA, and Vancouver, Canada)
1961	France and Switzerland, (Locarno, W)
1961	Denmark and Sweden (W)
1962	Italy (Diano Marina, W)
1963	Holland (biketrip Texel and Belgium, MVS camp, W)
1964	Switzerland, (W)
1965	Italy, (San Remo, W)
1966	Austria, (Youth retreat and skiing holiday, W)
1967	Spain, (Caribbean Islands, Tenerife, W)
1969	Russia, (Moscow and Leningrad, Wilf with parents and brother)
1969	Canada, (Vancouver engagement, W)
1969	Germany, France, Switzerland, Austria and Italy (H)
1970	Canada, (emigration W in May)
1970	Hawaii, (Honolulu, Maui, honeymoon, W&H)
1971	Germany (Christmas, W&H)
1972	USA, (Dallas Texas, W)
1972	USA, (Montana, W&H)
1972	England, (W&H)
1973	Germany, Bulgaria, Turkey, Switzerland, Italy, Vatican, Monaco, France and Holland (2 months, W&H)
1976	Germany (2 year stay from May 1976 to March 1978)
1976	Liechtenstein (coffee break in November, W&H)
1977	Switzerland (W&H with Hedy's parents)
1977	Spain, island of Ibiza (W&H with Hedy's and my parents)
1978	Canada (our return from 2 year stay in Germany)

1980	Germany, (family trip Christmas, see Christmas travel story)
1981	USA, (Oregon, Cannon Beach and Washington, w.fam)
1982	Germany, Austria, Switzerland (choir tour W&H)
1983	Jamaica, (company award trip, Jan., W&H)
1983	USA, Lake Chelan, WA (fam. / July, burned hand)
1983	Germany (W with Jeremy (Aug – Sept)
1984	Germany (W visiting father in hospital)
1984	Hawaii (award trip with family, July: Maui and Honolulu)
1984	USA, Las Vegas, (company award trip Nov. W&H)
1985	Barbados, (company trip Jan. W&H)
1985	Germany (with family, Christmas and Golden Wedding)
1985	England (with family, part of our trip to Germany)
1986	Bermuda (April, W&H)
1987	Mexico, (Acapulco, company trip, W&H)
1987	Germany (Berlin, Aug., H &R)
1988	Germany, (W with Adrian)
1988	Russia and Holland, (H)
1988	USA, New York, (company award trip, regional winner, W&H)
1988	USA, Montana, fam.
1989	Hawaii: Honolulu and Maui, (company trip, W&H)
1989	Germany, (May, W)
1989	Bermuda, (company regional award trip, W&H)
1990	Germany, (mother's birthday, Auerbach, August, W&H)
1990	Germany, (father's funeral, October, W only)
1991	USA, Palm Springs, CA, (Feb. Hedy with parents and Herta)
1991	USA, Florida, (Disneyworld w. family)
1991	Germany, (W and Adrian, Sylt)
1992	Portugal, (company trip, also Spain, Holland and Germany, June, W&H)
1992	USA, Leavenworh, WA, (August w. family)
1992	USA, Birch Bay, WA (November W&H)
1993	USA, Oregon, (July, timeshare, W&H)

1993	Germany, (mother's 85th birthday, Aug. W&H)
1994	Hawaii, Honolulu, (March, W& H)
1994	USA, WA, Leavenworth, (Oct. W&H)
1995	USA, WA, Discovery Bay (Timeshare, March; W&H)
1995	USA, FL, Miami (Cruise to St. Martin, July, W&H)
1995	Germany, (Sept. W&H)
1996	USA, Lake Chelan, Leavenworth, (March; W&H)
1996	Germany, (April, W&H)
1996	Germany, (Dec, W)
1997	USA, Florida, Naples, (March W& H)
1997	Germany (W&H)
1998	Mexico, Cabo San Lucas, timeshare, March, W&H)
1998	USA, WA, Leavenworth, (timeshare, Oct. W& H)
1999	Germany, (Helga's 60th birthday, Black Forest, April, W& H)
1999	USA, WA, Birch Bay, (timeshare, June/July, W&H)
1999	Hawaii: Maui, Kauai, Big island, (timeshare, July, W&H)
2000	Mexico, Puerto Vallarta, (Buenaventura Hotel, March, W& H)
2000	USA, WA, Leavenworth-Whidby Island, Oct. W&H
2000	Hawaii, (Nov, H visiting Adrian)
2001	USA, Maine, (visit Adrian at camp on our tour to Eastern Canada, Aug. W&H)
2001	Hawaii: Honolulu, (Oct.-Nov. W&H)
2003	Mexico, Cancun, (March, W&H)
2004	Hawaii, Maui, (March W&H)
2004	USA, Idaho, Montana, WA, return trip from Calgary (June W&H)
2005	Turkey, Greece and Israel (May-June, W&H)
2006	Mexico, Puerto Vallarta, (March, Family)
2007	USA, Nevada and Utah, (April, W&H)
2008	Mexico, Puerto Vallarta, (March with family)
2009	USA, Nevada, Las Vegas (Feb, W&H)
2009	South America: Peru, Brazil, Argentina, Paraguay (MWC July, W&H)
2010	Germany, Czech Republic (Sept, W&H)

2011	Mexico, P. Vallarta, Paradise Village (Feb. W&H)
2011	Ireland, Scotland, England (Aug. W&H)
2012	USA, Arizona, Tucson and Phoenix (March, W&H)
2012	USA, WA, Whidbey island, Leavenworth, Gig Harbour (Sept. W&H)
2012	Hawaii, (December, family)
2013	USA, WA, Lake Chelan, Leavenworth, (May, W&H)
2013	France, Switzerland, Germany (Sept., W&H)
2014	Hawaii, Kona (Jan-Feb, Hilton, W&H)
2014	USA, WA, Leavenworth (June, W&H)
2015	Mexico, Mazatlan (Feb. – March, W&H)
2015	USA, Eastern States: PA, MD, DC; VA, NJ, NY, CT, MA (July-Aug, W&H)
2015	Belgium, Austria, Hungary, Germany (Sept., W&H)
2016	Hawaii, Kona (Feb. Hedy)
2016	Dominican Rep. Punta Cana, (meeting with sponsored child, April, WH)
2017	China (April 6-16; Hedy)
2017	Mexico, P. Vallarta (April, Marival Resort and Suites, Wilf)

WILFRIED HEIN

Chronological List of Vacations Within Canada [23]

Year	Prov.	Vacations and trips within Canada
1971	BC	Van. Island: Victoria, (summer, W&H)
1972	AB, MB	(August, W&H)
1975	BC	Van. Island, Victoria, (summer, fam.)
1978	BC	Camp Squeah (July, fam.)
1979	BC, AB	Motorhome trip (W&H with my parents)
1980	BC	Penticton (summer, fam.)
1980	BC	Camp Squeah (July, fam. Music camp)
1982	BC	Van. Island, Victoria Easter holiday (April, fam.)
1983	BC	Osoyoos, BC (fam)
1987	BC, AB	Okanagan, Banff and Lake Louise (W. with Wolfgang and Jeremy)
1987	BC	Hatzic Lake, (fam. camping, Sept.)
1988	AB, MB	Edmonton and Winkler, (Wiebe reunion July w. fam.)
1990	BC	Big Bar Ranch and Bridge Lake (Aug. w. fam.)
1991	BC	Shuswap area, Pine Grove, Adams River, (w. family)
1992	BC	Whistler, Mini holiday
1993	BC	Kelowna, Sicamous, Nelson (May, W&H)
1993	BC	Ft. St. John (Tracie's wedding, Hedy w. Robert and Adrian)
1993	BC	Silverstar, (July, Wiebe reunion, w. fam.)
1994	BC	108 Mile House, Blue River, Helmcken Falls, (W& H)
1996	BC	Sicamous, Vernon, Penticton, (July, W&H)
1997	AB	Edmonton, (March, Hedy w. mother)
1997	BC	Penticton, (Aug. W&H)
1998	BC	Penticton, (July, W & H)
1998	AB, MB	Edmonton and Winnipeg, (Wiebe Reunion, July, H)
1998	BC	Whistler, (Christmas w. fam.)
1999	BC	Penticton, (Oct. W& H)

---

[23] Of our vacations within Canada, we spent nine holidays on Vancouver Island (including the Gulf Islands), eight in Pentiction, four both in Whistler and on the Sunshine Coast.

THINGS MY MOTHER TAUGHT ME

2000	BC, AB	Hedy picked me up in Canmore, trip through the Kootneys, July, W&H)
2000	MB	Winkler, (Bernie Zacharias funeral, July, Hedy only)
2001	BC	Penticton, (April, W&H)
2001	BC	Van. Island, Parksville and Tofino (June, W&H)
2001	East	Que, NB, NS, PEI, Ont. (Aug. W&H)
2002	BC	Van. Island, Victoria, (March, W&H)
2002	BC	Sunshine Coast, Powel River, (Aug. W&H)
2002	BC	Fort St. John (Julie wedding, Aug. H)
2002	BC	Whistler and Van. Island, Victoria, (W&H w. Eckart and Helga, Oct.)
2003	BC	Penticton, (July, W&H)
2003	BC	Sunshine Coast, Ruby lake, Sechelt, (Aug. W&H)
2003	AB	Banff and Lake Louise, 55 Plus Retreat (Oct, W&H)
2004	BC, AB	Kelowna, jasper, Lake Louise, Banff (June, W&H w. Eckart and Helga)
2005	BC	Van., Island, Victoria (March, W&H)
2005	BC	Westbank, Penticton (Aug, W&H)
2006	BC	Gulf islands Pender, Galiano, Gabriola (Aug, W&H)
2007	BC, AB	Edmonton, Drumheller, Radium Hot Springs, (Aug, W&H)
2008	BC	Gulf islands: Maine and Saltspring (Aug/Sept., W&H)
2009	BC	Van. Island, Victoria (May, W&H)
2009	BC	Sunshine Coast, Gibsons (July, W&H)
2009	BC	Camp Squeah, (Sept., Anabaptist Conference, W&H)
2010	BC	Van. Island, Victoria, (May, W&H)
2011	BC	Penticton (June, W&H)
2013	BC	Osoyoos (May, W&H)
2014	BC	Osoyoos (June, W&H)
2014	BC	Whistler, Crystal Lodge (Sept. W&H)
2016	BC	Kelowna, Summerland, Penticton (July, W&H)
2016	BC	Sunshine Coast, Gibsons, (August hot spell, W&H)
2016	BC	Harrison Hot Springs (New Year Eve, Fam.)
2017	BC	Whistler, Hilton (May, W&H)
2017	BC	Vancouver Island, Parksville, Courtenay, Qualicum Beach (Sept. W&H)

WILFRIED HEIN

Hedy's Postgraduate Workshops and Conferences

Hedy, who graduated with a bachelor of music in 1970, attended the following music workshops and conferences:

Year	Prov./ Country	Hedy's Music Workshops, Conferences and Music Related Trips
1971	BC	Music Camp at Shawnigan Lake School, Vancouver Island with well-known violinist Ruggiero Ricci (summer course- 3 weeks)
1983	MB	Winnipeg, Choral Music workshop (Jan.)
1983	AB	Calgary, Suzuki Institute (Aug)
1983	USA	Bellingham, WA, Suzuki Children course (Aug. Hedy took Jeremy and Robert there)
1984	USA	Schaumburg, IL, Suzuki Teachers conference (May)
1984	USA	Forest Grove, OR, Suzuki Institute (June)
1985	AB	Edmonton, Suzuki International conference (Aug)
1986	USA	Bellingham, WA, Suzuki Institute (Aug)
1986	BC	Vancouver, Starr Violine Workshop
1987	BC	Vancouver, string workshop w. Janos Starker (Feb)
1987	Germany	Berlin, International Suzuki Conference with Robert (Aug)
1987	BC	Langley, Can.-American Suzuki Institute (July)
1988	Russia	Choir trip to Ukraine and Siberia (June)
1988	USA	Bellingham, WA: Suzuki Institute (July – Aug)
1989	BC	Vancouver, Cello workshop (Feb)
1989	USA	Nampa, Idaho, Suzuki Institute (June-July)
1989	BC	Langley, Can.-American Suzuki Institute, TWU, (Aug. w. Robert and Adrian)
1990	USA	San Francisco, CA, Suzuki Violin Teachers Conference (May)
1990	BC	Fort Langley, Summer Music Camp (Aug)
1991	BC	Can. American Suzuki Institute, TWU, Langley (July)
1992	AB	Banff, Music Festival Canada 1992, (April, with Robert, MEI Razzberry Jam)
1994	USA	Chicago, Suzuki Teachers Conference (June)
1996	USA	Chicago, Suzuki Teachers Conference, (June)
1997	USA	Missoula, MT, Suzuki Cello Institute, (July)
1997	USA	Seattle, WA, Suzuki Cello Institute (Aug).
1999	USA	Deerfield, IL, Cello Teachers Training course (June-July)
2002	MB	Winkler, Girls' Choir reunion, (Sept.)
2003	MB	Winnipeg, Wiebe family CD Recording, CMU Winnipeg. (May)
2004	AB	Edmonton, Suzuki Teachers conference, (July)

Resources

Books:

Gerlach, Horst. *Bildband zur Geschichte der Mennoniten* (Uelzen-Oldenstadt, Germany, Druck und Verlag Guenther Preuschoff), article entitled "Die Kinderspeisungs-Aktion der Mennoniten in Ludwigshafen/Rhein."

Gesangbuch, Konferenz der Süddeutschen Mennonitengemeinden e.V. Ludwigsburg (Germany, 1972).

Harder, J. Bernhard. *Alexandertal, Die Geschichte der letzten deutschen Stammsiedlung in Russland* (Berlin, Kohnert Druckerei, 1955).

Hege, Christian. *Chronik der Familie Hege, Heft 1* (Frankfurt a.M., 1937).

Hege, Christian. *Chronik der Familie Hege, Heft 2* (Karlsruhe 1970).

Hein, Gerhard. *Vertrauen, Freuen, Danken* (Weisenheim am Berg, Germany, Agape Verlag, 1992).

Hein, Wilfried. *A Witness in Times of War and Peace* (Victoria, BC, Canada: Friesenpress, 2015).

Laendliche Heimvolkshochschule / Evangelische Bauernschule Hohebuch, *Hans Hege, 2. Februar 1885–2. Januar 1983, zum Gedächtnis* (Mai 1983).

Loewen, Harry, Elisabeth L. Wiens, Elke and Peter Foth. *Warum ich mennonitisch bin* (Hamburg, Germany: Kuempers Verlag, 1996).

Luther, Martin, Die Bibel, Württembergische Bibelanstalt (Germany, 1935).

Redekopp, Elsa. *Two Worlds for Jash* (Winnipeg, MB: Windflower Communications, 1991).

_____. *Wish and Wonder* (Winnipeg, MB: Reddell Publishing, 1982).

_____. *Dream and Wonder* (Winnipeg, MB: Kindred Press, 1986).

Schellenberg, Alfred, *The Legacy,* Philipp Wiebe and Anna Bestvater (Winnipeg, MB, July 1998).

Stockfleth Heinrich Arnold, *Gesangbuch,* Ludwigshafen, Konferenz der Süddeutschen Mennonitengemeinden, e.V. (1972).

Shelley, Bruce L., *Church History in Plain Language* (Dallas, TX, Word Publishing, 1995), 254.

Stuttgarter Biblisches Nachschlagewerk, Württembergische Bibelanstalt (1932).

Suderman, Erica, *WIEBE SCRAPBOOK from Generation to Generation,* in honour of Philipp Wiebe and Anna Bestvater (Abbotsford, BC, July 2003, also available as CD).

Willms Thielman, Susanne and Philip-Sherwood, *Susanne Remembers,* A Mennonite childhood in revolutionary Russia (Abbotsford, BC: Judson Lake House, 2009).

Articles:

Correll, Ernst. "Bibliographical and research Notes, Mennonite Quarterly Review." *The Hege-Hagey Family; Historical Notes and Comments,* XXXIV (July 1960).

Gerlach, Horst, Das Mennonitische Gemeindeideal, Eine kurze Beschreibung einer christlichen Freikirche, Traktat Christliche Mission der Mennoniten, Esch-Alzette, Luxemburg (No date given, probably 1956).

Hege, Albrecht, Praelat, Heilbronn, *Trauergottesdienst für Dr. h.c. Hans Hege, Ansprache in der Stadtkirche Waldenburg am 6. Januar 1983, Beerdigungsgottesdienst.*

Hege, Hans, Immigrant II, Photocopy p.29, source not given.

Hein, Lydia, *Emanzipation* (Emancipaton), Junge Gemeinde, 1/73, Januar/Februar 1973, 8–9 (original in German in the author's possession).

Handouts from talks:

Flint, Peter W., Director of the Dead Sea Scrolls Institute, Canada, *The Dead Sea Scrolls and the Reliability of Bibles used Today.* Seminar held on October 16, 2004 at Aldergrove United Church, BC.

DVDs:

Dueck, David Film Production, *and When They Shall Ask, A Doku-Drama of the Russian Mennonite Experience*, DVD, Winnipeg, MB, Mennonite Media Society, 2010.

CDs:

Ens, Phil (Executive Producer); Wiebe, George (Program structure, conductor); *Stimmt an, the Musical Heritage of the Philipp Wiebe Family,* CD: Winnipeg, recorded at CMU by Faith and Life Communications, 2003.

Websites:

https://en.wikipedia.org/wiki/List_of_Christians_martyred_during_the_reign_of_Diocletian

https://www.mwc-cmm.org/article/previous-assemblies

http://gameo.org/index.php?title=Alexandertal_Mennonite_Settlement(Samara_Oblast,_Russia)

Letters:

Hein, Lydia, more than six hundred personal letters to her son Wilfried have been reviewed and some excerpts of poems, wise sayings and Scripture verses have been translated and included in this memoir.

Bibliography of Wilf Hein

Books Published:

A Witness in Times of War and Peace: The Story of Gerhard Hein, a Mennonite Pastor who served in the Wehrmacht During World War II. Victoria, BC: FriesenPress, 2015.

Articles Published:

"Christmas Echos," A Christmas message delivered by Dr. Christian Neff (1863-1946) during World War II. (translated from German into English). *Roots and Branches.* Vol. 23, no. 1, February 2017.

Biography of Gerhard Hein, published on Global Anabaptist Mennonite Encyclopedia Online (Gameo, July 2016). It can be found on www.gameo.org and typing in Gerhard Hein or by clicking on the following link: http://gameo.org/index.php?title=Hein,_Gerhard_(1905%E2%80%931990).

"A Response to Helmut Foth's Essay, '*Wie die Mennoniten in die deutsche Volksgemeinschaft hineinwuchsen."* Roots and Branches.* Vol. 20, no. 4 (November 2014):7.

Book review of Peter P. Klassen's book: "Die deutsch-voelkische Zeit in er Kolonie-Fernheim, Chaco, Paraguay 1933-1944. Ein Beitrag zur Geschichte der auslandsdeutschen Mennoniten während des Dritten Reiches." *Roots and Branches.* Vol 20, no. 4 (November 2014):25.

"*Tankstelle*"—*Columbia Bible Camp*, Mennonitische Rundschau, September 20, 1972, 95. Jahrgang, Nummer 38, 12.

"*Explo '72*", Mennonitische Rundschau, July 12, 1972, 95. Jahrgang, Nummer 28, 9.

"*Family Camp Experience of 1972*" Invitation flyer for family camp at Columbia Bible Camp 1973.

Letters to Editors:

"There's nothing inspirational about killing unborn babies." Abbotsford News, October 17, 2008.

"Agrifair keeps me up." Abbotsford News, Week of August 3, 2008.

"Attack was 'malicious' and without merit." Abbotsford News, May, 24, 2007.

"We need to further reduce health risks." Abbotsford News, Feb. 17, 2007.

"Maybe we should look more to Creator." Abbotsford News, July 8, 2006.

"Now let's focus on the unborn." Abbotsford News, July 5, 2005.

"Go organic—stay healthy." Abbotsford News, January 8, 2005.

"The real Jesus." Mennonite Brethren Herald, April 19, 2002.

"Abbotsford really cares.", Abbotsford News November 15, 2001.

Lectures and Presentations:

March 20, 2016
Bakerview MB Church, BC / Current Issues Class: *Keeping the Faith in Nazi Germany.*

November 2, 2016
Reach Gallery, Abbotsford, BC: The Conflicts German *"Pacifists" Faced During the Third Reich."*

Aug 30, 2015
Together with another couple, my wife and I gave report about the Mennonite World Conference in Harrisburg to our Current Issues Sunday School Class on August 30, 2015.

INDEX

A

Adrian
  Family picture, Christmas 2016 341
  Mother's Day letter, 1991 197
  School essay, 1996 240
  Wedding, 2007 276
Afterword 345
Auerbach, mother's birtday pary, 1990 189
Award, first prize in nation, 1983 and 1984 151

B

Baptism, Wilf 55
Beringer, Klaus visiting my cousin in Ulm, 2015 332
Bibliography W. Hein 388
Birthday speech to mother 1993 218
Blessings experienced 79
Book launch, A Witness, Oct. 2015 394
Bread from Heaven story 246
Bulgaria, Italy and Berlin, 1973 110

C

Career in Germany, 1960-70 62
Christmas Travel Story 1980 135

D

Death of a believer, beautiful words 237
Dreams, comforting to my mother 206

E

Eckart
  Letter to mother after father passed away 192
Educational background Wilf 371
Emigration, May 1970 88
Engagement 85
England, 2011 310
Explo, Dallas, 1972 106

F

Family Tree, Lydia Hein 360
Family trips
  Hawaii, 2012/13 322
Father's teachings
  Faith 185
  Forgiveness 160
  Imperfection (Stueckwerk) 190, 204
  Source of strength 189
  Thankfulness 131
  Trust and submission 140
  Trust the Lord 131
  Try your best 130
France, 2013 311

G

Germany two years, 1976-78 122
Golden Wedding parents, 1986 162
Grandparents Hege picture 34
Greece, 2005 261

H

Hedy
  40th anniversy Victoria, 2010 298
  Fraser Valley Symphony Orchestra picture 282
  Graduation picture 92
Hege, Hans 357
Hege, Hegi, Hagey, ancestors 353
Hege Liesel quote 114
Home
  Clearbrook, 1975 118
  Coquitlam 115
  Spur Ave, 2012 321
Honeymoon Hawaii 97
Hus monument, Prague 294

I

Ireland, 2011 304
Israel, 2005 262

J

Jeremy
  Ama's letter to you 177
  Family picture, Christmas 2016 339

L

Letter to dad during his illness 78

M

Miracle 01
  Rescue from drowning 45
Miracle 02
  Mother's survival 46
Miracle 03
  Car accident near Berlin 75
Miracle 04
  Protection from car accident 76
Miracle 05
  How we met 83
Miracle 06
  Passing the Calculus course 106
Miracle 07
  Meeting an angel 119
Miracle 08
  A flight re-scheduled 120
Miracle 09
  Finding reliable renters for our home 122
Miracle 10
  Finding a place to live in Germany 123
Miracle 11
  Finding a job in Germany 123
Miracle 12
  Finding a suitable place near work 123
Miracle 13
  Difficulties turned into blessings 124
Miracle 14
  All expenses paid for 124
Miracle 15
  Getting rid of our stuff 128
Miracle 16
  Finding a new job in Canada 129
Miracle 17
  Healed by prayer 134
Miracle 18
  Surviving two near disasters 135
Miracle 19
  Winning top award 150
Miracle 20
  The Fall of the Wall 186
Moscow, 1969 74
Mother, 85th birtday 217
Mother's last letter 233
Mother's teachings
  Activity level, keep mentally active 184

Activity level, remain active 111
Aging 138
Anxiety 115
Encourage others 120
Eternal life, prepare for it 121
Faith 185
FAITH, keeping it 166
Feeding mind 230
GRACE definition in a poem 139
Happiness is a choice 175
Health challenges 210
Job problems 195
Learning, a life-long process 130
Loneliness 209
Love 87, 231
Love, no age limit 176
Morning contemplation 140
Positiveness, say good things about others 104
Qualities modelled 235
Serve others 105
Shortcomings 160
Thankfulness 111, 181, 224
Trust, a poem 343
Trust in the Lord 105

O

Obituaries
  Albert Willms 370
  Erica Suderman 367, 369, 370
  Jake Sawatzky 363
  Tina Sawatzky-Wiebe 365

P

Poems when biking through Holland 72
Prophetic words
  Future lifes partner 83

R

Resources used 385
Retirement BMS, 2002 243
Retirement from Propharma 271

Robert
  Berlin conference, 1987 170
  Family picture, Christmas 2015 340

S

Sawatsky, John visit in Connecticut, 2015 330
Sawatzky, Jake 244
Sawatzky, Tina 249
Silver wedding, Wilf & Hedy, 1995 238
South America, 2009 286
Switzerland, 2013 313

T

Travelog Wilf & Hedy 376
Turkey, 2005 258

U

USA trainee from 1959-60 69

V

Vienna, choir trip, 1982 145

W

Wedding, May 1970 92
Wilf's 65th birtday 268
Wittenberg, Germany, 2010 295

Book Reviews:

Robert Martens, *Roots and Branches*. Vol. 23, no. 1, February 2017, 26.

Mennonite Historia, Vol. 43, No 2, June 2017, 9-10.

Mennonitische Geschichtsblaetter, 74. Jahrgang 2017, 142.

Online Reviews:

1. Mark Janzen, professor of history at Bethel College in Kansas. Mennonite World Review Journal, January 2017 issue: http://mennoworld.org/2017/01/30/columns/book-review-a-witness-in-times-of-war-and-peace/.
2. Clif Hostetler, Kansas, USA: Listed under "goodreads.com," 5-Star. http://www.goodreads.com/book/show/27170321-a-witness-in-times-of-war-and-peace.
3. Elma Schemenauer, a Canadian author of seven books: https://www.amazon.com/review/R47GHFBVCQD8Y.

4. The online review by the Mennonite Historical Society can be found under the following link: http://www.mhsbc.com/bookreviews/hein_memoir.pdf.

Availability:

www.friesenpress.com, House of James, Abbotsford, BC; Wilf Hein, Abbotsford, BC.

ABOUT THE AUTHOR

Wilf Hein was born in 1940 in Germany, where he lived for thirty years. He was the younger of two sons of Gerhard and Lydia Hein, a Mennonite pastor couple. He graduated in Germany as "Drogist" and later received his API certificate from an Educational Institute for the German Pharmaceutical Industry. When he met his Canadian sweetheart, he decided to immigrate to Canada. After arriving there in 1970, Wilf continued his studies for three years at Douglas College and at the University of British Columbia (UBC). In addition, he wrote several exams in the medical and pharmaceutical area and took some computer and sales management courses. These helped him to excel in the pharmaceutical industry and win several top awards. After his retirement, he enrolled in correspondence courses through Briercrest College and Seminary, obtaining his certificate in the Bible Exploration Series, and then devoted his time to writing.

His recent book, a memoir of his father, a Mennonite pastor and historian, appeared under the title *A Witness in Times of War and Peace*. It is a translation of his father's life story entitled *A Russian German Experiences East and West* and tells among many other things the struggles he experienced when he was called to serve in the German army.

Wilf is married to Hedy Sawatzky, a violin teacher. They have three married sons and ten grandchildren. He is a member of Bakerview MB Church, where he served on the missions committee, as a care group leader, in the senior outreach ministry and in some other areas. He also served on the board of directors of the Central Academy of Music, Logos BTE, and the local chapter of Neighbourlink, on his residential strata council and as a Spiritual Care Volunteer at Fraser Health. Wilf holds memberships at the Mennonite Faith and Learning Society and the Mennonite Historical Societies in British Columbia., as well as in Germany, and at the Apollo Fitness Center in his hometown. His interests include reading, writing, studying history of Christianity, and traveling. He has traveled extensively, visiting thirty-five countries and includes some of his travel experiences in his memoir as well.

CPSIA information can be obtained
at www.ICGtesting.com
Printed in the USA
LVHW01s2350240518
578317LV00005B/8/P